The Lives of the Painters, Sculptors & Architects

Copyright © 2007 BiblioBazaar
All rights reserved

Giorgio Vasari

The Lives of the Painters, Sculptors & Architects

In Eight Volumes
VOLUME 1

BIBLIOBAZAAR

The Lives of the Painters, Sculptors & Architects

CONTENTS

Cimabue, Painter of Florence. 31
Arnolfo di Lapo, Florentine Architect. 39
Niccola and Giovanni Pisani, Sculptors and Architects. 52
Andrea Tafi, Florentine Painter. 68
Gaddo Gaddi, Florentine Painter. 73
Margaritone, Painter, Sculptor and Architect of Arezzo. 78
Giotto, Painter, Sculptor, and Architect of Florence. 83
Agostino and Agnolo, Sculptors and Architects of Siena. 107
Stefano, Painter of Florence, and Ugolino of Siena. 116
Pietro Laurati, Painter of Siena. 121
Andrea Pisano, Sculptor and Architect. 125
Buonamico Buffalmacco, Painter of Florence. 134
Ambruogio Lorenzetti, Painter of Siena. 150
Pietro Cavallini, Painter of Rome. 153
Simone Martini and Lippo Memmi, Painters of Siena. 157
Taddeo Gaddi, Painter of Florence. 165
Andrea di Cione Orcagna, Painter, Sculptor, and
    Architect of Florence. 174
Tommaso called Giottino, painter of Florence. 184
Giovanni da Ponte, Painter of Florence. 190
Agnolo Gaddi, Painter of Florence. 193
Berna, Painter of Siena. 199
Duccio, Painter of Siena. 202
Antonio, Painter of Venice. 205
Jacopo di Casentino, Painter. 210

Spinello, Painter of Arezzo...214
Gherardo Stamina, Painter of Florence. 225
Lippo, Painter of Florence. 228
Don Lorenzo, Monk of the Angeli of Florence, Painter. 231
Taddeo Bartoli, Painter of Siena. 235
Lorenzo di Bicci, Painter of Florence.......................................238

PREFACE TO THE LIVES

I am aware that it is commonly held as a fact by most writers that sculpture, as well as painting, was naturally discovered originally by the people of Egypt, and also that there are others who attribute to the Chaldeans the first rough carvings of statues and the first reliefs. In like manner there are those who credit the Greeks with the invention of the brush and of colouring. But it is my opinion that design, which is the creative principle in both arts, came into existence at the time of the origin of all things. When the Most High created the world and adorned the heavens with shining lights, His perfect intellect passing through the limpid air and alighting on the solid earth, formed man, thus disclosing the first form of sculpture and painting in the charming invention of things. Who will deny that from this man, as from a living example, the ideas of statues and sculpture, and the questions of pose and of outline, first took form; and from the first pictures, whatever they may have been, arose the first ideas of grace, unity, and the discordant concords made by the play of lights and shadows? Thus the first model from which the first image of man arose was a lump of earth, and not without reason, for the Divine Architect of time and of nature, being all perfection, wished to demonstrate, in the imperfection of His materials, what could be done to improve them, just as good sculptors and painters are in the habit of doing, when, by adding additional touches and removing blemishes, they bring their imperfect sketches to such a state of completion and of perfection as they desire. God also endowed man with a bright flesh colour, and the same shades may be drawn from the earth, which supplies materials to counterfeit everything which occurs in painting. It is indeed true that it is impossible to feel absolutely certain as to what steps men took for the imitation of the beautiful works of Nature in these arts before the flood, although it appears, most probable that even then they practised all manner of painting and sculpture; for Bel, son of the proud Nimrod, about 200 years after the flood, had a statue made, from which idolatry afterwards arose; and his celebrated daughter-in-law, Semiramis, queen of Babylon, in the building of that city, introduced among the ornaments there coloured representations from life of divers kinds of animals, as well as of herself and of her husband Ninus, with the bronze statues of her father, her mother-in-law, and her great-grandmother, as Diodorus relates, calling them Jove, Juno, and Ops—Greek names, which did not then exist. It was, perhaps, from these statues that the Chaldeans learned to make the images of their gods. It is recorded in Genesis how 150 years later, when Rachel was fleeing from Mesopotamia with her husband Jacob, she stole the idols of her father Laban. Nor were the Chaldeans singular in making statues, for the Egyptians also had theirs, devoting great pains to those arts, as is shown by the marvellous tomb of that king of remote antiquity, Osimandyas, described at length by Diodorus, and, as the severe command of Moses proves, when, on leaving Egypt, he gave orders that no images should be made to God, upon pain of death. Moses also, after having ascended the Mount, and having found a golden calf manufactured and adored by his people, was greatly troubled at seeing divine honours accorded to the image of a beast; so that he not only broke it to powder, but, in the punishment of so great a fault, caused the Levites to put to death many thousands of the false Israelites who had committed this idolatry. But as the sin consisted in adoring idols and not in making them, it is written in Exodus that the art of design and of making statues, not only in marble but in all kinds of metal, was given by the mouth of God himself to Bezaleel, of the tribe of Judah, and to Aholiab, of the tribe of Dan, who made the two cherubim of gold, the candles, the veil, and the borders of the sacerdotal vestments, together with a number of other beautiful things in the tabernacle, for no other purpose than that people should put them on for their own adornment and delight. From the things seen before the flood, the pride of man found the means to make statues of those who wished their fame in the world to be immortal; and the Greeks, who give a different origin to this, say that the Ethiopians found the first statues, according to Diodorus, the Egyptians imitated these, while the Greeks followed the Egyptians. From this time until Homer's day it is clear that sculpture and painting were perfect, as we may see from the description of Achilles' shield by that divine poet, who represents it with such skill that the image of it is presented to our minds as clearly as if we had seen the thing itself. Lactantius Firmianus attributes the credit of the invention to Prometheus, who like God formed the human form out of dust. But according to Pliny this art was introduced into Egypt by Gyges of Lydia, who on seeing his shadow cast by the fire, at once drew a representation of himself on the wall with a piece of coal. For some time after that it was the custom to draw in outline only, without any colouring, Pliny again being our authority. This was afterwards introduced by Philocles of Egypt with considerable pains, and also by Cleanthes and Ardices of Corinth and by Telephanes of Sicyon. Cleophantes of Corinth was the first of the Greeks to use colours, and Apollodorus was the first to introduce the brush. Polignotus of Thasos, Zeuxis and Timagoras of Chalcis, Pythia and Aglaphon followed them, all most celebrated, and after them came the renowned Apelles who was so highly esteemed and honoured for his skill by Alexander the Great, for his wonderful delineation of Calumny and Favour, as Lucian relates. Almost all the painters and sculptors were of high excellence, being frequently endowed by heaven, not only with the additional gift of poetry, as we read in Pacuvius, but also with that of philosophy. Metrodorus is an instance in point, for he was equally skilled as a philosopher and as a painter, and when Apelles was sent by the Athenians to Paulus Emilius to adorn his triumph he remained to teach philosophy to the general's sons. Sculpture was thus generally practised in Greece, where there flourished a number of excellent artists, among them being Phidias of Athens, Praxiteles and Polycletus, very great masters. Lysippus and Pyrgoteles who were of considerable skill in engraving, and Pygmalion in ivory carving in relief, it being recorded of him that he obtained life by his prayers for the figure of a maid carved by him. The ancient Greeks and Romans also honoured and rewarded painting, since they granted the citizenship and very liberal gifts to those who excelled in this art. Painting flourished in Rome to such an extent that Fabius gave a name to his house, subscribing himself in the beautiful things he did in the temple of safety as Fabius the painter. By public decree slaves were prohibited from practising painting, and so much honour was continually afforded by the people to the art and to artists that rare works were sent to Rome among the spoils to appear in the triumphs; excellent artists who were slaves obtained their liberty and received notable rewards from the republic. The Romans bore such a reverence for the art that when the city of Syracuse was sacked Marcellus gave orders that his men should treat with respect a famous artist there, and also that they should be careful not to set fire to a quarter in which there was a very fine picture. This was afterwards carried to Rome to adorn his triumph. To that city in the course of time almost all the spoils of the world were brought, and the artists themselves gathered there beside these excellent works. By such means Rome became an exceedingly beautiful city, more richly adorned by the statues of foreign artists than by those made by natives. It is known that in the little island city of Rhodes there were more than 30,000 statues, in bronze and marble, nor did the Athenians possess less, while those of Olympus and Delphi were more numerous still, and those of Corinth were without number, all being most beautiful and of great price. Does not every one know how Nicomedes, king of Lycia, expended almost all the wealth of his people owing to his passion for a Venus by the hand of Praxiteles? Did not Attalus do the same? who without an afterthought expended more than 6000 sesterces to have a picture of Bacchus painted by Aristides. This picture was placed by Lucius Mummius, with great pomp to adorn Rome, in the temple of Ceres. But although the nobility of this art was so highly valued, it is uncertain to whom it owes its origin. As I have already said, it is found in very ancient times among the Chaldeans, some attribute the honour to the Ethiopians, while the Greeks claim it for themselves. Besides this there is good reason for supposing that the Tuscans may have had it earlier, as our own Leon Batista Alberti asserts, and weighty evidence in favour of this view is supplied by the marvellous tomb of Porsena at Chiusi, where not long ago some tiles of terracotta were found under the ground, between the walls of the Labyrinth, containing some figures in half-relief, so excellent and so delicately fashioned that it is easy to see that art was not in its infancy at that time, for to judge by the perfection of these specimens it was nearer its zenith than its origin. Evidence to the same purport is supplied every day by the quantity of pieces of red and black Aretine vases, made about the same time, to judge by the style, with light carvings and small figures and scenes in bas-relief, and a quantity of small round masks, cleverly made by the masters of that age, and which prove the men of the time to have been most skilful and accomplished in that art. Further evidence is afforded by the statues found at Viterbo at the beginning of the pontificate of Alexander VI., showing that sculpture was valued and had advanced to no small state of perfection in Tuscany. Although the time when they were made is not exactly known, yet from the style of the figures and from the manner of the tombs and of the buildings, no less than by the inscriptions in Tuscan letters, it may be conjectured with great reason that they are of great antiquity, and that they were made at a time when such things were highly valued. But what clearer evidence can be desired than the discovery made in our own day in the year 1554 of a bronze figure representing the Chimæra of Bellerophon, during the excavation of the fortifications and walls of Arezzo. This figure exhibits the perfection of the art attained by the Tuscans. Some small letters carved on a paw are presumed, in the absence of a knowledge of the Etruscan language, to give the master's name, and perhaps the date. This figure, on account of its beauty and antiquity, has been placed by Duke Cosimo in a chamber in his palace in the new suite of rooms which contains my paintings of the deeds of Pope Leo X. The Duke also possesses a number of small bronze figures which were found in the same place. But as the antiquity of the works of the Greeks, Ethiopians, Chaldeans, and Tuscans is enveloped in darkness, and because it is necessary in such matters to base one's opinions on conjectures, although these are not so ill founded that one is in danger of going very far astray, yet I think that anyone who will take the trouble to consider the matter carefully will arrive at the same conclusion as I have, that art owes its origin to Nature herself, that this beautiful creation the world supplied the first model, while the original teacher was that divine intelligence which has not only made us superior to the other animals, but like God Himself, if I may venture to say it. In our own time it has been seen, as I hope to show quite shortly, that simple children, roughly brought up in the woods, have begun to draw by themselves aided by the vivacity of their intellect, instructed solely by the example of these beautiful paintings and sculptures of Nature. Much more then is it probable that the first men, being less removed from their divine origin, were more perfect, possessing a brighter intelligence, and that with Nature as a guide, a pure intellect for master, and the lovely world as a model, they originated these noble arts, and by gradually improving them brought them at length, from small beginnings, to perfection. I do not deny that there must have been an originator, since I know quite well that there must have been a beginning at some time, due to some individual. Neither will I deny that it is possible for one person to help another, and to teach and open the way to design, colour, and relief, because I know that our art consists entirely of imitation, first of Nature, and then, as it cannot rise so high of itself, of those things which are produced from the masters with the greatest reputation. But I will say that an attempt to determine the exact identity of such men is a very dangerous task, and the knowledge when gained would probably prove unprofitable, since we have seen the true and original root of all. But the life and fame of artists depend upon their works which are destroyed by time one after the other in the order of their creation. Thus the artists themselves are unknown as there was no one to write about them and could not be, so that this source of knowledge was not granted to posterity. But when writers began to commemorate things made before their time, they were unable to speak of those of which they had seen no notice, so that those who came nearest to these were the last of whom no memorial remains. Thus Homer is by common consent admitted to be the first of the poets, not because there were none before him, for there were although they were not so excellent, and in his own works this is clearly shown, but because all knowledge of these, such as they were, had been lost two thousand years before. But we will now pass over these matters which are too vague on account of their antiquity and we will proceed to deal with clearer questions, namely, the rise of the arts to perfection, their decline and their restoration or rather renaissance, and here we stand on much firmer ground. The practice of the arts began late in Rome, if the first figures were, as reported, the image of Ceres made of the money of Spurius Caasius, who was condemned to death without remorse by his own father, because he was plotting to make himself king. But although the arts of painting and sculpture continued to flourish until the death of the last of the twelve Cæsars, yet they did not maintain that perfection and excellence which had characterised them before, as is seen as seen in the buildings of the time. The arts declined steadily from day to day, until at length by a gradual process they entirety lost all perfection of design. Clear testimony to this is afforded by the works in sculpture and architecture produced in Rome in the time of Constantine, notably in the triumphal arch made for him by the Roman people at the Colosseum, where we see, that for lack of good masters not only did they make use of marble works carved in the time of Trajan, but also of spoils brought to Rome from various places. These bas-reliefs, statues, the columns, the cornices and other ornaments which belong to another epoch only serve to expose the defects in those parts of the work which are entirely due to the sculptors of the day and which are most rude. Very rude also are some scenes of small figures in marble under the circles and the pediment, representing victories, while between the side arches there are some rivers also very crude and so poor that they leave one firmly under the impression that the art of sculpture had been in a state of decadence for a long while. Yet the Goths and the other barbarous and foreign nations who combined to destroy all the superior arts in Italy had not then appeared. It is true that architecture suffered less than the other arts of design. The bath erected by Constantine at the entrance of the principal portico of the Lateran contains, in addition to its porphyry columns, capitals carved in marble and beautifully carved double bases taken from elsewhere, the whole composition of the building being very well ordered. On the other hand, the stucco, the mosaic and some incrustations of the walls made by the masters of the time are not equal to those which had been taken away for the most part from the temples of the gods of the heathen, and which Constantine caused to be placed in the same building. Constantine observed the same methods, according to report, with the garden of Æquitius in building the temple which he afterwards endowed and gave to Christian priests. In like manner the magnificent church of S. John Lateran, built by the same emperor, may serve as evidence of the same fact, namely, that sculpture had already greatly declined in his time, because the figures of the Saviour and of the twelve apostles in silver, which he caused to be made, were very base works, executed without art and with very little design. In addition to this, it is only necessary to examine the medals of this emperor, and other statues made by the sculptors of his day, which are now at the Capitol, to clearly perceive how far removed they are from the perfection of the medals and statues of the other emperors, all of which things prove that sculpture had greatly declined long before the coming of the Goths to Italy. Architecture, as I have said, maintained its excellence at a higher though not at the highest level. Nor is this a matter for surprise, since large buildings were almost entirely constructed of spoils, so that it was easy for the architects to imitate the old in making the new, since they had the former continually before their eyes. This was an easier task for them than far the sculptors, as the art of imitating the good figures of the ancients had declined. A good illustration of the truth of this statement is afforded by the church of the chief of the apostles in the Vatican, which is rich in columns, bases, capitals, architraves, cornices, doors and other incrustations and ornaments which were all taken from various places and buildings, erected before that time in very magnificent style. The same remarks apply to S. Croce at Jerusalem, which Constantine erected at the entreaty of his mother, Helena; of S. Lorenzo outside the wall, and of S. Agnesa, built by the same emperor at the request of his daughter Constance. Who also is not aware that the font which served for the baptism of the latter and of one of her sisters, was ornamented with fragments of great antiquity? as were the porphyry pillar carved with beautiful figures and some marble candelabra exquisitely carved with leaves, and some children in bas-relief of extraordinary beauty? In short, by these and many other signs, it is clear that sculpture was in decadence in the time of Constantine, and with it the other superior arts. If anything was required to complete their ruin it was supplied by the departure of Constantine from Rome when he transferred the seat of government to Byzantium, as he took with him to Greece not only all the best sculptors and other artists of the age, such as they were, but also a quantity of statues and other beautiful works of sculpture.

After the departure of Constantine, the Caesars whom he left in Italy, were continually building in Rome and elsewhere, endeavouring to make these works as good as possible, but as we see, sculpture, painting and architecture were steadily going from bad to worse. This arose perhaps from the fact that when human affairs begin to decline, they grow steadily worse until the time comes when they can no longer deteriorate any further. In the time of Pope Liberius the architects of the day took considerable pains to produce a masterpiece when they built S. Maria Maggiore, but they were not very happy in the result, because although the building, which is also mostly constructed of spoils, is of very fair proportions, it cannot be denied that, not to speak of other defects, the decoration of the church with stucco and painting above the columns is of very poor design, and that many other things to be seen there leave no doubt as to the degradation of the arts. Many years later, when the Christians were suffering persecution under Julian the Apostate, a church was erected on the Celian Hill to SS. John and Paul, the martyrs, in so inferior a style to the others mentioned above that it is quite clear that at that time, art had all but entirely disappeared. The edifices erected in Tuscany at the same time bear out this view to the fullest extent. The church outside the walls of Arezzo, built to St Donato, bishop of that city, who suffered martyrdom with Hilarion the monk, under the same Julian the Apostate, is in no way superior to the others, and this is only one of many. It cannot be contended that such a state of affairs was due to anything but the lack of good architects, since the church in question, which is still standing, has eight sides, and was built of the spoils of the theatre, colosseum and other buildings erected in Arezzo before it was converted to the Christian faith. No expense has been spared, its columns being of granite and porphyry and variegated marble which, had formerly adorned the ancient buildings. For my own part, I have no doubt, seeing the expense incurred, that if the Aretines had been able to employ better architects they would have produced something marvellous, since what they actually accomplished proves that they spared themselves nothing in order to make this building as magnificent and complete as possible. But as architecture had lost less of its excellence than the other arts, as I have often said before, some good things may be seen there. At the same period the church of S. Maria in Grado was enlarged in honour of St Hilarion, who had lived in the city a long time before he accompanied Donato to receive the palm of martyrdom. But as Fortune, when she has brought men to the top of the wheel, either for amusement or because she repents, usually turns them to the bottom, it came to pass after these things that almost all the barbarian nations rose in divers parts of the world against the Romans, the result being the abasement of that great empire in a short time, and the destruction of everything, notably of Rome herself. That fall involved the complete destruction of the most excellent artists, sculptors, painters and architects who abandoned their profession and were themselves buried and submerged under the debris and ruins of that most celebrated city. The first to go were painting and sculpture, as being arts which served rather for pleasure than for utility, the other art, namely architecture, being necessary and useful for the welfare of the body, continued in use, but not in its perfection and purity. The very memory of painting and sculpture would have speedily disappeared had they not represented before the eyes of the rising generation, the distinguished men of another age. Some of them were commemorated by effigies and by inscriptions placed on public and private buildings, such as amphitheatres, theatres, baths, aqueducts, temples, obelisks, colosseums, pyramids, arches, reservoirs and treasuries, yes, and even on the very tombs. The majority of these were destroyed and obliterated by the barbarians, who had nothing human about them but their shape and name. Among others there were the Visigoths, who having made Alaric their king, invaded Italy and twice sacked Rome without respect for anything. The Vandals who came from Africa with Genseric, their king, did the like. But he, not content with his plunder and booty and the cruelties he inflicted, led into servitude the people there, to their infinite woe, and with them Eudoxia the wife of the Emperor Valentinian, who had only recently been assassinated by his own soldiers. These men had greatly degenerated from the ancient Roman valour, because a great while before, the best of them had all gone to Constantinople with the Emperor Constantine, and those left behind were dissolute and abandoned. Thus true men and every sort of virtue perished at the same time; laws, habits, names and tongues suffered change, and these varied misfortunes, collectively and singly, debased and degraded every fine spirit and every lofty soul. But the most harmful and destructive force which operated against these fine arts was the fervent zeal of the new Christian religion, which, after long and sanguinary strife, had at length vanquished and abolished the old faith of the heathen, by means of a number of miracles and by the sincerity of its acts. Every effort was put forth to remove and utterly extirpate the smaller things from which errors might arise, and thus not only were the marvellous statues, sculptures, paintings, mosaics and ornaments of the false pagan gods destroyed and thrown down, but also the memorials and honours of countless excellent persons, to whose distinguished merits statues and other memorials had been set up by a most virtuous antiquity. Besides all this, in order to build churches for the use of the Christians, not only were the most honoured temples of the idols destroyed, but in order to ennoble and decorate S. Peter's with more ornaments than it then possessed, the mole of Hadrian, now the castle of S. Angelo, was despoiled of its stone columns, as well as of many other things which are now seen in ruins.

Now, although the Christian religion did not act thus from any hatred for talent, but only because of its contempt for the heathen gods, yet the utter ruin of these honourable professions, which entirely lost their form, was none the less entirely due to this burning zeal. That nothing might be wanting to these grave disasters there followed the rage of Totila against Rome, who destroyed the walls, ruined all the most magnificent and noble buildings with fire and sword, burned it from one end to another, and having stripped it of every living creature left it a prey to the flames, so that for the space of eighteen days not a living soul could be found there. He utterly destroyed the marvellous statues, paintings, mosaics and stuccos, so that he left Rome not only stripped of every trace of her former majesty, but destitute of shape and life. The ground floors of the palaces and other building had been adorned with paintings, stuccos and statues, and these were buried under the debris, so that many good things have come to light in our own day. Those who came after, judging everything to be ruined, planted vines over them so that these ruined chambers remained entirely underground, and the moderns have called them grottos and the paintings found there grotesques. The Ostrogoths being exterminated by Narses, the ruins of Rome were inhabited in a wretched fashion when after an interval of a hundred years there came the Emperor Constans of Constantinople, who was received in a friendly manner by the Romans. However he wasted, plundered and carried away everything that had been left in the wretched city of Rome, abandoned rather by chance than by the deliberate purpose of those who had laid it waste. It is true that he was not able to enjoy this booty, for being driven to Sicily by a storm at sea, he was killed by his followers, a fate he richly deserved, and thus lost his spoils, his kingdom and his life. But as if the troubles of Rome had not been sufficient, for the things which had been taken away could never return, there came an army of Saracens to ravage that island, who carried away the property of the Sicilians and the spoils of Rome to Alexandria, to the infinite shame and loss of Italy and of all Christendom. Thus what the popes had not destroyed, notably St Gregory, who is said to have put under the ban all that remained of the statues and of the spoils of the buildings, finally perished through the instrumentality of this traitorous Greek. Not a trace or a vestige of any good thing remained, so that the generations which followed being rough and material, particularly in painting and sculpture, yet feeling themselves impelled by nature and inspired by the atmosphere of the place, set themselves to produce things, not indeed according to the rules of art, for they had none, but as they were instructed by their own intelligence.

The arts of design having arrived at this pitch, both before and during the time that the Lombards ruled Italy, they subsequently grew worse and worse, until at length they reached the lowest depths of baseness. An instance of their utter tastelessness and crudeness may be seen in some figures over the door in the portico of S. Peter's at Rome, in memory of some holy fathers who had disputed for Holy Church in certain councils. Further evidence is supplied by a number of examples in the same style in the city and in the whole of the Exarchate of Ravenna, notably some in S. Maria Rotonda outside that city, which were made shortly after the Lombards were driven from Italy. But I will not deny that there is one very notable and marvellous thing in this church, and that is the vault or cupola which covers it, which is ten braccia across and serves as the roof of the building, and yet is of a single piece and so large that it appears impossible that a stone of this description, weighing more than 200,000 pounds, could be placed so high up. But to return to our point, the masters of that day produced nothing but shapeless and clumsy things which may still be seen to-day. It was the same with architecture, for it was necessary to build, and as form and good methods were lost by the death of good artists and the destruction of good buildings, those who devoted themselves to this profession built erections devoid of order or measure, and totally deficient in grace, proportion or principle. Then new architects arose who created that style of building, for their barbarous nations, which we call German, and produced some works which are ridiculous to our modern eyes, but appeared admirable to theirs. This lasted until a better form somewhat similar to the good antique manner was discovered by better artists, as is shown by the oldest churches in Italy which are not antique, which were built by them, and by the palaces erected for Theoderic, King of Italy, at Ravenna, Pavia, and Modena, though the style is barbarous and rather rich and grand than well conceived or really good. The same may be said of S. Stefano at Rimini and of S. Martino at Ravenna, of the church of S. Giovanni Evangelista in the same city built by Galla Placida about the year of grace 438, of S. Vitale which was built in the year 547, and of the abbey of Classi di fuori, and indeed of many other monasteries and churches built after the time of the Lombards. All these buildings, as I have said, are great and magnificent, but the architecture is very rude. Among them are many abbeys in France built to S. Benedict and the church and monastery of Monte Casino, the church of S. Giovanni Battista built by that Theodelinda, Queen of the Goths, to whom S. Gregory the Pope wrote his dialogues. In this place that queen caused the history of the Lombards to be painted. We thus see that they shaved the backs of their heads, and wore tufts in front, and were dyed to the chin. Their clothes were of broad linen, like those worn by the Angles and Saxons, and they wore a mantle of divers colours; their shoes were open to the toes and bound above with small leather straps. Similar to the churches enumerated above were the church of S. Giovanni, Pavia, built by Gundiperga, daughter of Theodelinda, and the church of S. Salvatore in the same city, built by Aribert, the brother of the same queen, who succeeded Rodoaldo, husband of Gundiberta, in the government; the church of S. Ambruogio at Pavia, built by Grimoald, King of the Lombards, who drove from the kingdom Aribert's son Perterit. This Perterit being restored to his throne after Grimoald's death built a nunnery at Pavia called the Monasterio Nuovo, in honour of Our Lady and of St Agatha, and the queen built another dedicated to the Virgin Mary in Pertica outside the walls. Cunibert, Perterit's son, likewise built a monastery and church to St George called di Coronato, in a similar style, on the spot where he had won a great victory over Alahi. Not unlike these was the church which the Lombard king Luit-prand, who lived in the time of King Pepin, the father of Charlemagne, built at Pavia, called S. Piero, in Cieldauro, or that which Desiderius, who succeeded Astolf, built to S. Piero Clivate in the diocese of Milan; or the monastery of S. Vincenzo at Milan, or that of S. Giulia at Brescia, because all of them were very costly, but in a most ugly and rambling style. In Florence the style of architecture was slightly improved somewhat later, the church of S. Apostolo built by Charlemagne, although small, being very beautiful, because the shape of the columns, although made up of pieces, is very graceful and beautifully made, and the capitals and the arches in the vaulting of the side aisles show that some good architect was left in Tuscany, or had arisen there. In fine the architecture of this church is such that Pippo di Ser Brunnellesco did not disdain to make use of it as his model in designing the churches of S. Spirito and S. Lorenzo in the same city. The same progress may be noticed in the church of S. Mark's at Venice, not to speak of that of S. Giorgio Maggiore erected by Giovanni Morosini in the year 978. S. Mark's was begun under the Doge Giustiniano and Giovanni Particiaco next to S. Teodosio, when the body of the Evangelist was brought from Alexandria to Venice. After the Doge's palace and the church had suffered severely from a series of fires, it was rebuilt upon the same foundations in the Byzantine style as it stands to-day, at a great cost and with the assistance of many architects, in the time of the Doge Domenico Selvo, in the year 973, the columns being brought from the places where they could be obtained. The construction was continued until the year 1140, M. Piero Polani being then Doge, from the plans of several masters who were all Greeks, as I have said. Erected at the same time, and also in the Byzantine style, were the seven abbeys built in Tuscany by Count Hugh, Marquis of Brandenburg, such as the Badia of Florence, the abbey of Settimo, and the others. All these structures and the vestiges of others which are not standing bear witness to the fact that architecture maintained its footing though in a very bastard form far removed from the good antique style. Further evidence is afforded by a number of old palaces erected in Florence in Tuscan work after the destruction of Fiesole, but the measurements of the doors and the very elongated windows and the sharp-pointed arches after the manner of the foreign architects of the day, denote some amount of barbarism. In the year after 1013 the art appears to have received an access of vigour in the rebuilding of the beautiful church of S. Miniato on the Mount in the time of M. Alibrando, citizen and bishop of Florence, for, in addition to the marble ornamentation both within and without, the façade shows that the Tuscan architects were making efforts to imitate the good ancient order in the doors, windows, columns, arches and cornices, so far as they were able, having as a model the very ancient church of S. Giovanni in their city. At the same period, pictorial art, which had all but disappeared, seems to have made some progress, as is shown by a mosaic in the principal chapel of the same church of S. Miniato.

From such beginnings design and a general improvement in the arts began to make headway in Tuscany, as in the year 1016 when the Pisans began to erect their Duomo. For in that time it was a considerable undertaking to build such a church, with its five aisles and almost entirely constructed of marble both inside and out. This church, built from the plans and under the direction of Buschetto, a clever Greek architect from Dulichium, was erected and adorned by the Pisans when at the zenith of their power with an endless quantity of spoils brought by sea from various distant parts, as the columns, bases, capitals, cornices and other stones there of every description, amply demonstrate. Now since all these things were of all sizes, great, medium, and small, Buschetto displayed great judgment in adapting them to their places, so that the whole building is excellently devised in every part, both within and without. Amongst other things he devised the façade, which is made up of a series of stages, gradually diminishing toward the top and consisting of a great number of columns, adorning it with other columns and antique statues. He carried out the principal doors of that façade in the same style, beside one of which, that of the Carroccio, he afterwards received honourable burial, with three epitaphs, one being in Latin verse, not unlike other things of the time:

> *Quod vix mille boum possent juga juncta movere*
> *Et quod vix potuit per mare ferre ratis*
> *Buschetti nisu, quod erat Mirabile visu*
> *Dena puellarum turba levavit onus.*

As I have mentioned the church of S. Apostolo at Florence above, I will here give an inscription which may be read on a marble slab on one of the sides of the high altar, which runs:

> VIII. v. Die vi. Aprilis in resurrectione Domini Karolus Francorum Rex Roma revertens, ingressus Florentiam cum magno gaudio et tripudio succeptus, civium copiam torqueis aureis decoravit. Ecclesia Sanctorum Apostolorum in altari inclusa est laminea plumbea, in qua descripta apparet praefacta fundatio et consecration facta per Archiepiscopum Turpinum, testibus Rolando et Uliverio.

The edifice of the Duomo at Pisa gave a new impulse to the minds of many men in all Italy, and especially in Tuscany, and led to the foundation in the city of Pistoia in 1032 of the church of S. Paolo, in the presence of S. Atto, the bishop there, as a contemporary deed relates, and indeed of many other buildings, a mere mention of which would occupy too much space.

I must not forget to mention either, how in the course of time the round church of S. Giovanni was erected at Pisa in the year 1060, opposite the Duomo and on the same piazza. A marvellous and almost incredible statement in connection with this church is that of an ancient record in a book of the Opera of the Duomo, that the columns, pillars and vaulting were erected and completed in fifteen days and no more. The same book, which may be examined by any one, relates that an impost of a penny a hearth was exacted for the building of the temple, but it does not state whether this was to be of gold or of base metal. The same book states that there were 34,000 hearths in Pisa at that time. It is certain that the work was very costly and presented formidable difficulties, especially the vaulting of the tribune, which is pear-shaped and covered outside with lead. The exterior is full of columns, carving, scenes, and the middle part of the frieze of the doorway contains figures of Christ and the twelve apostles in half-relief and in the Byzantine style.

About the same time, namely in 1061, the Lucchese, in emulation of the Pisans, began the church of S. Martino at Lucea, from the designs of some pupils of Buschetto, there being no other artists then in Tuscany. The façade has a marble portico in front of it containing many ornaments and carvings in honour of Pope Alexander II., who had been bishop of the city just before he was raised to the pontificate. Nine lines in Latin relate the whole history of the façade and of the Pope, repeated in some antique letters carved in marble inside the doors of the portico. The façade also contains some figures and a number of scenes in half-relief below the portico relating to the life of St Martin executed in marble and in the Byzantine style. But the best things there, over one of these doors, were done by Niccola Pisano, 170 years later, and completed in 1233, as will be related in the proper place, Abellenato and Aliprando being the craftsmen at the beginning, as some letters carved in marble in the same place fully relate. The figures by Niccola Pisano show to what an extent the art was improved by him. Most of the buildings erected in Italy from this time until the year 1250 were similar in character to these, for architecture made little or no apparent progress in all these years, but remained stationary, the same rude style being retained. Many examples of this may be seen to-day, but I will not now enumerate them, because I shall refer to them again as the occasion presents itself.

The admirable sculptures and paintings buried in the ruins of Italy remained hidden or unknown to the men of this time who were engrossed in the rude productions of their own age, in which they used no sculptures or paintings except such as were produced by the old artists of Greece, who still survived, making images of clay or stone, or painting grotesque figures and only colouring the first lineaments. These artists were invited to Italy for they were the best and indeed the only representatives of their profession. With them they brought the mosaics, sculptures, and paintings which they themselves produced and thus they taught their methods to the Italians, after their own rough and clumsy style. The Italians practised the art in this fashion up to a certain time, as I shall relate.

As the men of the age were not accustomed to see any excellence or greater perfection than the things thus produced, they greatly admired them, and considered them to be the type of perfection, base as they were. Yet some rising spirits aided by some quality in the air of certain places, so far purged themselves of this crude style that in 1250 Heaven took compassion on the fine minds that the Tuscan soil was producing every day, and directed art into its former channels. And although the preceding generations had before them the remains of arches, colossi, statues, pillars or stone columns which were left after the plunder, ruin and fire which Rome had passed through, yet they could never make use of them or derive any profit from them until the period named. Those who came after were able to distinguish the good from the bad, and abandoning the old style they began to copy the ancients with all ardour and industry. That the distinction I have made between old and ancient may be better understood I will explain that I call ancient the things produced before Constantine at Corinth, Athens, Rome and other renowned cities, until the days of Nero, Vaspasian, Trajan, Hadrian and Antoninus; the old works are those which are due to the surviving Greeks from the days of St Silvester, whose art consisted rather of tinting than of painting. For the original artists of excellence had perished in the wars, as I have said, and the surviving Greeks, of the old and not the ancient manner, could only trace profiles on a ground of colour. Countless mosaics done by these Greeks in every part of Italy bear testimony to this, and every old church of Italy possesses examples, notably the Duomo of Pisa, S. Marco at Venice and yet other places. Thus they produced a constant stream of figures in this style, with frightened eyes, outstretched hands and on the tips of their toes, as in S. Miniato outside Florence between the door of the sacristy and that of the convent, and in S. Spirito in the same city, all the side of the cloister towards the church, and in Arezzo in S. Giuliano and S. Bartolommeo and other churches, and at Rome in old S. Peter's in the scenes about the windows, all of which are more like monsters than the figures which they are supposed to represent. They also produced countless sculptures, such as those in bas-relief still over the door of S. Michele on the piazza Padella at Florence, and in Ognissanti, and in many places, in tombs and ornaments for the doors of churches, where there are some figures acting as corbels to carry the roof, so rude and coarse, so grossly made, and in such a rough style, that it is impossible to imagine worse.

 Up to the present, I have discoursed exclusively upon the origin of sculpture and painting, perhaps more at length than was necessary at this stage. I have done so, not so much because I have been carried away by my love for the arts, as because I wish to be of service to the artists of our own day, by showing them how a small beginning leads to the highest elevation, and how from so noble a situation it is possible to fall to utterest ruin, and consequently, how the nature of these arts resembles nature in other things which concern our human bodies; there is birth, growth, age, death, and I hope by this means they will be enabled more easily to recognise the progress of the renaissance of the arts, and the perfection to which they have attained in our own time. And again, if ever it happens, which God forbid, that the arts should once more fall to a like ruin and disorder, through the negligence of man, the malignity of the age, or the ordinance of Heaven, which does not appear to wish that the things of this world should remain stationary, these labours of mine, such as they are (if they are worthy of a happier fate), by means of the things discussed before, and by those which remain to be said, may maintain the arts in life, or, at any rate, encourage the better spirits to provide them with assistance, so that, by my good will and the labours of such men, they may have an abundance of those aids and embellishments which, if I may speak the truth freely, they have lacked until now.

But it is now time to come to the life of Giovanni Cimabue, who originated the new method of design and painting, so that it is right that his should be the first of the Lives. And here I may remark that I shall follow the schools rather than a chronological order. And in describing the appearance and the arts of the artists, I shall be brief, because their portraits, which I have collected at great expense, and with much labour and diligence, will show what manner of men they were to look at much better than any description could ever do. If some portraits are missing, that is not my fault, but because they are not to be found anywhere. If it chance that some of the portraits do not appear to be exactly like others which are extant, it is necessary to reflect that a portrait of a man of eighteen or twenty years can never be like one made fifteen or twenty years later, and, in addition to this, portraits in black and white are never so good as those which are coloured, besides which the engravers, who do not design, always take something from the faces, because they are never able to reproduce those small details which constitute the excellence of a work, or to copy that perfection which is rarely, if ever, to be found in wood engravings. To conclude, the reader will be able to appreciate the amount of labour, expense, and care which I have bestowed upon this matter when he sees what efforts I have made in my researches.

CIMABUE,
PAINTER OF FLORENCE.

The endless flood of misfortunes which overwhelmed unhappy Italy not only ruined everything worthy of the name of a building, but completely extinguished the race of artists, a far more serious matter. Then, as it pleased God, there was born in the year 1240 in the city of Florence, Giovanni, surnamed Cimabue, of the noble family of the Cimabui, to shed the first light on the art of painting. As he grew up he appeared to his father and others to be a boy of quick intelligence, so that he was accordingly sent to receive instruction in letters to a relation, a master at S. Maria Novella, who then taught grammar to the novices of that convent. Instead of paying attention to his lessons, Cimabue spent the whole day in drawing men, horses, houses, and various other fancies on his books and odd sheets, like one who felt himself compelled to do so by nature. Fortune proved favourable to this natural inclination, for some Greek artists were summoned to Florence by the government of the city for no other purpose than the revival of painting in their midst, since that art was not so much debased as altogether lost. Among the other works which they began in the city, they undertook the chapel of the Gondi, the vaulting and walls of which are to-day all but destroyed by the ravages of time. It is situated in S. Maria Novella, next the principal chapel. In this way Cimabue made a beginning in the art which attracted him, for he often played the truant and spent the whole day in watching the masters work. Thus it came about that his father and the artists considered him so fitted to be a painter that, if he devoted himself to the profession, he might look for honourable success in it, and to his great satisfaction his father procured him employment with the painters. Then, by dint of continual practice and with the assistance of his natural talent, he far surpassed the manner of his teachers both in design and in colour. For they had never cared to make any progress, and had executed their works, not in the good manner of ancient Greece, but in the rude modern style of that time. But although Cimabue imitated the Greeks he introduced many improvements in the art, and in a great measure emancipated himself from their awkward manner, bringing honour to his country by his name and by the works which he produced. The pictures which he executed in Florence bear testimony to this, such as the antipendium to the altar of St Cecilia, and a Madonna in S. Croce, which was then and still is fastened to a pillar on the right hand side of the choir. Subsequently he painted on a panel a St Francis, on a gold ground. He drew this from nature, to the best of his powers, although it was a novelty to do so in those days, and about it he represented the whole of the saint's life in twenty small pictures full of little figures, on a gold ground. He afterwards undertook a large picture for the monks of Vallombrosa in their abbey of S, Trinita at Florence. This was a Madonna with the child in her arms, surrounded by many adoring angels, on a gold ground. To justify the high opinion in which he was already held, he worked at it with great industry, showing improved powers of invention and exhibiting our lady in a pleasing attitude. The painting when finished was placed by the monks over the high altar of the church, whence it was afterwards removed to make way for the picture of Alesso Baldovinetti, which is there to-day. It was afterwards placed in a small chapel of the south aisle in that church. Cimabue next worked in fresco at the hospital of the Porcellana, at the corner of the via Nuova which leads to the Borgo Ognissanti. On one side of the façade, in the middle of which is the principal door, he represented an Annunciation, and on the other side, Jesus Christ with Cleophas and Luke, life-size figures. In this work he abandoned the old manner, making the draperies, garments, and other things somewhat more life-like, natural and soft than the style of the

Greeks, full as that was of lines and profiles as well in mosaics as in painting. The painters of those times had taught one another that rough, awkward and common-place style for a great number of years, not by means of study but as a matter of custom, without ever dreaming of improving their designs by beauty of colouring or by any invention of worth. After this was finished Cimabue again received a commission from the same superior for whom he had done the work at S. Croce. He now made him a large crucifix of wood, which may still be seen in the church. The work caused the superior, who was well pleased with it, to take him to their convent of S. Francesco at Pisa, to paint a picture of St Francis there. When completed it was considered most remarkable by the people there, since they recognised a certain quality of excellence in the turn of the heads and in the fall of the drapery which was not to be found in the Byzantine style in any work executed up to that time not only in Pisa but throughout Italy.

For the same church Cimabue afterwards painted a large picture of Our Lady with the child in her arms, surrounded by several angels, on a gold ground. In order to make room for the marble altar which is now there it was soon afterwards removed from its original situation and placed inside the church, near the door on the left hand. For this work he was much praised and rewarded by the Pisans. In Pisa also he painted a panel of St Agnes surrounded by a number of small figures representing scenes from her life, at the request of the Abbot of S. Paolo in Ripa d'Arno. The panel is to-day over the altar of the Virgin in that church.

The name of Cimabue having become generally known through these works, he was taken to Assisi, a city of Umbria, where, in conjunction with some Greek masters, he painted a part of the vaulting of the lower Church of S. Franceso, and on the walls, the life of Jesus Christ and that of St Francis. In these paintings he far surpassed the Greek masters, and encouraged by this, he began to paint the upper church in fresco unaided, and on the large gallery over the choir, on the four walls, he painted some subjects from the history of Our Lady, that is to say, her death, when her soul is carried to Heaven by Christ on a throne of clouds, and when He crowns her in the midst of a choir of angels, with a number of saints beneath. These are now destroyed by time and dust. He then painted several things at the intersections of the vaulting of that church, which are five in number. In the first one over the choir he represented the four Evangelists, larger than life-size, and so well done, that even to-day they are acknowledged to possess some merit; and the freshness of the flesh colouring shows, that by his efforts, fresco-painting was beginning to make great progress. The second intersection he filled with gilt stars on an ultramarine field. In the third he represented Jesus Christ, the Virgin his mother, St John the Baptist and St Francis in medallions, that is to say, a figure in each medallion and a medallion in each of the four divisions of the vault. The fourth intersection like the second he painted with gilt stars on ultramarine. In the fifth he represented the four Doctors of the church, and beside each of them a member of the four principal religious orders. This laborious undertaking was carried out with infinite diligence. When he had finished the vaults he painted the upper part of the walla on the left side of the church from one end to the other, also in fresco. Near the high altar between the windows and right up to the vaulting he represented eight subjects from the Old Testament, starting from the beginning of Genesis and selecting the most noteworthy incidents. In the space flanking the windows to the point where they terminate at the gallery which runs round the inside of the church, he painted the remainder of the Old Testament history in eight other subjects. Opposite these and corresponding to them he painted sixteen subjects representing the deeds of Our Lady and of Jesus Christ, while on the end wall over the principal entrance and about the rose window above it, he painted the Ascension and the descent of the Holy Spirit upon the apostles. This work which is most extraordinary for richness and beauty, must, in my opinion, have astounded the people of those times, painting having been in such blindness for so long a apace. When I saw it again in the year 1563 it seemed most beautiful, as I reflected how marvellous it was that

Cimabue should see so much light in the midst of so great darkness. But it is worthy of note that of all these paintings those of the vaults are much the best preserved since they are less injured by the dust and other accidents. When these works were finished Giovanni set about painting the walls beneath, namely those beneath the windows, and he did some things there, but as he was summoned to Florence on some affairs of his own, he did not pursue the task, which was finished by Giotto many years after, as will be related when the time comes.

Cimabue having thus returned to Florence painted in the cloister of S. Spirito, where the whole length of wall towards the church is done in the Byzantine style by other masters, events from the life of Christ, in three arches, with considerable excellence of design. At the same time, he sent to Empoli some things executed by him in Florence, which are held in great reverence to this day in the Pieve of that town. He next painted a picture of Our Lady for the church of S. Maria Novella, where it hangs high up between the chapel of the Rucellai and that of the Bardi of Vernio. The figure was of a larger size than any which had been executed up to that time, and the angels about it show that, although be still had the Byzantine style, he was making, some progress towards the lineaments and methods of modern times. The people of that day, who had never seen anything better, considered this work so marvellous, that they carried it to the church from Cimabue's house in a stately procession with great rejoicing and blowing of trumpets, while Cimabue himself was highly rewarded and honoured. It is reported, and some records of the old painters relate that while Cimabue was painting this picture in some gardens near the gate of S. Piero, the old king Charles of Anjou passed through Florence. Among the many entertainments prepared for him by the men of the city, they brought him to see the picture of Cimabue. As it had not then been seen by anyone, all the men and women of Florence flocked thither in a crowd, with the greatest rejoicings, so that those who lived in the neighbourhood called the place Borgo Allegri (Joyful Quarter), because of the rejoicing there. This name it has ever afterwards retained, being in the course of time enclosed within the walls of the city.

At S. Francesco, at Pisa, where Cimabue executed some other works, which have been mentioned above, in the cloister, at a corner beside the doorway leading into the church, is a small picture in tempera by his hand, representing Christ on the cross, surrounded by some angels who are weeping, and hold in their hands certain words written about the head of Christ, and which they are directing towards the ears of our Lady, who is standing weeping on the right hand side; and on the other side to St John the Evangelist, who is there, plunged in grief. The words to the Virgin are: *"Mulier, ecce filius tuus,"* and those to St John: *"Ecce mater tua."* Another angel, separated from these, holds in its hands the sentence: *"Ex illa hora accepit eam discipulus in suam."* In this we perceive how Cimabue began to give light and open the way to inventions, bringing words, as he does here, to the help of his art in order to express his meaning, a curious device certainly and an innovation.

By means of these works Cimabue had now acquired a great name and much profit, so that he was associated with Arnolfo Lapi, an excellent architect of that time, in the building of S. Maria del Fiore, at Florence. But at length, when he had lived sixty years, he passed to the other life in the year 1300, having achieved hardly less than the resurrection of painting from the dead.

He left behind a number of disciples, and among others Giotto, who was afterwards an excellent painter. Giotto dwelt in his master's old house in the via del Cocomero after Cimabue's death. Cimabue was buried in S. Maria del Fiore, with this epitaph made for him by one of the Nini:—

> "Credidit ut Clmabos picturæ castra tenere
> Sic tenuit vivens, nunc tenet astra poli."

I must not omit to say that if the greatness of Giotto, his pupil, had not obscured the glory of Cimabue, the fame of the latter would have been more considerable, as Dante points out in his Commedia in the eleventh canto of the Purgatorio, with an allusion to the inscription on the tomb, where he says:

> "Credette Cimabue nella pintura
> Tener lo campo, ed ora ha Giotto il grido
> Si che la fama di colui oscura."

A commentator on Dante, who wrote during Giotto's lifetime, about 1334, some ten or twelve years after the poet's death, in his explanation of these lines, says the following words in speaking of Cimabue: "Cimabue was a painter of Florence in the time of our author, a man of unusual eminence and so arrogant and haughty withal, that if any one pointed out a fault or defect in his work, or if he discovered any himself, since it frequently happens that an artist makes mistakes through a defect in the materials which he employs, or because of some fault in the instrument with which he works, he immediately destroyed that work, however costly it might be. Giotto was, and is, the most eminent among the painters of the same city of Florence, as his works testify, at Rome, Naples, Avignon, Florence, Padua, and many parts of the world," etc. This commentary is now in the possession of the Very Rev. Vincenzio Borghini, prior of the Innocents, a man distinguished for his eminence, piety and learning, but also for his love for and skill in all the superior arts, so that he has well deserved his judicious selection by Duke Cosimo to be the ducal representative in our academy of design.

Returning to Cimabue, Giotto certainly overshadowed his renown, just as a great light eclipses a much smaller one, and although Cimabue was, as it were, the first cause of the revival of the art of painting, yet Giotto, his disciple, moved by a praiseworthy ambition, and aided by Heaven and by Nature, penetrated deeper in thought, and threw open the gates of Truth to those who afterwards brought art to that perfection and grandeur which we see in our own age. In fact the marvels, miracles, and impossibilities executed at the present time by those who practise this art, and which are to be seen every day, have brought things to such a pitch, that no one marvels at them although they are rather divine than human, and those who make the most praiseworthy efforts may consider themselves fortunate, if, instead of being praised and admired, they escape censure, and even disgrace. The portrait of Cimabue by the hand of Simone of Siena may be seen in the chapter-house of S. Maria Novella, executed in profile in the picture of the Faith. The face is thin the small beard is somewhat red and pointed, and he wears a hood after the fashion of the day, bound gracefully round his head and throat. The one beside him is Simone himself, the designer of the work, who drew himself with the aid of two mirrors placed opposite each other, which have enabled him to draw his head in profile. The soldier in armour between them is said to be Count Guido Novello, lord of Poppi. In concluding this life I have to remark that I have some small things by Cimabue's hand in the beginning of a book in which I have collected drawings by the hand of every artist, from Cimabue onwards. These little things of Cimabue are done like miniatures, and although they may appear rather crude than otherwise to modern eyes, yet they serve to show to what an extent the art of design profited by his labours.

ARNOLFO DI LAPO, FLORENTINE ARCHITECT.

In the preface to these lives I have spoken of some edifices in the old but not antique style, and I was silent respecting the names of the artists who executed the work, because I did not know them. In the introduction to the present life I propose to mention some other buildings made in Arnolfo's time, or shortly before, the authors of which are equally unknown, and then to speak of those which were erected during his lifetime, the architects of which are known, either because they may be recognised through the style of the buildings, or because there is some notice of them in the writings and memorials left by them in the works done. This will not be beside the point, for although the buildings are neither beautiful nor in good style, but only very large and magnificent, yet they are none the less worthy of some consideration.

In the time of Lapo, and of Arnolfo his son, many buildings of importance were erected in Italy and outside, of which I have not been able to find the names of the architects. Among these are the abbey of Monreale in Sicily, the Piscopio of Naples, the Certosa of Pavia, the Duomo of Milan, S. Pietro and S. Petrodio of Bologna, and many others, which may be seen in all parts of Italy, erected at incredible cost. I have seen and examined all these buildings, as well as many sculptures of these times, particularly at Ravenna, but I have never found any memorial of the masters, and frequently not even the date when they were erected, so that I cannot but marvel at the simplicity and indifference to fame exhibited by the men of that age. But to return to our subject. After the buildings just enumerated there arose some persons of a more exalted temper, who, if they did not succeed in lighting upon the good, at least made the attempt.

The first was Buono, of whom I knew neither the country nor the surname, since he himself has put nothing beyond his simple name to the works which he has signed. He was both a sculptor and architect, and he worked at first in Ravenna, building many palaces and churches, and executing some sculptures, in the year of grace 1152. Becoming known by these things, he was summoned to Naples, where he began the Castel Capoano and the Castel dell' Uovo, although they were afterwards finished by others, as will be related. Subsequently, in the time of the Doge Domenico Morosini, he founded the campanile of S. Marco at Venice, with much prudence and good judgment, and so well did he drive the piles and lay the foundations of that tower, that it has never moved a hair's breadth, as many buildings erected in that city before his time may be seen to have done. Perhaps it was from him that the Venetians learned their present method of laying the foundations of the rich and beautiful edifices which are erected every day to adorn that most noble city. At the same time it must be admitted that the tower has no other excellence of its own, either in style or decoration, or indeed anything which is worthy of much praise. It was finished under the Popes Anastasius IV. and Adrian IV. in the year 1154. Buono was also the architect of the Church of S. Andrea at Pistoia, and a marble architrave over the door, full of figures executed in the Gothic style, is his work; On this architrave his name is carved, as well as the date at which the work was done by him, which was in the year 1166. Being afterwards summoned to Florence, he prepared the design for enlarging the Church of S. Maria Maggiore, which was carried out. The church was then outside the city, and was held in veneration, because Pope Pelagius had consecrated it many years before, and because it was in size and style a building of considerable merit.

Buono was next invited by the Aretines to their city, where he built the old residence of the lords of Arezzo, a palace in the Gothic style, and near it a tower for a bell. This building, which was very tolerable for that style, was thrown down in 1533 because it was opposite and too near the fortifications of the city.

The art now began to receive some amount of improvement through the works of a certain Guglielmo, a German by race, as I believe, and some buildings were erected at a great expense and in a slightly better style. In the year 1174 this Guglielmo, in conjunction with Bonanno, a sculptor, is said to have founded the campanile of the Duomo at Pisa, where the following words are carved:

A.D. M..C. 74 campanile hoc fuit fundatum Mense Aug.

But these two architects had not much experience in laying foundations in Pisa, and since they did not drive in piles as they should have done, before they were half through the work, there was a subsidence on one side, and the building leant over on its weaker side, so that the campanile hangs 6-1/2 braccia out of the straight according to the subsidence on that side, and although this appears slight from below, it is very apparent above, so that one is filled with amazement that the tower can stand thus without falling and without the walls being cracked. The reason is that the building is round both within and without, and the stones are so arranged and bound together, that its fall is all but impossible, and it is supported moreover by foundations raised 3 braccia above the ground level, which were made to maintain it after the subsidence had taken place, as may be seen. Had it been square; I am convinced that it would not be standing, to-day, as the corners of the square would have pushed out the sides so that they would have fallen, a thing which frequently happens. And if the Carisenda tower at Bologna, which is square, leans without falling, that is because it is lighter and does not hang over so much, nor is it nearly so heavy a structure as this campanile, which is praised, not because of its design or good style, but simply by reason of its extraordinary position, since to a spectator it does not appear possible that it can remain standing. The Bonanno mentioned above, while he was engaged on the campanile, also executed in 1180 the principal door of the Duomo of Pisa in bronze. On it may be seen these words:

*Ego Bonannus Pis, mea arle hanc portam uno anno perfeci
tempore Benedicti operarii.*

That the art was making steady progress may be seen by the walls of S. Giovanni Lateran at Rome, which were constructed of the spoils of antiquity under Popes Lucius III. and Urban III., when the Emperor Frederick was crowned by the latter, because certain small temples and chapels there, made with these spoils, possess considerable merit of design and contain some things which are worth notice, and this, among others, that the vaults were made of small tubes with compartments of stucco, so as not to overload the side walls of the buildings, a very praiseworthy contrivance for those times. The cornices and other parts show that the artists were helping one another to find the good.

Innocent III. afterwards caused two palaces to be erected on the Vatican hill, and from what can be seen of them they appear to have been in a fairly good style, but since they were destroyed by other popes, and especially by Nicholas V., who pulled down and rebuilt the greater part of the palace, I will say no more about them, except that a part of them may be seen in the great round tower, and a part in the old sacristy of St Peter's. This Innocent III., who wore the tiara for nineteen years, took great delight in architecture, and erected many buildings in Rome, notably the tower of the Conti, so called after the name of his family, from designs by Marchionne, an architect and sculptor of Arezzo. In the year that Innocent died this artist completed the Pieve of Arezzo, as well as the campanile. He adorned the front of the church with three rows of columns, one above the other, in great variety, not only in the shape of the capitals and bases, but even in the shafts, some being heavy, others slender, some bound together in pairs, others in fours. In like manner some are covered with representations of the vine, while others are made to become supporting figures, variously carved. He further introduced many animals of different kinds, which carry the weight of the columns on their backs, the whole exhibiting the strangest and most extravagant fantasies imaginable, not only altogether removed from the excellent antique order, but opposed to all good and reasonable proportion. Yet in spite of all this, anyone who will justly consider the matter will see that he was making strenuous efforts to do well, and possibly he imagined that he had discovered the way in this manner of work and in this wondrous variety. The same artist carved a rather large God the Father, with certain angels in half-relief in the arch over the door of that church in a rude style, together with the twelve months of the year, adding underneath his name, cut in round letters, as was customary, and the date, 1216. It is said that Marchionne also erected for Pope Innocent the old building and church of the hospital of S. Spirito in Sassia, in the Borgo Vecchio at Rome, where some part of the old work may still be seen. Indeed the old church remained standing to our own day, when It was restored in the modern style, with more ornament and design, by Pope Paul III. of the house of the Farnese. In S. Maria Maggiore, also in Rome, he made the marble chapel, which contains the manger of Jesus Christ, in which he placed a portrait of Pope Honorius III., drawn from life. He also made that Pope's tomb, decorating it with ornaments which were somewhat better than, and very different from, the style then prevalent throughout Italy. At the same time also Marchionne made the lateral door of S. Pietro at Bologna, which truly was a very great work for those times, because of the number of sculptures which are seen in it, such as lions in relief, which sustain columns, with men and other animals, also bearing burdens. In the arch above he made the twelve months in relief, with varied fancies, each month with its zodiacal sign, a work which must have been considered marvellous in those times.

    About the same time the order of the friars minors of St Francis was established, which, after it had been confirmed by Pope Innocent

III., increased the general devoutness and the number of friars, not only in Italy, but in every part of the world, to such an extent, that there was scarcely a city of note which did not build churches and convents for them at very great cost, each one according to its ability. Thus brother Elias, who was superior of that order at Assisi, founded a church, dedicated to Our Lady in that place, two years before the death of St Francis, while the saint, as general of the order, was away preaching. After the death of St Francis all Christendom crowded to visit the body of a man, who, both in life and in death, was known to have been so much beloved of God. As every man did alms to the saint according to his ability, it was determined that the church begun by friar Elias should be made much larger and more magnificent. But since there was a scarcity of good architects, and as the work demanded an excellent one, it being necessary to erect the building on a very high hill, round the base of which runs a torrent called Tescio, a German master named Jacopo was brought to Assisi after much deliberation, as being the best man who was then to be found. After he had examined the site and understood the wishes of the friars, who held a chapter general at Assisi for the purpose, he designed a most beautiful church and convent, making it in three stories. One of these was underground, while the two others served as churches, the lower one to be a vestibule with a portico of considerable size about it, the other as the church proper. The ascent from the first to the second was managed by means of a very convenient arrangement of steps, which encircled the chapel and which were divided into two flights for the sake of greater comfort, leading up to the second church. He built this in the form of the letter T, making it five times as long as it was broad, dividing one nave from the other by great stone pillars, uniting them with stout arches, between which he set up the vaulting. This truly monumental work then was carried out from such plans in every detail, except that he did not use the Cross vaulting on the walls between the body of the church and the principal chapel, but employed barrel vaulting for the sake of greater strength. He afterwards placed the altar before the principal chapel of the lower church, and when this was finished he deposited the body of St Francis beneath, after a most solemn translation. And because the tomb of the glorious saint is in the first or lower church, where no one ever goes, and which has its doors walled up, there is a magnificent iron railing about the altar, richly adorned with marble and mosaic which permits the tomb to be seen. On one side of the building were erected two sacristies and a lofty campanile, five times as high as it is broad. Above it there was originally a lofty spire of eight sides, but it was removed because it threatened to fall down. The work was brought to a conclusion in the space of four years and no more by the ability of Master Jacopo the German, and by the industry of friar Elias. After the friar's death twelve strong towers were erected about the lower church in order that the vast erection should never be destroyed; in each of these is a spiral staircase ascending from the ground to the summit. In the course of time, moreover, several chapels were added and other rich ornaments, of which it is not necessary to speak further, as enough has been said about the matter for the present, especially as it is in the power of every one to see how much that is useful, ornamental, and beautiful has been added to this beginning of Master Jacopo, by popes, cardinals, princes, and many other great persons of all Europe.

And now to return to Master Jacopo. By means of this work he acquired such renown throughout Italy that he was invited to Florence by the government of the city, and was afterwards received there with the utmost goodwill. But the Florentines, in accordance with a custom of abbreviating names which they practised then as they do now, called him not Jacopo, but Lapo, all his life, for he settled permanently in that city with all his family. And although at divers times he went away to erect a number of buildings in Tuscany his residence was always at Florence. As examples of such buildings I may cite the palace of the Poppi at Casentino which he built for the count there, who had married the beautiful Gualdrada, with the Casentino as her dower; the Vescovado for the Aretines, and the Palazzo Vecchio of the lords of Pietramela. It was at Florence that he laid the piles of the ponte alla Carraia, then called the ponte Nuovo, in 1218, and finished them in two years. A short while afterwards it was completed in wood, as was then the custom. In the year 1221 he prepared plans for the church of S. Salvadore del Vescovado which was begun under his direction, as was the church of S. Michele on the piazza Padella where there are some sculptures in the style of those days. He next designed a system of drainage for the city, raised the piazza S. Giovanni, and in the time of M. Rubaconte da Mandella of Milan, constructed the bridge which still bears his name. It was he who discovered the useful method of paving the streets with stone, when they had previously been paved only with bricks. He designed the existing Podesta palace, which was originally built for the *amziani*, and finally, after he had designed the tomb of the Emperor Frederick for the abbey of Monreale in Sicily, by the order of Manfred, he died, leaving Arnolfo, his son, heir to his ability, no leas than to his fortune.

Arnolfo, by whose talents architecture was no less improved than painting had been by Cimabue, was born in the year 1232, and was thirty-two years of age at his father's death. He was at that time held in very great esteem, because, not only had he learned all that his father had to teach, but had studied design under Cimabue in order to make use of it in sculpture, so that he was reputed the best architect in Tuscany. Thus not only did the Florentines found, under his direction, the last circuit of the walls of their city in the year 1284, but they also built, after his design, the loggia and pillars of Or San Michele, where grain is sold, constructing it of brick with a simple roof above. It was also in conformity with his advice that when the cliff of the Magnoli fell, on the slope of S, Giorgio above S. Lucia in the via dei Bardi, a public decree was issued the same year that no walls or edifices should ever more be erected in that place seeing that they would always be in danger owing to the undermining of the rock by water. That this is true has been seen in our day in the fall of many buildings and fine houses of the aristocracy. The year after, 1285, he founded the loggia and piazza of the priors, and in the Bödia of Florence he constructed the principal chapel and those on either side of it, restoring both the church and choir, which had originally been built on a much smaller scale by Count Ugo, the founder. For the cardinal Giovanni degli Orsini, papal legate in Tuscany, he built the campanile of that church, which woo some praise among the works of those times, but it did not receive its stone finishing until after the year 1303. His next work was the foundation, in 1294, of the church of S, Croce, where the friars minors are. Arnolfo designed the nave and side aisles of this church on such a large scale that he was unable to vault the space under the roof owing to the great distances, so with much judgment he made arches from pillar to pillar, and on these he placed the roof with stone gutters along the top of the arches to carry off the water, inclined at such an angle that the roof should be safe, as it is, from the danger of damp. This thing was so novel and ingenious that it well deserves the consideration of our day. He next prepared plans for the first cloisters of the old convent of that church, and shortly after he removed from the outside of the church of S. Giovanni all the arches and tombs of marble and stone which were there and put a part of them behind the campanile in the façade of the Canonical Palace, beside the oratory of S. Zanobi, when he proceeded to incrust all the eight sides of the exterior of the church with black Prato marble, removing the rough stone which was originally used with the antique marbles.

In the meantime the Florentines were desirous of erecting buildings in Valdarno above the castle of S. Giovanni and Castelfranco for the convenience of the city and for the supply of victuals to their markets. Arnolfo prepared the plan for this in the year 1295, and gave such general satisfaction, as indeed he had in his other works, that he was awarded the citizenship of Florence.

After these things the Florentines took counsel together, as Giovanni Villani relates in his History, to build a principal church for their city, and to make it so grand and magnificent that nothing larger or finer could be desired by the industry and power of man; and thus Arnolfo prepared the plans for the church of S. Maria del Fiore, a building which it is impossible to praise too highly. He provided that the exterior should be entirely incrusted with polished marble, with all the cornices, pillars, columns, carvings of leaves, figures, and other things which may be seen to-day, and which were brought very near completion, although not quite. But the most marvellous circumstance of all in this undertaking was the care and judgment with which he made the foundations, for in clearing the site, which is a very fine one, other small churches and houses about S. Reparata were involved beside that edifice itself. He made the foundations of this great structure both broad and deep, filling them with good materials, such as gravel and lime, with large stones at the bottom, so that they have been able without difficulty to bear the weight of the huge dome with which Filippo di Ser Brunellesco vaulted the church, as may be seen to-day. The excellence of this initial work was such that the place is still called Lungo i Fondamenti (beside the foundations). The laying of the foundations and the initiation of so great a church was celebrated with much ceremony. The first stone was laid on the day of the Nativity of Our Lady 1298 by the cardinal legate of the Pope, in the presence not only of many bishops and of all the clergy, but also of the podesta, captains, priors, and other magistrates of the city, and indeed of all the people of Florence, the church being called S. Maria del Fiore. Now, as it was estimated that the expenses of this work would be very heavy, as they afterwards proved to be, a tax of four deniers the pound was imposed at the chamber of the commune on everything exported from the city, as well as a tax of two soldi per head yearly. In addition to this, the Pope and the legate offered the most liberal indulgences to those who would contribute alms towards the work. I must not omit to mention, however, that besides the broad foundations of 15 braccia deep, buttresses were, with great foresight, placed at each angle of the eight sides, and it was the presence of these which encouraged Brunellesco to impose a much greater weight there than Arnolfo had originally contemplated.

It is said that when Arnolfo began the two first lateral doors of S. Maria del Fiore, he caused some fig leaves to be carved in a frieze, which were the armorial bearings of his father Lapo, from which it may be inferred that the family of the Lapi, now among the nobility of Florence, derives its origin from him. Others say that Filippo di Ser Brunellesco was also among the descendants of Arnolfo. But I let this pass for what it is worth, and return to Arnolfo, for there are some who say that the Lapi originally came from Figaruolo, a castle situated at the mouth of the Po. I say that for this magnificent achievement he deserved unstinted praise and an immortal renown, since he caused the exterior of the building to be incrusted with marble of various colours, and the interior with hard stone, making even the most insignificant corners of the building of the same stone. But, in order that every one may know the proportions of this marvellous edifice, I will add that from the doorway to the far end of the chapel of St Zanobi the length is 260 braccia, the breadth at the transepts is 166 braccia, that of nave and aisles 66. The nave is 72 braccia high, and the aisles 48. The external circumference of the entire church is 1280 braccia; the cupola, from the ground to the base of the lantern, is 154 braccia; the lantern, without the ball, is 36 braccia high, the ball 4 braccia high, and the cross 8 braccia; the entire cupola, from the ground to the top of the cross, is 202 braccia. But to return to Arnolfo, I say that he was considered so excellent, and so much confidence was felt in him, that nothing of importance was discussed without his advice being first asked. Thus the foundation of the final circuit of the city walls having been finished that same year by the community of Florence, the commencement of which was referred to above, and also the gate towers, and the work being well forward, he began the palace of the Signori, making it similar in design to that which his father Lapo had erected for the counts of Poppi. But he was unable to realise the grand and magnificent conception which he had formed in that perfection which his art and judgment required, because a piazza had been made by the dismantling and throwing down of the houses of the Uberti, rebels against the Florentine people and Ghibellines, and the blind prejudice of certain persons prevailed against all the arguments brought forward by Arnolfo to such an extent that he could not even obtain permission to make the palace square, because the rulers of the city were most unwilling to allow the building to have its foundations in the land of the Uberti, and they would rather suffer the destruction of the south nave of S. Piero Scheraggio than give him free scope in the space designated. They were also desirous that he should include and adapt to the palace the tower of the Fieraboschi, called the Torre della Vacca (Cow Tower), 50 braccia in height, in which the great bell was hung, together with some houses bought by the commune for such a building. For these reasons it is no marvel if the foundations of the palace are awry and out of the square, as, in order to get the tower in the middle and to make it stronger, he was obliged to surround it with the walls of the palace. These were found to be in excellent condition in the year 1561 by Giorgio Vasari, painter and architect, when he restored the palace in the time of Duke Cosimo, Thus, as Arnolfo filled the tower with good materials, it was easy for other masters to erect upon it the lofty campanile which we see to-day, since he himself finished no more than the palace in the space of two years. It was in later years that the building received those improvements to which it owes its present grandeur and majesty.

After all these things, and many others not less useful than beautiful, Arnolfo died at the age of seventy, in the year 1300, about the time when Giovanni Villani began to write the general history of his times. And since he left S. Maria del Fiore not only with its foundations laid, but saw three principal apses under the cupola vaulted in, to his great praise, he deserves the memorial set up to him in the church on the side opposite the campanile, with these lines carved in the marble in round letters:—

> "Anno millenis centum bis octo nogenis
> Venit legatus Roma bonitate donatus
> Qui lapidem fixit fundo, simul et benedixit

Praesule Francisco, gestante pontificatum
Istud ab Arnolpho templum fuit aedificatum
Hoc opus insigne decorans Florentia digne
Reginæ coeli construxit mente fideli
Quam tu, Virgo pia, semper defende, Maria,"

    I have written the life of Arnolfo with the greatest possible brevity because, although his works do not nearly approach the perfection of those of the present time, yet he none the less deserves to be remembered with affection, since, in the midst of so great darkness, he pointed out the road to perfection to those who came after him. The portrait of Arnolfo, by the hand of Giotto, may be seen in S. Croce, next to the principal chapel, where the friars are mourning the death of St Francis. He is represented in the foreground as one of the two men who are talking together. A representation of the exterior of the church of S. Maria del Fiore, with the dome, by the hand of Simon of Siena, may be seen in the chapter-house of S. Maria Novella. It was taken from the actual model of wood which Arnolfo made. From this representation it is clear that Arnolfo proposed to begin to vault his space, starting immediately above the first cornice, whilst Filippo di Ser Brunellesco, desiring to lighten the weight and make the appearance of the structure more graceful, added above this the whole of the space which contains the round windows before he began his vaulting. This matter would be even more obvious than it is had not the negligence and carelessness of those who had charge of the works of S. Maria del Fiore in past years allowed Arnolfo's own model, as well as those of Brunellesco and others, to be lost.

NICCOLA AND GIOVANNI PISANI, SCULPTORS AND ARCHITECTS.

Having discussed the arts of design and painting in dealing with Cimabue, and that of architecture in the life of Arnolfo Lapo, we now propose to treat of sculpture, and of the very important architectural works of Niccola and Giovanni Pisani. Their achievements in both sculpture and architecture are alike remarkable for the manner in which they have been conceived as well as for the style in which they are executed, since to a great extent they emancipated themselves from the clumsy and ill-proportioned Byzantine style in both arts, showing more originality in the treatment of their subjects and arranging their figures in better postures.

Niccola Pisani was originally associated with some Greek sculptors who were engaged upon the figures and other ornaments in relief for the Duomo at Pisa and the church of San Giovanni there. Among the spoils brought home by the Pisan fleet was a very fine sarcophagus on which was an admirable representation of the chase of Meleager, hunting the Calydonian boar. Both the nude and the draped figures of this composition are executed with much skill, while the design is perfect. This sarcophagus, on account of its beauty, was afterwards placed by the Pisans in the façade of the Duomo opposite S, Rocco, against the principal door on that side. It originally served as a tombstone for the mother of the Countess Matilda, if we may credit the inscription cut in the marble:

Anno Domini MCXVI. Kal. Aug. obiit D. Matilda felisis memoriae comitissa, quae pro anima genetricis suae D. Beatricis comitissae venerabilis in hoc tumba honorabili quiescents in multis partis mirificc hanc dotavit ecclesiam, quarum animae requiescent in pace.

And then follows:

Anno Domini MCCCIII. sub dignissimo optrario Burgundio Tadi occasione graduum fiendorum per ipsum circa ecclesiam supradictam tumba superius notata bis trantlata fuit, nunc de sedibus primis in ecclesiam, nunc de ecclesia in hunc locum, ut cernitis eccelentem.

Niccola, considering the excellence of this work, which greatly delighted him, applied such diligence in imitating that style, studying carefully both the sarcophagus and other excellent sculptures on other antique sarcophagi, that before long he was considered the best sculptor of his time. There was indeed, after Arnolfo, no other sculptor of repute in Tuscany except Fuccio, a Florentine architect and sculptor. Fuccio designed S. Maria sopra Arno at Florence in 1229, putting his name over the door. The marble tomb of the queen of Cyprus in the church of St Francis of Assisi is also his work. It contains a number of figures, the principal one being the queen herself, seated on a lion, as emblematical of her strength of mind. She had bequeathed a large sum of money for the completion of these works.

Niccola having proved himself a much greater master than Fuccio, was summoned to Bologna in 1225 to make a marble tomb for St Domenic Calagora, founder of the order of the Friars Preachers, then recently deceased. Having, arranged with those who had charge of the work, he designed a tomb full of figures, as may be seen at this day. The task was completed in 1231, and the finished tomb was greatly praised, it being considered a remarkable work, and the best piece of sculpture executed up to that time. He further made plans for the church there and for a great part of the convent. On returning to Tuscany, he learned that Fuccio had set out from Florence and was gone to Rome, at the time when the Emperor Frederick was crowned there by Honorius. From Rome Fuccio accompanied Frederick to Naples, where he finished the castle of Capoana, now called "la Vicheria," where all the courts of that kingdom are held. He also completed the Castel del' Uovo, founding the towers, made the gate on the side of the River Volturno at Capua, constructed a park near Gravina for fowling, enclosing it by a wall, and made another at Amalfi for winter hunting, besides many other things which are omitted for the sake of brevity.

Meanwhile Niccola was staying at Florence, obtaining practice not only in sculpture but also in architecture by means of the works which were in progress throughout Italy, but especially in Tuscany, with some amount of good design. Thus he contributed not a little to the abbey of Settimo, left unfinished by the executors of Count Hugh of Brandenburg, as the other six had been, as we have noticed above. For although an inscription on the campanile of the abbey reads *"Gugliel me fecit"* yet it is clear from the style of the work that it was carried out under the control of Niccola. At the same time he was building the old palace of the *anziani* at Pisa. This building has been dismantled at the present time by Duke Casino, who has used a part of the old edifice for the erection of the magnificent palace and convent of the new order of the knights of St Stephen, after the designs of Giorgio Vasari, Aretine painter and architect, who has done his best with the old walls, to adapt them to the modern style. Niccola designed many other palaces and churches at Pisa, and he was the first, after the loss of good methods of construction, who introduced the founding of buildings at Pisa upon pillars connected by arches, first driving piles in under the pillars. This method renders the building absolutely secure, as is shown by experience, whereas without the piles, the foundations are liable to give way, causing the walls to fall down. The church of S. Michele in Borgo of the monks of Gamaldoli was also built after his plans. But the most beautiful, ingenious and fanciful piece of architecture that Niccola ever constructed was the campanile of S. Niccola at Pisa, where the friars of St Augustine are. Outside it is octagonal, but the interior is round with a winding staircase rising to the top leaving the middle space void like a well, while on every fourth step there are columns with lame arches, which follow the curve of the building. The spring of the vaulting rests upon these arches, and the ascent is of such sort that anyone on the ground always sees those who are going up, those who are at the top see those who are on the ground, while those who are in the middle see both those who are above and those below. This curious invention was afterwards adopted by Bramante in a better style with more balanced measurements and richer ornamentation, for Pope Julius II. in the Belvedere at Rome, and by Antonio da Sangallo for Pope Clement VII. in the well at Orvieto, as will be said when the time comes.

To return to Niccola who excelled no less as a sculptor than as an architect. For the church of S. Martino at Lucca he executed a deposition from the Cross, which is under the portico above the minor doorway on the left hand as one enters the church. It is executed in marble, and is full of figures in half relief, carried out with great care, the marble being pierced through, and the whole finished in such style as to give rise to hopes in those who first practised this art with the most severe labour, that one would soon come who would give them more assistance with greater ease. It was Niccola also who in the year 1240 designed the church of S. Jacopo at Pistoia, and set some Tuscan masters to work there in mosaic, who did the vaulting of the apse. But although it was considered a difficult and costly thing at the time, it rather moves one to laughter and compassion to-day, and not to admiration, oh account of the poorness of the design, a defect which was prevalent not only in Tuscany, but throughout Italy, where the number of buildings and other things erected without method and without design betray the poverty of their minds no less than the bountiful riches lavished on them by the men of their day; a wasteful expenditure of wealth, because there was no masters capable of executing in a good style the things which they made for them. Now Niccola was steadily increasing his renown in both sculpture and architecture, and was of greater account than the sculptors and architects who were then at work in the Romagna, as one may see in S. Ippolito and S. Giovanni at Faenza, in the Duomo of Ravenna, in S.

Francesco, in the houses of the Traversari, and in the church of Prato, and at Rimini, in the public palace, in the houses of the Malatesti, and in other buildings which are much worse than the old buildings erected in Tuscany at the same time; and what is here said of the Romagna, may be repeated with even more truth of a part of Lombardy. It is only necessary to see the Duomo of Ferrara and the other buildings erected for the Marquis Azzo, to perceive at once how different they are from the Santo of Padua, built from Niccola's model, and from the church of the friars minors at Venice, both of them magnificent and famous buildings.

In Niccola's day there were many moved by a laudable spirit of emulation, who applied themselves more diligently to sculpture than they had done before, especially in Milan, where many Lombards and Germans were gathered for the building of the Duomo. These were afterwards scattered throughout Italy by the dissensions which arose between the Milanese and the Emperor Frederick. They then began to compete among themselves, both in carving marble and in erecting buildings, and produced works of some amount of excellence. The same thing happened in Florence after the works of Arnolfo and Niccola were seen. The latter, while the little church of the Misericordia on the piazza S. Giovanni was being built after his designs, carved a marble statue of Our Lady with St Domenic and another saint on either side, which may still be seen on the façade of that church. It was also in Niccola's time that the Florentines began to demolish many towers, erected previously in a rude style in order that the people should suffer less by their means in the frequent collisions between the Guelphs and Ghibellines, or for the greater security of the commonweal. One of these, the tower of Guardamorto, situated on the piazza S; Giovanni, presented unusual difficulty to those who wished to destroy it because the walls were so well knit that the stones could not be removed with the pickaxe, and also because the tower was a very high one. Niccola, however, caused a piece to be cut out of one of the sides of the tower and closed the gap with wooden supports, a braccia and a half long, he then set fire to the props, and so soon as these were consumed the tower fell down and was totally destroyed. The idea seemed so ingenious and so well adapted for such emergencies, that it afterwards came into general use, so that whenever it was necessary to destroy a building, the task was speedily accomplished in this most facile manner.

Niccola was present when the foundations of the Duomo of Siena were laid, and he designed the Church of S. Giovanni in that city. He went back to Florence in the year of the return of the Guelphs, and designed the church of S. Trinita, and the women's convent at Faenza, pulled down in recent years to make the citadel. Being subsequently summoned to Naples, and not wishing to abandon his enterprises in Tuscany, he sent thither his pupil Maglione, sculptor and architect, who in the time of Conrad afterwards built the church of S. Lorenzo at Naples, finished a part of the Vescorado, and made some tombs there, in which he closely imitated the manner of his master, Niccola. In the meantime Niccola went to Volterra, in the year that the people of that place came under the dominion of the Florentines (1254), in response to a summons, because they wished him to enlarge their Duomo, which was small; and although it was very irregular, he improved its appearance, and made it more magnificent than it was originally. Then at length he returned to Pisa and made the marble pulpit of S. Giovanni, devoting all his skill to it, so that he might leave a memory of himself in his native place. Among other things in it he carved the Last Judgment, filling it with a number of figures, and if they are not perfectly designed they are at any rate executed with patience and diligence, as may be seen; and because he considered that he had completed a work which was worthy of praise, as indeed he had, he carved the following lines at the foot:

> "Anno milleno bis centum bisque trideno.
> Hoc opus insigne sculpsit Nicola Pisanus."

The people of Siena, moved by the fame of this work, which greatly delighted not only the Pisans, but whoever saw it, assigned to Niccola the task of making for their Duomo the pulpit from which the gospel is sung, at the time when Guglielmo Mariscotti was praetor. In this Niccola introduced a number of subjects from the life of Jesus Christ, especially remarkable for the figures which they contain, which stand out in high relief, all but severed from the background, a work of great difficulty. He likewise designed the church and convent of S. Domenico at Arezzo, for the lords of Pietramela who built it, and at the request of the bishop Ubertini he restored the Pieve of Cortona, and founded the church of S. Margherita for the friars of St Francis, on the highest ground in that city. The fame of Niccola was continually on the increase, owing to these works, so that in 1267 he was invited by Pope Clement IV. to Viterbo, where, among many other things he restored the church and convent of the Friars Preachers. From Viterbo he went to Naples to King Charles, who having defeated and slain Curradino on the plain of Tagliacozzo, founded a wealthy church and abbey on the spot, for the burial-place of the large number of men who had fallen on that day, ordaining that prayers should be offered for their souls both day and night by many monks. King Charles was so delighted with the work of Niccola in this building that he loaded him with honours and rewards. On the way back from Naples to Tuscany Niccola stayed to take part in the building of S. Maria at Orvieto, where he worked in the company of some Germans, making figures in high relief in marble for the front of that church, and more particularly a Last Judgment, comprising both Paradise and Hell; and as he took the greatest pains to render the souls of the blessed in Paradise as beautifully as he possibly could, so he introduced into his Hell the most fantastic shape of devils imaginable, all intent on tormenting the souls of the damned. In this work not only did he surpass the Germans who were working there, but even himself, to his great glory, and because he introduced a great number of figures and spared no pains, it has been praised even to our own day by those whose judgment does not extend beyond such circumstances.

Among other children Niccola had a son called Giovanni, who was always with his father, and under his care learned both sculpture and architecture, so that in the course of a few years he became not only the equal of his father, but his superior in some things. Thus, as Niccola was already old, he withdrew to Pisa and lived quietly there, leaving the control of everything to his son. At the death in Perugia of Pope Urban IV., Giovanni was sent for to make the tomb, which he executed in marble; but it was afterwards thrown down, together with that of Pope Martin IV., when the Perugians enlarged their Vescovado, so that only a few remains may be seen to-day dispersed about the church. At the same time the Perugians, thanks to the skill and industry of a friar of the Silvestrini, had brought to their city from the hill of Pacciano, two miles away, an abundance of water. The ornamentation of the fountain in both bronze and marble was entrusted to Giovanni, so that he thereupon set his hand to the work, making three basins, one above the other, two in marble and one in bronze. The first is placed at the top of a flight of steps of twelve faces, the second rests on some pillars which rise from the centre of the first, while the third, which is of bronze, is supported by three figures; and in the middle are griffins, also of bronze, which throw out water on every side. And as Giovanni considered that he had executed an excellent piece of work, he put his name to it. The arches and conduits of this fountain, which cost 160,000 gold ducats, were found to be very much worn and broken about the year 1560, but Vincenzio Danti, sculptor of Perugia, contrived a means, to his great glory, of bringing water to the fountain in the original way, without rebuilding the arches, which would have been very costly. When the work was finished Giovanni felt anxious to return to see his old father, who was sick, and he set out from Perugia intending to return to Pisa; but on his way through Florence he was compelled to stay there, to assist with others at the mills of the Arno, which were being made at S. Gregorio, near the piazza dei Mozzi. But at length receiving word that his father Niccola was dead, he departed for Pisa, where he was received with great honour by all the city, on account of his worth, since everyone rejoiced that although Niccola was lost to them, yet they still possessed Giovanni, who inherited his father's ability as well as his property. Nor were they deceived in him when the time of testing arrived, for when it was necessary to do some few things for the tiny but highly-ornate church of S. Maria della Spina, the task was entrusted to Giovanni. He therefore put his hand to the work and brought the ornamentation of that oratory to the state of perfection which it possesses to-day, the more so as he introduced the portrait of Niccola, taken from life, executed to the best of his ability. When the Pisans had seen this they decided to entrust him the construction of the Campo Santo, which is against the piazza del Duomo towards the walls, as they had long desired and talked of having a place for the burial of all their dead, both gentle and simple, so that the Duomo should not be filled with tombs, or for other reasons. Thus Giovanni with good designs and great judgment erected the building as we now see it, in style, size, and marble ornamentation, and as no expense was spared, it was roofed with lead. On the outside of the principle entrance may be read these words, carved in the marble:

> "A.D. MCCLXXVIII. tempore Domini Federigi archiepiscopi Pisani, et Domini Terlati potestatis operario Orlando Sardella, Johanne magistro aedificante."

In the completion of this work, 1283, Giovanni went to Naples, where he erected the Castel Nuovo for King Charles; and in order to enlarge it and add to its strength, he was compelled to pull down a number of houses and churches, among them a convent of the friars of St Francis, which was afterwards rebuilt on a larger and grander scale at some distance from the castle, with the title of S. Maria della Nuova. After these building had been set on foot and were well advanced, Giovanni left Naples to return to Tuscany, but when he reached Siena he was not allowed to go farther, but was induced to design the façade of the Duomo of that city, which was subsequently erected from his plans in a very rich and magnificent style. In the following year, 1286, while the bishop's palace at Arezzo was being built from the design of Margaritone, architect of Arezzo, Giovanni was fetched from Sienna to that city by Guglielmo Ubertini, the bishop there. He there executed in marble the table of the high altar, full of figures cut in relief of leaves and other ornaments, dividing the work into compartments by fine mosaics and enamels on silver plates, fixed into the marble with great care. In the midst is Our Lady with the child at her neck, and on one side of her is St Gregory the Pope (which is a portrait of Pope Honorius IV. drawn from life), and on the other side St Donato, the bishop and protector of that city, whose body, with those of St Antilia and other saints, rest under that same altar. And as the altar stands out by itself, the sides are decorated with small representations in bas-relief from the life of St Donato, and the work is crowned with a series of niches, full of marble figures in relief, of exquisite workmanship. On the Madonna's breast is an ornament shaped like a gold casket, containing, if report be true, jewels of great value, although it is believed that they, as well as some other small figures on the top and about the work, were taken away by the soldiers, who do not often respect the even most Holy Sacrament. On these works the Aretines expended 30,000 florins, as is found in some records. Nor does this appear impossible, because at that time it was considered to be a thing of the most precious and rare description, so that when Frederick Barbarossa returned from his coronation at Rome, and was passing through Arezzo many years after its completion, he praised and admired it infinitely, and indeed with good cause, since the joints are constructed of tiny pieces so excellently welded together, that to an inexperienced eye, the whole work seems to be made in one piece. In the same church Giovanni made the chapel of the Ubertini, a noble family, and lords of a castle, as they still are, though they were formerly of greater estate. He adorned this with many marble ornaments, which are to-day covered over by many large ornaments of stone, placed there in the year 1535, after plans by Giorgio Vasari, for the support of an organ of extraordinary excellence and beauty which rests upon them. Giovanni Pisano also designed the church of S. Maria dei Servi, which has been destroyed in our day, together with many palaces of the noblest families of the city, for the reasons mentioned above. I must not omit to note that in the construction of the marble altar Giovanni was assisted by some Germans, who associated with him, rather for the sake of learning the art, than for gain, and who profited so much by his instruction, that when they went to Rome, after the completion of that work, they served Pope Boniface VIII. in many works of sculpture executed for St Peter's, and also in architecture, when he made Civita Castellana. They were, moreover, sent by that Pope to S. Maria at Orvieto, where they made a number of marble figures for the façade of the church, which were very tolerable for those times. But among the others who assisted Giovanni in his undertakings for the Vescovado at Arezzo, were Agostino and Agnolo, sculptors and architects of Siena, who far surpassed all the others, as will be said in the proper place. But to return to Giovanni. When he left Orvieto he came to Florence to see Arnolfo's building of S. Maria del Fiore, and also to see Giotto, of whom he had heard a great deal elsewhere; but no sooner had he arrived in Florence than he was appointed by the intendants of the fabric of S. Maria del Fiore to make the Madonna, which stands between two small angels above the door of that church, which leads into the canons' quarters, a work much praised at the time. He next made the small font for S. Giovanni, containing representations from the life of that saint in half-relief. Proceeding thence to Bologna he directed the construction of the principal chapel of the church of St Domenico, in which he was also commissioned to make the marble altar by Teodorico Borgognoni of Lucca, then bishop, a friar of that order. Later on (1298), in the same place, he made the marble table in which are Our Lady and eight other figures, all of very tolerable workmanship. In the year 1300, when Niccola da Prato was at Florence as cardinal legate of the Pope, for the purpose of settling the discords among the Florentines, he caused Giovanni to build a nunnery for him at Prato, which was called S. Niccola after him, and in the same district he made him restore the convent of S. Domenico, as well as that of Pistoia, in both of which the arms of that cardinal may still be seen. And since the Pistolese held the name of Niccola, Giovanni's father, in great respect, because he had displayed his talents in that city, they commissioned Giovanni to make a marble pulpit for the church of S. Andrea, similar to that which he had made for the Duomo of Siena, and in competition with one which had been made shortly before for the church of S. Giovanni Evangelista by a German, which had been much praised. Giovanni finished his task in four years, dividing the work into four subjects from the life of Jesus Christ, and further introducing a Last Judgment, working with the utmost diligence in order to equal, and perhaps surpass, that celebrated pulpit of Orvieto. About the pulpit above some columns which support it and in the architrave he carved the following lines, since he thought that he had completed a great and beautiful work, as indeed he had, considering the attainments of the age:

> Hoc opus sculpsit Johannes, qui res non egit inanes.
> Nicoli natus . . . meliora beatus
> Quam genuit Pisa, doctum super omnia visa.

At the same time Giovanni made the holy water vessel in marble for the same church of S. Giovanni Evangelista, borne by three figures, Temperance, Prudence and Justice, and as it was then considered a work of great beauty, it was placed in the middle of the church as a remarkable object. Before he left Pistoia he made the model for the campanile of S. Jacopo, the principal church of the city, although the work was not then begun. The tower is situated beside the church in the piazza of S. Jacopo, and bears the date A.D. 1301. On the death of Pope Benedict IX. at.

Perugia, Giovanni was sent for to make his tomb, which he executed in marble in the old church of S. Domenico of the Friars Preachers, placing the Pope's effigy, taken from life, and in his pontifical habit, upon the sarcophagus with two angels holding a curtain, one on either side, and Our Lady above, between two saints, executed in relief, as well as many other ornaments carved on the tomb. Similarly in the new church of the same order he made the tomb of M. Niccolo Guidalotti of Perugia, bishop of Recanati, who was the founder of the new University of Perugia. In this same new church, which had been previously founded by others, he directed the construction of the principal nave, and this part of the building was much more securely founded than the rest, which leans over to one side, and threatens to fall down, owing to the faulty laying of the foundations. And in truth he who undertakes to build or perform any things of importance ought always to take the advice, not of those who know little, but of those most competent to help him, so that he may not afterwards have to repent with loss and shame that he was ill-directed when he was in most need of assistance.

When he had completed his labours in Perugia, Giovanni wished to go to Rome to learn from the few antique things there, as his father had done, but being hindered by good reasons, he was never able to fulfil his desire, chiefly because he heard that the court had just gone to Avignon. So he returned to Pisa, where Nello di Giovanni Falconi, craftsman, entrusted to him the great pulpit of the Duomo, which is fixed to the choir on the right hand side as one approaches the high altar. He set to work on this, and on a number of figures in full relief, three braccia high, which he intended to use for it, and little by little he brought it to its present form, resting in part on the said figures and in part upon lions, while on the sides he represented scenes from the life of Jesus Christ. It is truly a sin that so much money, such diligence and labour should not be accompanied by good design, and that it should lack that perfection, invention, grace, and good style which any work of our own day would possess, even were it executed at much less cost and with less difficulty.

Yet it must have excited no small admiration among the men of the time, who had only been accustomed to see the rudest productions. It was finished in the year 1320, as appears in certain lines which run round the pulpit and read thus:

> "Laudo Deum verum, per quem sunt optima rerum
> Qui dedit has puras homini formate figuras;
> Hoc opus, his annis Domini sculpsere Johannis
> Arte manus sole quandam, natique Nicole.
> Cursis undenis tercentum milleque plenis."

There are thirteen other lines, which I do not write here, because I do not wish to weary the reader, and because these are sufficient to show not only that the pulpit is by the hand of Giovanni, but that the men of that time were alike in their shortcomings. A Madonna between St John the Baptist and another saint may be seen over the principal of the door of the Duomo; it is in marble, and by the hand of Giovanni, and the figure kneeling at her feet is said to be Piero Gambacorti, the warden. However this may be, the following words are cut in the pedestal, on which the image of Our Lady stands:

> "Sub Petri cura haec pia fuit scutpta figura
> Nicoli nato sculptore Johanne vocato."

Moreover there is another marble Madonna, by Giovanni, over the side door, which is opposite the campanile, while on one side of her kneel a lady and two children, representing Pisa, and on the other side the Emperor Henry. On the base are these words:

> Ave gratia plena, Dominus teum,

and then—

> Nobilis arte manus sculpsit Johannes Pisanus
> Sculpsit sub Burgundio Tadi benigno.

And about the base of Pisa:

> Virginis ancilla sum Pisa quieta sub illa,

and about the base of Henry:

> Imperat Henricus qui Cliristo fertur amicus.

In the old Pieve at Prato, beneath the altar of the principal chapel, was preserved for many years the girdle of Our Lady, which Michele da Prato had brought back with him from the Holy Land, and had deposited it with Uberto, provost of the church, who laid it in the said place, where it was always held in great veneration. In the year 1312 an attempt to steal it was made by a native of Prato, a man of a most evil life, another Ser Ciappelletto, but he was discovered and put to death for sacrilege. Moved by this deed, the people of Prato proposed to make a strong and suitable receptacle in which the girdle should be kept with greater security, and sent for Giovanni, who was now an old man. Acting upon his advice, they constructed the chapel in the principal church, where Our Lady's girdle now reposes. They then greatly increased their church also from his plans, and incrusted both the church and the campanile with white and black marble on the outside, as may be seen. At length Giovanni died at a ripe old age in the year 1320, after having completed many works in sculpture and architecture besides those which are mentioned here. And in truth a great debt is due to him and to Niccola his father, since in an age which lacked every element of good design, in the midst of all the darkness they threw so much light on those arts in which they were really excellent.

Giovanni was honourably buried in the Campo Santo, in the same tomb in which his father Niccola was laid. Many disciples of his flourished after him, but especially Lino, sculptor and architect of Siena, who made the chapel which contains the body of St Ranieri in the Duomo of Pisa, richly decorated with marble; and also the baptismal font of that cathedral which bears his name. Let no one marvel that Niccola and Giovanni executed so many works, for besides the fact that they lived to a good age, they were the foremost masters in Europe of their time, so that nothing of importance was undertaken without their taking part in it, as may be seen in many inscriptions besides those which have been quoted. Whilst speaking of these two sculptors and architects, I have often referred to Pisa, so that I do not hesitate at this stage to quote some words written on the pedestal of a vase mounted on a column of porphyry and supported by a lion, which is situated on the steps of the new hospital there. They are as follows:

"This is the talent which the Emperor Cæesar gave to Pisa, to the intent that the tribute which they rendered to him should be regulated thereby. The talent was set upon this column and lion in the time of Giovanni Rosso, master of the work of S. Maria Maggiore, Pisa, A.D. MCCCXIII., the second Indiction, in March."

ANDREA TAFI, FLORENTINE PAINTER.

Just as the works of Cimabue excited no small amount of wonder in the men of that time, since he introduced a better design and form into the art of painting, whereas they had only been accustomed to see things executed on the Byzantine style, so the mosaics of Andrea Tafi, who was a contemporary, were much admired and even considered divine, for the people of that day, who had not been used to see anything different did not think that it was possible to produce better works in that art. But in truth, as he was not the most capable man in the world, and having reflected that working in mosaic was more valued on account of its greater durability, be left Florence for Venice, where some Greek painters were working in mosaic at S. Marco. There he formed a close intimacy with them, and by dint of persuasion, money, and promises he at length contrived to bring to Florence Master Apollonio, a Greek painter, who taught him how to bake the glass of the mosaic, and how to make the cement in which to fix it. With him Andrea worked at the tribune of S. Giovanni, doing the upper part which contains the Dominions, Principalities, and Powers. Afterwards when he had gained more experience, he did the Christ which is in the same church above the principal chapel as will be related below. But as I have mentioned S. Giovanni, I will take this opportunity of saying that that ancient sanctuary is incrusted both within and without with marbles of the Corinthian order, and not only is it perfectly proportioned and finished in all its parts, but most beautifully adorned with doors and windows. Each face is supplied with two columns of granite, 11 braccia high, forming three compartments, above which are the architraves, which rest on the columns, to carry the whole weight of the double roof, which is praised by modern architects as a remarkable thing, and justly, because this church helped to demonstrate to Filippo di Ser Brunellesco, Donatello, and the other masters of their time what possibilities there were in that art. They all studied architecture from this building and from the church of S. Apostolo at Florence, a work of such a good style that it approaches the true antique, since, as I have said before, all the columns are measured and arranged with such care that much may be learned from a careful examination of the entire structure. But I will refrain from saying more about the good architecture of this church, though much might be added to what precedes, and I will content myself by saying that those who rebuilt the marble façade of the church of S. Miniato del Monte, deviated widely from this model and from this excellent style. This work was carried out in honour of the conversion of the blessed Giovanni Gualberto, citizen of Florence and founder of the congregation of the monks of Vallombrosa, because these and many other works erected afterwards are not to be compared for excellence to those two buildings. The art of sculpture experienced a similar fate because all the masters of the time who were then working in Italy, as has been said in the preface to the lives, were very rude. This may be seen in many places, but especially in S. Bartolommeo of the regular canons at Pistoia where there is a pulpit very rudely executed by Guido da Como, containing the beginning of the life of Jesus Christ, with these words inscribed there by the artist himself in the year 1199:

> "Sculptor laudatur, quod doctus in arte probatur,
> Guido da Como me cunctis carmine promo."

But to return to S. Giovanni, I pass by the history of its foundation because that has been written by Giovanni Villani and other authors, and, as I have already remarked that the good architecture in use to-day is derived from that building, I will now add that, to judge by appearances, the tribune is of a later date. At the time when Alesso Baldovinetti, succeeding the Florentine painter Lippo, repaired the mosaics it appeared as if it had anciently been painted in red, the designs being executed on the stucco. Now Andrea Tafi and Apollonius the Greek, in their scheme for the decoration of the tribune, divided it into compartments. Starting from the top of the vault next to the lantern these became gradually larger until they reached the cornice below. The upper part is divided into rings representing various subjects. The first contains all the ministers and performers of the Divine will, such as the Angels, Archangels, Cherubim, Seraphim, Dominions, Principalities, Powers. The second, in which the mosaics are executed in the Byzantine style, are the principal acts of God from the creation of light to the flood. The circle underneath this which descends with increased space to the eight faces of the tribune contains the history of Joseph and his twelve brethren. These are followed by other spaces of the same size and a like situation containing the life of Jesus Christ in mosaic from the Conception of Mary to the Ascension. Next, following the same order, under the three friezes, is the life of St John the Baptist, beginning with the apparition of the angel to Zacharias the priest and continuing to John's beheading and the burial of his body by the disciples. All these things are rude, without design and without art, and they are no advance upon the Byzantine style of the time so that I cannot praise them absolutely, though they merit some commendation, when one considers the methods in use at the time and the imperfect state in which pictorial art then was. Besides, the work is sound and the pieces of mosaic are very well set. In short, the latter part of the work is much better or rather less bad than is the beginning, although the whole, when compared with the works of to-day rather excites laughter than pleasure or admiration. Ultimately Andrea made the Christ, 7 braccia high, for the tribune on the wall of the principal chapel, which may be seen there to-day, and this he did by himself without the aid of Apollonio, to his great glory. Having become famous throughout Italy by these works and being reputed excellent in his own land, he received the richest honours and rewards. It was certainly a great good fortune for Andrea to be born at a time when only rude works were produced, so that things which should have been considered of very slight account or even worthless, were held in reasonable repute. The same thing happened to fra Jacopo da Turrita, of the order of St Francis, who received extraordinary rewards for the mosaics which he executed for the small choir behind the altar of S. Giovanni, although they deserved little praise, and he was afterwards invited to Rome as a great master, where he was employed on some works in the chapel of the high altar of S. Giovanni Lateram and in that of S. Maria Maggiore. He was next invited to Pisa, where he did the Evangelists and other things which are in the principal tribune of the Duomo, in the same style as the other things which he executed, although he was assisted by Andrea Tafi and Gaddo Gaddi. These were finished by Vicino, for Jacopo left them in a very imperfect state. The works of these masters obtained credit for some time, but when the productions of Andrea, Cimabue, and the rest had to bear comparison with those of Giotto, as will be said when the time comes, people came to recognise in which direction perfection in art lay, for they saw how great a difference there was between the first manner of Cimabue and that of Giotto in the delineation of figures, a difference equally strongly marked in the case of their pupils and imitators. From this time others gradually sought to follow in the footsteps of the better masters, surpassing each other more and more every day, so that art rose from these humble beginnings to that summit of perfection to which it has attained to-day. Andrea lived eighty-one years and died before Cimabue in 1294. The reputation and honour which he won by his mosaics, because it was he who had first brought to Tuscany the better manner of executing and who had taught it to the men of that province, led to the execution of the excellent works in that art by Gaddo Gaddi, Giotto, and the rest, which have brought them fame and immortality. After Andrea's death his merits were magnified in the following inscription:

Here lies Andrea, who produced graceful and beautiful works
In all Tuscany. Now he has gone.
To adorn the realm of the stars.

Buonamico Buffalmacco was a pupil of Andrea, and played many pranks on him when a youth. From his master Buonamico had the portraits of Pope Celestine IV. and Innocent IV., both of which he afterwards introduced in the paintings which he made in S. Paolo a Ripa d'Arno at Pisa. Another pupil was Antonio di Andrea Tafi, who may possibly have been his son. He was a fair painter, but I have not been able to find any works by his hand, and there is nothing beyond a bare mention of him in the old book of the company of artists in design.

But Andrea Tafi deserves a high place among the old masters, because, although he learned the principles of mosaic from the craftsman whom he brought from Venice to Florence, yet he introduced such improvements into the art, uniting the pieces with great care, and making his surfaces as smooth as a table (a very important thing in mosaics), that he prepared the way for Giotto among others, as will be said in that artist's life; and not for Giotto alone, but for all those who have since practised this branch of pictorial art to our own day. Thus it may be asserted with perfect truth that the marvellous works in mosaic, which are now being carried out in S. Marco, at Venice, owe their origin to Andrea Tafi.

GADDO GADDI, FLORENTINE PAINTER.

Gaddo, painter of Florence, who flourished at this same time, showed more design in the works which he produced in the Byzantine style, and which he executed with great care, than did Andrea Tafi and the other painters who preceded him. This was possibly due to his close friendship and intercourse with Cimabue, for, whether it was through congeniality of disposition or through the goodness of their hearts, they became very much attached to each other, and their frequent conversations together, and their friendly discussions upon the difficulties of the arts, gave rise to many great and beautiful ideas in their minds. This came to pass the more readily, because they were aided by the quality of the air of Florence, which usually produces ingenious and subtle spirits, and which made them strangers to that ruggedness and coarseness from which Nature cannot entirely free herself even when assisted by the rivalry of the good craftsmen and the precepts laid down by them in every age. It is, indeed, abundantly clear that, when things have been talked over in a friendly way, without any reserve of convention, although this rarely happens, they may be brought to a great state of perfection. The same remark applies to those who study the sciences; for, by discussing difficulties among themselves when they arise, they remove them, rendering the path so clear and easy, that the greatest glory may be won thereby. But, on the other hand, there are some who, with devilish arts, and led by envy and malice, make profession of friendship under the guise of truth and affection, give the most pernicious advice, so that the arts do not attain to excellence so soon as they do where the minds of noble spirits are united by such a bond of love as that which drew together Gaddo and Cimabue, and, in like manner, Andrea Tafi and Gaddo. It was Andrea who took Gaddo into his companionship to finish the mosaics of S. Giovanni. Here Gaddo learned so much, that he was able, without assistance, to make the prophets, which may be seen round the walls of that sanctuary, in the squares under the windows; and, as he executed these unaided and in a much improved style, they brought him great renown. Encouraged by this, he prepared himself to work alone, and devoted himself constantly to the study of the Byzantine style, combined with that of Cimabue. By such means, it was not long before he became an excellent artist; so that the wardens of S. Maria del Fiore entrusted to him the semi-circular space within the building above the principal entrance, where he introduced a Coronation of the Virgin, in mosaic. Upon its completion, it was pronounced by all the foreign and native masters to be the finest work of its kind that had yet been seen in Italy, for they recognised that it possessed more design and more judgment, and displayed the results of more study, than were to be found in all the remaining works in mosaic then in existence in the peninsula. Thus, his fame being spread abroad by this work, he was summoned to Rome by Clement V. in the year 1308,—that is to say, in the year following the great fire, in which the church and palaces of the Lateran were destroyed. There he completed for the Pope some works in mosaic, which had been left unfinished by Jacopo da Turrita.

His next work, also in mosaic, was in the church of St Peter's, where he executed some things in the principal chapel and for other parts of the church; but especially a God the Father, of large size with many figures, which he did for the façade. He also assisted in the completion of some mosaics on the façade of S. Maria Maggiore, somewhat improving the style, and departing slightly from the Byzantine manner, which was entirely devoid of merit. On his return to Tuscany, he did some work in mosaic for the Tarlati, lords of Pietramala, in the old Duomo, outside Arezzo, in a vault entirely constructed of spungite. He covered the middle part of this building with mosaics; but the church fell down in the time of Bishop Gentile Urbinate, because the old stone vaulting was too heavy for it, and it was afterwards rebuilt in brick by that bishop. On his departure from Arezzo, Gaddo went to Pisa, where he made, for a niche in the chapel of the Incoronata in the Duomo, the Ascension of Our Lady into Heaven, where Jesus Christ is awaiting her, with a richly appareled throne for her seat. This work was executed so well and so carefully for the time, that it is in an excellent state of preservation to-day. After this, Gaddo returned to Florence, intending to rest. Accordingly he amused himself in making some small mosaics, some of which are composed of egg-shells, with incredible diligence and patience, and a few of them, which are in the church of S. Giovanni at Florence, may still be seen. It is related that he made two of these for King Robert, but nothing more is known of the matter. This much must suffice for the mosaics of Gaddo Gaddi. Of pictures he painted a great number, among them that which is on the screen of the chapel of the Minerbetti in S. Maria Novella, and many others sent to different places in Tuscany. Thus, by producing now mosaics and now paintings, he executed many very tolerable works in both mediums, which will always assure him good credit and reputation. There is a great deal more which I might say about Gaddo, but I will pass it over in silence, because the manner of the painters of those days cannot be of great assistance to artists; and I shall dwell at greater length upon the lives of those who may be of some help, because they introduced improvements into the art.

Gaddo lived seventy-three years, and died in 1312. He was honourably buried in S. Croce by his son Taddeo. This Taddeo, who had Giotto for his godfather, was the only one of all Gaddo's children who became a painter, learning the rudiments of the art from his father and the rest from Giotto. Besides Taddeo, a Pisan painter named Vicino was also a pupil of Gaddo. He did some excellent work in mosaic for the great tribune of the Duomo of Pisa, where the following words still testify to his authorship:

"Tempore Domini Johannis Rossi operarii istius ecclesiæ, Vicinus pictor incepit et perfecit hanc imaginem B. Mariæ, sed Majestatis, et Evangelistae per alios inceptæ, ipse complevit et perfecit. Anno Domini 1321. De mense Septembris. Benedictum sit nomen Domini Dei nostri Jesu Christi. Amen."

The portrait of Gaddo, by the hand of Taddeo his son, may be seen in the Baroncelli chapel in the church of S. Croce, where he stands by the side of Andrea Tafi, in the marriage of the Virgin. In the book, which I have mentioned above, there is a miniature by Gaddo, like those of Cimabue, and which serves to show his ability as a draughtsman.

Now, because an old book from which I have extracted these few notices about Gaddo Gaddi, speaks of the building of the church of S. Maria Novella in Florence for the Friars Preachers, a truly magnificent and imposing structure, I will take this opportunity of relating the circumstances of its erection. While St Dominic was at Bologna, the place of Ripoli outside Florence was granted to him. Accordingly he sent twelve friars thither under the care of the blessed Giovanni da Salerno. Not many years after they came to Florence, to the church and place of S. Pancrazio, and established themselves there. When Dominic himself came to Florence they left it, and went to stay in the church of S. Paolo, as he wished them to do. Subsequently when the place of S. Maria Novella and all its possessions were granted to Blessed Giovanni by the papal legate and by the bishop of the city, they entered into possession and began to live in that place on the last day of October 1221. But as this church was rather small, with a western aspect and the entrance on the old piazza, the friars, who had increased in numbers and who were in great credit in the city, began to think of enlarging their church and convent. So, having collected a great sum of money, and many people of the city having promised every assistance, they began the construction of a new church on St Luke's day, 1278, when the first stone was laid with great ceremony by the Cardinal Latino degli Orsini, legate of Pope Nicholas III. to the

Florentines. The architects of the church were fra Giovanni of Florence, and fra Ristoro of Campi, lay brethren of the order, who had restored the ponte alia Carraia, and that of S. Trinita, after their destruction by the flood of October 1264. The greater part of the land covered by the church and convent was given to the friars by the heirs of M. Jacopo, de' Tornaquinci knight. The cost, as has been said, was defrayed partly by alms, partly by the money of various persons who gave assistance readily, but especially by the good offices of friar Aldobrandino Cavalcanti, who was, afterwards bishop of Arezzo, and who is buried over the gate of the Virgin. Besides other things this friar is said to have collected by his industry all the labour and materials required for the church. It was completed when fra Jacopo Passavanti was prior of the convent, who thus deserved his marble tomb which is on the left hand side in front of the principal chapel. The church was consecrated by Pope Martin V. in the year 1470, as appears by an inscription on marble on a pillar on the right of the principal chapel, which runs:

> Anno Domini 1420 die Septembris, Dominus Martinus divina providentia Papa V personaliter hanc ecclesiam consecravit, et magnas indulgentias contulit visitantibus eamdem.

All these things and many more are related in a chronicle of the building of this church, which is in the possession of the fathers of S. Maria Novella, as well as in the history of Giovanni Villani. I did not wish to omit these few particulars, because the church is one of the finest and most important in Florence, and also because it contains many excellent works of the most famous artists of a later time, as will be related hereafter.

MARGARITONE, PAINTER, SCULPTOR AND ARCHITECT OF AREZZO.

Among the other painters of old time, in whom the well-deserved praise accorded to Cimabue and his pupil Giotto aroused a great deal of fear, for their good workmanship in painting was hailed throughout Italy, was one Margaritone, painter of Arezzo, who recognised equally well with the others who previously occupied the foremost positions in painting in that unhappy age, that the work of these two men would probably all but obliterate his own reputation. Margaritone was considered excellent among the painters of the age who worked in the Byzantine style, and he did a number of pictures in tempera at Arezzo. He worked in fresco also, painting almost the whole of the church of S. Clemente, an abbey of the order of the Camaldolites, but these occupied him a long time and cost him much trouble. The church is entirely destroyed to-day, together with many other buildings, including a strong fortress called S. dementi, because the Duke Cosimo de' Medici not only here, but round the whole circuit of the city, pulled down many buildings and the old walls which had been restored by Guido Petramalesco, a former bishop and lord of the city, in order to reconstruct them with curtains and bastions much stronger and of less circuit than the former ones had been, and consequently more easy to defend with a smaller number of men. Margaritone's pictures in this church contained many figures both small and great, and although they were executed in the Byzantine style, yet they were admitted to show evidence of having been executed with good judgment and with love of art, as may be inferred from the works of this painter which are still extant in that city. Of these the principal is a picture, now in the chapel of the Conception in S. Francesco, representing a Madonna with modern ornamentation, which is held in great veneration by the friars there. In the same church he did a large crucifix, also in the Byzantine style, which is now placed in the chapel where the quarters of the superintendent are situated. The Saviour is delineated upon the axes of the cross, and Margaritone made many such crucifixes in that city. For the nuns of S. Margherita he painted a work which is now placed in the transept of their church. This is canvas stretched on a panel, containing subjects from the life of Our Lady and of St John the Baptist in small figures, executed in a much better style, and with more diligence and grace than the large ones. This work is noteworthy, not only because the little figures in it are so carefully finished that they resemble the work of an illuminator, but because it is a wonderful thing that a picture on canvas should have lasted three hundred years. He did an extraordinary number of pictures for all the city, and a St Francis drawn from life at Sargiano, a convent of the bare-footed friars. To this he placed his name, because he considered that it was more than usually well done. He afterwards made a large crucifix in wood, painted in the Byzantine manner, and sent it to Florence to M. Farinata degli Uberti, a most famous citizen who, in addition to many other notable exploits, had saved his native city from imminent danger and ruin. This crucifix is now in S. Croce, between the chapel of the Peruzzi and that of the Giugni. In S. Domenico, at Arezzo, a church and convent built by the lords of Pietramela in the year 1275, as their coat of arms proves, he did many things before returning to Rome, where he had already given great satisfaction to Pope Urban IV. by doing some things in fresco for him in the portico of St Peter's; for although in the Byzantine style of the time, they were not without merit. After he had finished a St Francis at Ganghereto, a place above Terranuova in the Valdarno, he devoted himself to sculpture, as he was of an ambitious spirit, and he studied with such diligence that he succeeded much better than he had done in painting; for although his first sculptures were in the Byzantine style, as may be seen in four figures in wood of a Deposition from the Cross in the Pieve, and some other figures in relief which are in the chapel of St Francis above the baptismal font, yet he adopted a much better manner after he had visited Florence and had seen the works of Arnolfo, and of the other more celebrated sculptors of the time. In the year 1275 he returned to Arezzo in the suite of Pope Gregory, who passed through Florence on his journey from Avignon to Rome. Here an opportunity presented itself to make himself better known, for the Pope died at Arezzo after having given 30,000 scudi to the Commune wherewith to finish the building of the Vescovado which had been begun by Master Lapo, and had made but little progress. The Aretines therefore ordained that the chapel of St Gregory should be made in memory of the Pope in the Vescovado, in which Margaritone afterwards placed a picture, and in addition that Margaritone should make a marble tomb for the Pope in the Vescovado. He set to work upon the task and brought it to such a successful completion, introducing the Pope's portrait from life both in marble and in painting, that it was considered to be the best work which he had ever produced.

Margaritone then set to work to complete the Vescovado, following the design of Lapo, and he displayed great activity; but he did not complete it, for a few years later, in 1289, war broke out again between the Florentines and Aretines, through the fault of Guglielmo Ubertini, bishop and lord of Arezzo, aided by the Tarlati of Pietramela and by the Pazzi of Val d'Arno, when all the money left by the Pope for the building of the Vescovado was expended upon the war, while evil befell the leaders, who were routed and slain at Campaldino. The Aretines then ordained that the tolls paid by the surrounding country, called a *dazio*, should be set aside for the use of the building, and this toll has lasted to our own day. To return to Margaritone, he seems to have been the first, so far as one can judge by his works, who thought it necessary to take precautions, when painting on wood, that the joints should be secure, so that no cracks or fissures should appear after the completion of the painting, and it was his practice to cover the panel completely with canvas, fastened on by a strong glue made of shreds of parchment and boiled in the fire; he then treated the surface with gypsum, as may be seen in many of his own pictures and in those of others. Over the gypsum, thus mixed with the glue, he made lines and diadems and other rounded ornaments in relief; and it was he who invented the method of grounding in bolar-moniac, on which he laid gold leaf which he afterwards burnished. All these things which had never been seen before may be noticed in his works, especially in an antependium in the Pieve of Arezzo, which contains scenes from the life of St Donate, and also in S. Agnesa and S. Niccolo in the same city.

Margaritone produced many works in his own country which were sent out of it, part of which were at Rome in S. Giovanni and in St Peter's, and some at S. Caterina at Pisa, where there is a St Catherine of his over an altar in the transept, containing many small figures in a representation of her life, and also a panel of St Francis with many subjects from his life, on a gold ground. In the upper church of S. Francesco at Assisi is a crucifix by his hand painted in the Byzantine style, on a beam which spans the church. All these works were greatly prized by the people of the time, although they are not valued to-day, except as being curious on account of their age; indeed they could only be considered good in an age when art was not at its zenith, as it is to-day. Margaritone also paid some attention to architecture, although I have not mentioned any things made from his designs because they are of slight importance. However, I must not forget to say that he designed the palace of the governors of the city of Ancona, as I have found, in 1270, in the Byzantine style; and what is more, he carved in sculpture eight windows for the façade, each of which has two columns in the middle, which support two arches. Over each window is a representation in half relief, occupying the space between the arches and the top of the window, of an Old Testament subject, carved in a species of stone found in the country. Under the windows and on the façade are some letters, the purport of which must be conjectured, so badly are they done, which give the date and time at which the work was executed. The design of the church of S. Ciriaco at Ancona was also by his hand. Margaritone died at the age of seventy-seven, regretting, it is said, that he had lived long enough to see the changes of the age and the honours accorded to the new artists. He was buried in the old Duomo of Arezzo, in a tomb of Travertine, which has been destroyed in our own time by the demolition of that church. The following epitaph was written for him:

> Hic jacet ille bonus pictura Margaritonus,
> Cui requiem Dominus tradat uhique plus.

Margaritone's portrait was in the old Duomo by the hand of Spinello, in the Adoration of the Magi, and was copied by me before the church was pulled down.

GIOTTO, PAINTER, SCULPTOR, AND ARCHITECT OF FLORENCE.

The debt which painters owe to Nature, which serves continually as an example to them, that from her they may select the best and finest parts for reproduction and imitation, is due also to the Florentine painter, Giotto; because, when the methods and outlines of good painting had been buried for so many years under the ruins caused by war, he alone, although born in the midst of unskilful artists, was able, through God's gift in him, to endow art with a proper form after it had been revived in a bad style. Certainly it was nothing short of a miracle, in so gross and unskilful an age, that Giotto should have worked to such purpose that design of which the men of the time had little or no conception, was revived to a vigorous life by his means. The birth of this great man took place in the year 1276, fourteen miles from Florence, in the town of Vespignano, his father, who was a simple field labourer, being named Bondone. He brought up Giotto as well as his position in life allowed. When the boy had attained the age of ten years he exhibited, in all his childish ways, an extraordinary quickness and readiness of mind, which made him a favourite, not only with his father, but with all who knew him, both in the village and beyond it. Bondone then set him to watch a few sheep, and while he was following these from place to place to find pasture, he was always drawing something from nature or representing the fancies which came into his head, with a stone on the ground or on sand, so much was he attracted to the art of design by his natural inclination. Thus one day when Cimabue was going on some business from Florence to Vespignano, he came upon Giotto, who, while his sheep were grazing, was drawing one of them from life with a pointed piece of stone upon a smooth surface of rock, although he had never had any master but nature. Cimabue stopped in amazement at the sight, and asked the boy if he would like to come and stay with him. Giotto replied he would go willingly if his father would consent. Cimabue lost no time in finding Bondone, who joyfully consented and allowed his son to accompany Cimabue to Florence. After his arrival there, assisted by his natural talent and taught by Cimabue, the boy not only equalled his master's style in a short time, but became such a good imitator of nature that he entirely abandoned the rude Byzantine manner and revived the modern and good style of painting, introducing the practice of making good portraits of living persons, a thing which had not been in use for more than two hundred years. And although there were some few portraits made in this manner, as has been said above, yet they had not been very successful, nor were they nearly so well executed as those of Giotto. Among other portraits which he made, the chapel of the Podesta palace at Florence still contains that of Dante Aligheri, his close companion and friend, no less famous as a poet than Giotto then was as a painter. This poet has been warmly praised by M. Giovanni Boccaccio in the introduction to the story of M. Forese da Rabatta. In this same chapel Giotto has also painted his own portrait as well as those of Ser Brunetto Latini, Dante's master, and M. Corso Donati, a famous citizen of the time. Giotto's first paintings were in the chapel of the high altar of the Badia at Florence, in which he made a number of things which were considered beautiful, but especially an Annunciation. In this he has represented with extraordinary truth the fear and astonishment of the Virgin Mary at the salutation of Gabriel, who, in her terror seems ready to run away. The picture of the high altar in the same chapel is also by Giotto's hand, and it has continued to retain its position there, rather because of a certain reverence which is felt for the work of such a man than for any other reason. In S. Croce there are four chapels decorated by his hand, three between the sacristy and the principal chapel, and one on the other side. In the first of these, that of M. Ridolfo de' Bardi, in which the bell ropes hang, is the life of St Francis, at whose death a number of friars exhibit the effect of weeping with considerable fidelity to nature. In the second, which is that of the family of the Peruzzi, are two subjects from the life of St John the Baptist, to whom the chapel is dedicated. Here is a very life-like representation of the dancing of Herodias, and of the promptitude with which some servants are performing the service of the table. In the same chapel are two miracles of St John the Evangelist, the one representing the raising of Drusiana, the other his being caught up into Heaven. The third chapel, that of the Giugni and dedicated to the Apostles, contains representations by Giotto of the martyrdom of many of them. In the fourth, that of the Tosinghi and Spinelli, which is on the north side of the church and is dedicated to the Assumption of Our Lady, Giotto painted the Nativity of the Virgin, her marriage, the Annunciation, the adoration of the Magi, and the presentation of the Christ child to Simeon. This last is a most beautiful thing, for not only is the warmest love depicted in the face of the old man as he receives the Christ, but the action of the child, who is afraid of him and stretches out his arms to return to his mother, could not be represented with more tenderness or greater beauty. In the Death of Our Lady the Apostles are represented with a number of very beautiful angels. The Baroncelli chapel in the same church contains a painting in tempera by Giotto's hand, in which he has represented with great care the coronation of Our Lady. It contains a very large number of small figures and a choir of angels and saints, produced with great diligence. On this work he has written his name and the date in gold letters. Artists who reflect that at this time Giotto was laying the foundations of the proper method of design and of colouring, unaided by the advantages of seeing the light of the good style, will be compelled to hold him in the highest veneration. In the same church of S. Croce there are in addition a crucifix above the marble tomb of Carlo Marzuppini of Arezzo, Our Lady with St John and the Magdalene at the foot of the cross, and opposite on the other side of the building an Annunciation towards the high altar over the tomb of Lionardo Aretino, which has been restored by modern artists with great lack of judgment. In the refectory he has done the history of St Louis, a Last Supper, and a Tree of the Cross, while the presses of the sacristy are decorated with some scenes from the lives of Christ and of St Francis in small figures. At the church of the Carmine in the chapel of St John the Baptist he represented the whole of that saint's life in several pictures; and in the Palazzo della parte Guelfa at Florence there is the history of the Christian faith painted admirably by him in fresco, and containing the portrait of Pope Clement IV., who founded that monastery to which he gave his arms, retained by them ever since.

After these works Giotto set out from Florence for Assisi in order to finish what Cimabue had begun there. On his way through Arezzo he painted the chapel of St Francis, which is above the baptistery in the Pieve there, and a St Francis and a St Dominic, portraits from life, on a round pillar near to a most beautiful antique Corinthian capital. In the Duomo outside Arezzo he decorated the interior of a large chapel with the Stoning of St Stephen, an admirable composition of figures. On completing these things he proceeded to Assisi, a city of Umbria, whither he was summoned by fra Giovanni di Muro della Marca, at that time general of the friars of St Francis. In the upper church of this town he painted a series of thirty-two frescoes of the life of St Francis, under the corridor which traverses the windows, sixteen on each side, with such perfection that he acquired the highest reputation thereby. In truth the work exhibits great variety, not only in the postures of the different figures, but in the composition of each subject, besides which it is very interesting to see the various costumes of those times and certain imitations and observations of Nature. One of the most beautiful of these represents a thirsty man, whose desire for water is represented in the most lively manner as he kneels on the ground to drink from a spring, with such wonderful reality that one might imagine him to be a real person. There are many other things most worthy of notice into which I will not enter now, because I do not wish to be tedious. Let it suffice to say that by these works Giotto acquired the highest reputation for the excellence of his figures, for his arrangement, sense of proportion, fidelity to Nature, and his innate facility which he had greatly increased by study, while in addition to this he never failed to express his meaning clearly. Giotto indeed was not so much the pupil of any human master as of Nature herself, for in addition to his splendid natural gifts, he studied Nature diligently, arid was always contriving new things and borrowing ideas from her.

When these works were completed Giotto painted in the lower church of the same place the upper part of the walls beside the high altar, and all four angles of the vaulting over the spot where the body of St Francis lies, the whole displaying his beautiful and inventive imagination. The first contains St Francis glorified in Heaven, surrounded by those Virtues which are required of those who wish to be perfect in the sight of God. On the one side Obedience puts a yoke on the neck of a friar who kneels before her, the bands of which are drawn by hands to Heaven. With one finger on her mouth she signifies silence, and her eyes are turned towards Jesus Christ, who is shedding blood from his side. Beside her are Prudence and Humility to show that where true obedience exists, there also will be humility and prudence, causing everything to prosper. In the second angle is Chastity, who will not allow herself to be won by the kingdoms, crowns, or palms which are being offered to her. At her feet stands Purity who is washing the naked, while Fortitude is bringing others to be washed and cleansed. On one side of Chastity is Penitence, chasing a winged Love with the cord of discipline and putting to flight Uncleanness. Poverty occupies the third space, treading on thorns with her bare feet; behind her barks a dog, while a boy is throwing stones at her and another is pushing thorns into her legs with a stick. Poverty here is espoused by St Francis, while Jesus Christ holds her hand in the mystical presence of Hope and Chastity. In the fourth and last of these places is a St Francis in glory, clothed in the white tunic of a deacon, in triumph and surrounded by a multitude of angels who form a choir about him and hold a banner on which are a cross and seven stars, while over all is the Holy Spirit. In each of these angles are some Latin words explanatory of the subject. Besides these four angles the paintings on the side walls are most beautiful, and deserve to be highly valued both for the perfection which they exhibit and because they were produced with such skill that they are in an excellent state of preservation to-day. These paintings contain an excellent portrait of Giotto himself, and over the door of the sacristy is a fresco by his hand of St Francis receiving the stigmata, so full of tenderness and devotion that it seems to me to be the most excellent painting that Giotto has produced here, though all are really beautiful and worthy of praise.

When S. Francesco was at length finished Giotto returned to Florence, where he painted with extraordinary care, a picture of St Francis in the fearful desert of Vernia, to be sent to Pisa. Besides a landscape full of trees and rocks, a new thing in those days, the attitude of the saint, who is receiving the stigmata on his knees with great eagerness, exhibits an ardent desire to receive them and an infinite love towards Jesus Christ, who is in the air surrounded by seraphim granting them to him, the varied emotions being all represented in the most telling manner imaginable. The predella of the picture contains three finely executed subjects from the life of the same saint. The work may now be seen in S. Francesco at Pisa, on a pillar beside the high altar, where it is held in high veneration in memory of so great a man. It led the Pisans, on the completion of their Campo Santo from the plan of Giovanni di Niccola Pisano, as already related, to entrust to Giotto the painting of a part of the walls. For as the exterior of the walls was incrusted with marble and sculptures at a great cost, the roof being of lead, and the interior filled with antique sarcophagi and tombs of Pagan times, gathered together in that city from all parts of the world, the Pisans wished the walls to be decorated with a series of noble paintings. Accordingly Giotto went to Pisa, and beginning at the end of one of the walls of the Campo Santo he depicted the life of the patient Job in six frescoes. Now it occurred to him that the marbles of the part of the building in which he was at work were turned towards the sea, and being exposed to the south-east wind, they are always moist and throw out a certain saltness, as do nearly all the bricks of Pisa, and because the colours and paintings are eaten away by these causes, and as he wished to protect his work from destruction as far as possible, he prepared a coating for the whole of the surface on which he proposed to paint his frescoes, which consisted of a plaster or incrusture made up of lime, chalk and brick-dust. This device has proved so successful, that the paintings which he subsequently executed on this surface, have endured to this day, and they would have stood better had not the neglect of those who should have taken care of them, allowed them to be much damaged by the damp. The want of attention to this detail, which would have involved little trouble, has caused the pictures to suffer a great deal in some places where the damp has converted the crimsons into black and caused the plaster to fall off. Besides this it is the nature of chalk when mixed with lime to become corroded and to peel, whence it happens that the colours are destroyed, although they may originally appear to take well. These frescoes contain the portrait of M. Farinata degli Uberti, besides many fine figures, among which one may remark some countrymen, who in bringing the sad news to Job, exhibit the utmost sorrow for the lost animals and the other misfortunes. There is also much grace in the figure of a servant, who with a fan of branches stands near the bowed figure of Job, abandoned by everyone else, for in addition to the figure being well executed in every particular, his attitude is wonderful, as with one hand he drives away the flies from his leprous and noisome master, and holds his nose with the other with disgust, to escape the smell. Very fine also are the other figures of these pictures and the heads of both men and women, and the delicate treatment of the drapery, so that it is small wonder that the work brought Giotto such renown in that city and elsewhere; that Pope Benedict IX., who was proposing to decorate St Peter's with some paintings, sent a courtier from Treviso to Tuscany, to see what manner of man Giotto was, and to report on the quality of his work. On the way the courtier learned that there were other excellent masters in painting and mosaic in Florence, and he interviewed a number of artists at Siena. When he had received designs from these, he proceeded to Florence. Entering Giotto's shop one morning, as he was at work, the envoy explained to him the Pope's intention, and the manner in which he wished to make use of his work, and finally asked Giotto for some small specimen of work to send to His Holiness. Giotto, who was always courteous, took a sheet of paper and a red pencil, pressed his arm to his side to make a compass of it, and then with a turn of his hand, produced a circle so perfect in every particular that it was a marvel to see. This done, he turned smiling to the courtier and said: "Here is the design." The latter, who thought he was joking, said: "Am I to have no other design but this?" "It is enough and more than enough," replied Giotto; "send it in with the others and you will see if it is recognised." The messenger perceived that he would obtain nothing else, and left in a state of considerable dissatisfaction, imagining that he had been laughed at. However, when he sent in the other designs with the names of their authors, he included that of Giotto, and related how the artist had executed it without moving his arm and without compasses. From this the Pope and all the courtiers present recognised to what an extent Giotto surpassed all the other painters of the time in excellence. When the story became public it gave rise to a saying which is still used for people of dull wits: "You are more round *(tondo)* than Giotto's O." This proverb deserves to be considered a good one, not only from the circumstances out of which it arose, but much more for its meaning, which is due to the two-fold significance of the word *tondo* in Tuscany, that of a perfect circle, and slowness and heaviness of mind. Accordingly the Pope sent for Giotto to Rome, where he received him with great honour, and recognised his worth. He caused him to paint for the tribune of St Peter's five subjects from the life of Christ, and the principal picture for the sacristy, all of which were executed with great care, nothing in tempera ever leaving his hands before it was perfectly finished; thus he richly deserved the reward of 600 gold ducats which the delighted Pope gave to him, bestowing many other favours upon him, so that it became the talk of all Italy.

As I do not wish to omit a memorable circumstance concerning art, I will notice here that there happened to be in Rome at this time a great friend of Giotto named Oderigi d'Aggobbio, an excellent illuminator of the day, who adorned many books for the Pope for the palace library, though they are now mostly destroyed by time. In my own book of old designs there are some remnants by his hand, and he certainly was a clever artist. But a much better master than he was Francis, an illuminator of Bologna, who did some very fair things for the Pope for the same library at that very time, in a like style, as may be seen in my book, where I have some designs by his hand, both for painting and illuminations, among them an eagle, excellently done, and a fine lion tearing up a tree. These two excellent illuminators are referred to by Dante in the passage on the vainglorious in the eleventh chapter of the Purgatorio, in these lines:

> "Oh, dissi lui, non se' tu Oderisi
> L'onor d'Aggobbio e l'onor di quell' arte
> Ch' alluminare è chimata in Parisi?
> Frate, diss' egli, più ridon le carte,
> Che pennelleggia Franco Bolognese
> L'onor è tutto or suo, e mio in parte."

When the Pope had seen these works he was so enchanted by Giotto's style that he commissioned him to surround the walls of St Peter's with scenes from the Old and New Testaments. Giotto therefore began these, and painted the fresco of the angle, seven braccia high, which is above the organ, and many other paintings, of which some have been restored by other artists in our own day, and some have been either destroyed or carried away from the old building of St Peter's during the founding of the new walls and set under the organ. Among these was a representation of Our Lady on a wall. In order that it might not be thrown down with the rest, it was cut out, supported by beams and iron, and so taken away. On account of its great beauty, it was afterwards built into a place selected by the devotion of M. Niccolo Acciancoli, a Florentine doctor enthusiastic over the excellent things of art, who has richly adorned it with stucco and other modern paintings. Giotto is also the author of the mosaic known as the Navicella, which is over the three doors of the portico in the courtyard of St Peter's. This is a truly marvellous work, well deserving its high reputation among all persons of taste. In addition to its excellent design, the apostles are admirably disposed, toiling in different ways in the midst of the tempest, while the winds fill the sail, which bellies out exactly like a real one; and yet it is a difficult task so to unite those pieces of glass to form the light and shade of so real a sail, which, even with the brush, could only be equalled by a great effort. Besides all this, there is a fisherman who is standing on a rock and fishing with a line, whose attitude is expressive of the extreme patience proper to that art, while his face betrays his hope and desire to catch something. Beneath the Navicella are three small arches painted in fresco, but as they are almost entirely effaced, I will say no more about them. All artists, however, unite in praise of these works.

At last, when Giotto had painted a large crucifix in tempera in the Minerva, a church of the Friars Preachers, which was then much admired, he returned to his own country, from which he had been absent for six years. But soon after Pope Clement V. was elected at Perugia, on the death of Pope Benedict IX., and Giotto was obliged to accompany the new pontiff to his court at Avignon to execute some works there. Thus, not only in Avignon, but in several other places of France, he painted many very beautiful frescoes and pictures, which greatly delighted the Pope and all his court. When he at length received his dismissal, he was sent away kindly with many gifts, so that he returned, home no less rich than honoured and famous. Among other things which he brought away with him was the Pope's portrait, which he afterwards gave to Taddeo Gaddi, his pupil. The date of this return to Florence was the year 1316. But he was not long permitted to remain in Florence, as he was invited to Padua to do some work for the lords della Scala, for whom he painted a beautiful chapel in the Santo, a church built in those times. He thence proceeded to Verona, where he did some pictures for the palace of Messer Cane, particularly the portrait of that lord, and a picture for the friars of S. Francesco. On the completion of these things he was detained at Ferrara, on his way back to Tuscany, to paint for the lords of Esti in their palace and S. Agostino some things which may be seen there to this day. When the news of Giotto's presence at Ferrara reached the Florentine poet Dante, he succeeded in inducing his friend to visit Ravenna, where the poet was exiled, and caused him to paint some frescoes about the church of S. Francesco for the lords of Polenta, which are of considerable merit. From Ravenna Giotto proceeded to Urbino, and did a few things there. Afterwards he happened to be passing through Arezzo, and being unable to refuse a favour to Piero Saccone, who had been very kind to him, he executed in fresco, on a pillar of the principal chapel of the Vescovado, a St Martin, who is cutting his mantle in two and giving part of it to a beggar who is all but naked. Then, when he had painted in tempera a large crucifix in wood for the Abbey of S. Fiore, which is now in the middle of that church, he at length reached Florence. Here, among many other things, he painted some pictures in fresco and tempera for the Nunnery of Faenza, which no longer exist owing to the destruction of that house.

In 1321 occurred the death of Giotto's dearest friend Dante, to his great grief; and in the following year he went to Lucca, where, at the request of Castruccio, then lord of that city, his birthplace, he made a picture of St Martin, with Christ above in the air, and the four patron saints of the city—St Peter, St Regulus, St Martin, and St Paulinus—who seem to be presenting a pope and an emperor, believed by many to be

Frederick of Bavaria and the anti-Pope Nicholas V. There are also some who believe that Giotto designed the impregnable fortress of the Giusta at S. Fridiano at Lucca. When Giotto had returned to Florence, King Robert of Naples wrote to his eldest son Charles, King of Calabria, who was then in that city, to use every means to induce the painter to go to Naples, where the king had just completed the building of the Nunnery of S. Chiara and the royal church, which he wished to have decorated with noble paintings. When Giotto learned that he was wanted by so popular and famous a king, he departed to serve him with the greatest alacrity, and on his arrival he painted many scenes from the Old and New Testaments in some chapels of the monastery. It is said that the scenes from the Apocalypse which he made in one of those chapels were suggested by Dante, as also perchance were some of the much-admired works at Assisi, of which I have already spoken at length; and although Dante was dead at this time, it is possible that they had talked over these things, as friends frequently do. To return to Naples, Giotto did many works in the Castel dell' Uovo, especially in the chapel, which greatly delighted the king, who became so fond of him that he often came to talk with the artist while he was at work, and took delight in seeing him at work and in listening to his conversation. Giotto, who always had a jest ready or some sharp retort, entertained the king with his hand in painting and with his tongue by his pleasant discourse. Thus it once happened that the king told him it was his intention to make him the first man in Naples, to which Giotto replied: "No doubt that is why I am lodged at the Porta Reale to be the first man in Naples." Another day the king said to him: "Giotto, if I were you, this hot day, I would leave off painting for a while." He answered: "So I should, certainly, if I were you." Being thus on very friendly terms with the king, he painted a good number of pictures for him in the chamber which King Alfonso I. pulled down to make the castle, and also in the Incoronata, and among those in the chamber were the portraits of many famous men, Giotto among the number. One day, by some caprice, the king asked Giotto to paint his kingdom. It is said that Giotto painted for him a saddled ass, with another new saddle at its feet at which it was sniffing, as if he wished for it in place of the one he had on. On each saddle were the royal crown and the sceptre of power. When the king asked Giotto for the meaning of this picture, he replied: "Such are your subjects and such is the kingdom, where every day they are wanting to change their master."

On his departure from Naples for Rome, Giotto stayed at Gaeta, where he was constrained to paint some subjects from the New Testament in the Nunziata, which have suffered from the ravages of time, but not to such an extent that it is not possible to distinguish a portrait of Giotto himself near a large crucifix of great beauty. This done, he remained a few days at Rome, in the service of the Signor Malatesta, whom he could not refuse this favour, and then he went on to Rimini, of which city Malatesta was lord, and there in the church of S. Francesco he painted a large number of pictures, which were afterwards destroyed by Gismondo, son of Pandolfo Malatesta, who rebuilt the whole of that church. In the cloister of the same church, towards the church front, he painted in fresco the life of the Blessed Michelina, which ranks with the best things which he ever did, on account of the many fine things which he took into consideration in executing it, for, quite apart from the beauty of the drapery and the grace and vigour of the heads, which are truly marvellous, there is a young woman of the most exquisite beauty, who in order to free herself from an accusation of adultery, takes a most solemn oath upon a book, keeping her eyes fixed on those of her husband, who has made her swear because his suspicions had been aroused by her giving birth to a black son, whom he could not be persuaded to acknowledge as his own. Just as the husband shows his anger and mistrust in his face, so his wife betrays, to those who look carefully at her, her innocence and simplicity, by the trouble in her face and eyes, and the wrong which is done to her in making her swear and in proclaiming her publicly as an adulteress. Giotto has also expressed with great realism a man afflicted with sores, as all the women who are about him, disgusted by the stench, turn away with various contortions in the most graceful manner imaginable. Then again the foreshortening in a picture containing a number of lame beggars is highly praiseworthy, and should be much prized by artists, since it is from these works that the origin of foreshortening is derived; and when it is remembered that they are the first, they must be considered very tolerable achievements. But the most remarkable thing of all in this series is the action of the saint with regard to certain usurers who are paying her the money realised by the sale of her possessions, which she intends to give to the poor. Her face displays contempt for money and other earthly things, which she seems to abhor, while the usurers are the very picture of human avarice and greed. Similarly the face of one who is counting the money, which he appears to be communicating to the notary who is writing, is very fine, for although his eyes are turned towards the notary, yet he keeps his hand over the money, thus betraying his greed, avarice, and mistrust. Also the three figures in the air representing Obedience, Patience, and Poverty, who are holding up the habit of St Francis, are worthy of the highest praise, chiefly on account of the natural folds of the drapery, showing that Giotto was born to throw light on the art of painting. Finally he has introduced into this work a portrait of the Signor Malatesta in a ship, which is most life-like; and his excellence is also displayed in the vigour, disposition, and posture of the sailors and other people, particularly of one figure who is speaking with others and putting his hand to his face spits into the sea. Certainly these things may be classed among the very best works in painting produced by the master, because, in spite of the large number of figures, there is not one which is not produced with the most consummate art, being at the same time exhibited in an attractive posture. Accordingly there is small need for wonder that the Signor Malatesta loaded him with rewards and praise. When Giotto had completed his works for this Signor, he did a St Thomas Aquinas reading to his brethren for the outside of the church door of S. Cataldo at Rimini at the request of the prior, who was a Florentine. Having set out thence he returned to Ravenna, where he executed a much admired painting in fresco in a chapel of S. Giovanni Evangelista. When he next returned to Florence, laden with honours and riches, he made a large wooden crucifix in tempera for S. Marco, of more than life-size, with a gold ground, and it was put on the right-hand side of the church. He made another like it for S. Maria Novella, in which his pupil Puccio Capanna collaborated with him. This is now over the principal entrance to the church, on the right-hand side, above the tomb of the Gaddi. For the same church he made a St Louis, for Paolo di Lotto Ardinghelli, with portraits of the donor and his wife at the saint's feet. This picture is placed on the screen.

In the following year, 1327, occurred the death of Guido Tarlati da Pietramala, bishop and lord of Arezzo, at Massa di Maremma, on his return from Lucca, where he had been visiting the Emperor. His body was brought to Arezzo, where it received the honour of a stately funeral, and Pietro Saccone and Dolfo da Pietramala, the bishop's brother, determined to erect a marble tomb which should be worthy of the greatness of such a man, who had been both spiritual and temporal lord and the leader of the Ghibelline party in Tuscany. Accordingly they wrote to Giotto, desiring him to design a very rich tomb, as ornate as possible; and when they had supplied him with the necessary measurements, they asked him to send them at once the man who was, in his opinion, the most excellent sculptor then living in Italy, for they relied entirely upon his judgment. Giotto, who was very courteous, prepared the design and sent it to them, and from it the tomb was made, as will be said in the proper place. Now Pietro Saccone was a great admirer of Giotto's worth, and when, not long after, he took the Borgo a S. Sepolero, he brought from that place to Arezzo a picture by the artist's hand, of small figures, which was afterwards broken into fragments; but Baccio Gondi, a Florentine of gentle birth, a lover of the noble arts and of every kind of virtue, made a diligent search for the pieces of this picture when he was commissioner at Arezzo, and succeeded in finding some. He brought them to Florence, where he holds them in great veneration, as well as some other things in his possession, also by Giotto, who produced so much that an enumeration of all his works would excite incredulity. It is not many years since that I happened to be at the hermitage of Camaldoli, where I have done a number of things for the fathers, and in a cell to which I was taken by the Very Rev. Don Antonio da Pisa, then general of the congregation of Camaldoli, I saw a very beautiful crucifix, on a gold ground, by Giotto, with his signature. I am informed by the Rev. Don Silvano Razza, a Camaldolian monk, that this crucifix is now in the cell of the principal, where it is treasured for its author's sake as a most precious thing, together with a very beautiful little picture by the hand of Raphael of Urbino.

For the Umiliati brethren of Ognissanti at Florence Giotto painted a chapel and four pictures, one of them representing Our Lady surrounded by a number of angels, with the child at her neck, on a large crucifix of wood, the design of which was subsequently copied by Puccio Capanna, and reproduced in every part of Italy, for he closely followed Giotto's style. When this work of the Lives was printed for the first time, the screen of that church contained a picture painted in tempera by Giotto, representing the death of Our Lady, surrounded by the apostles, while Christ receives her soul into His arms. The work has been much praised by artists, and especially by Michelagnolo Buonarotti who declared, as is related elsewhere, that it was not possible to represent this scene in a more realistic manner. This picture, being as I say held in great esteem, has been carried away since the publication of the first edition of this work, by one who may possibly have acted from love of art and reverence for the work, which may have seemed then to be too little valued, and who thus from motives of pity showed himself pitiless, as our poet says. It is certainly a marvel that Giotto should have produced such beautiful paintings in those times, especially when it is considered that he may in a certain sense be said to have learned the art without a master.

After these things, in the year 1334, on the ninth day of July, he began work on the campanile of S. Maria del Fiore, the foundations of which were laid on a surface of large stones, after the ground had been dug out to a depth of 20 braccia, the materials excavated being water and gravel. On this surface he laid 12 braccia of concrete, the remaining 8 braccia being filled up with masonry. In the inauguration of this work the bishop of the city took part, laying the first stone with great ceremonial in the presence of all the clergy and magistrates. As the work was proceeding on its original plan, which was in the German style in use at the time, Giotto designed all the subjects comprised in the ornamentation, and marked out with great care the distribution of the black, white, and red colours in the arrangement of the stones and lines. The circuit of the tower at the base was 100 braccia, or 25 braccia on each side, and the height 144 braccia. If what Lorenzo di Cione Giberti has written be true, and I most firmly believe it, Giotto not only made the model of this campanile, but also executed some of the marble sculptures in relief, which represent the origin of all the arts. Lorenzo asserts that he had seen models in relief by the hand of Giotto, and particularly those of these works, and this may readily be credited, since design and invention are the father and mother of all the fine arts, and not of one only. According to Giotto's model, the campanile should have received a pointed top or quadrangular pyramid over the existing structure, 50 braccia in height, but because it was a German thing, and in an old-fashioned style, modern architects have always discountenanced its construction, considering the building to be better as it is. For all these things Giotto received the citizenship of Florence, in addition to a pension of one hundred gold florins yearly from the Commune of Florence, a great thing in those days. He was also appointed director of the work which was carried on after him by Taddeo Gaddi, as he did not live long enough to see its completion.

While the campanile was in progress, Giotto made a picture for the nuns of S. Giorgio, and three half-length figures in the Badia of Florence, in an arch over the doorway inside, now whitewashed over to lighten the church. In the great hall of the podesta at Florence, he painted a representation of the Commune, which has been appropriated by many people. The figure represents a judge, seated with a sceptre in his hand, over whose head are the scales, equally poised to indicate the just measures meted out by him, while he is assisted by four Virtues, Fortitude with the soul, Prudence with the laws, Justice with arms, and Temperance with words; a fine painting, and an appropriate and plausible idea.

Giotto made a second visit to Padua, where besides painting a number of chapels and other things, he executed a famous series of pictures in the place of the Arena, which brought him much honour and profit. In Milan also he left a few things which are scattered about the city, and which are considered very beautiful to this day. At length, shortly after his return from Milan, he rendered his soul to God in the year 1336, to the great grief of all his fellow-citizens, and of all those who had known him or even heard his name, for he had produced so many beautiful works in his life, and was as good a Christian as he was an excellent painter. He was buried with honour, as his worth deserved, for in his life he was beloved by everyone, and especially by distinguished men of every profession. Besides Dante, of whom we have spoken above, he and his works were highly esteemed by Petrarch, who in his will left to Signor Francesco da Carrara, lord of Padua, among other things which were held in the greatest veneration, a Madonna by Giotto's hand, as a rare thing, and the gift most worthy to be offered to him. The words of this part of the will ran thus:—*Transeo ad dispositionem aliarum rerum; et predicto igitur domino meo Paduano, quia et ipse per Dei gratiam nan eget, et ego nihil aliud habeo dignum se, mitto tabulam meam sive historiam Beatæ Virginis Mariae, operis Jocti pictoris egregii, quæ mihi ab amico meo Michaele Vannis de Florentia missa est, in cujus pulchritudinem ignorantes non intelligunt, magistri autem artis stupent: hanc iconem ipsi domino lego, ut ipsa Virgo benedicta sibi sit propitia apud filium suum Jesum Christum, &c.* It was Petrarch also who said the following words in the fifth book of his Familiari written to his intimate friends: *Atque (ut a veteribus ad nova, ab externis ad nostra transgrediar) duos ego novi pictores egregios, nec formosos, Jottum Florentinorum civem, cujus inter modernos fama urgens est, et Simonem Sanensem. Novi scultores aliquot, &c.* Giotto was buried in S. Maria del Fiore, on the left hand as one enters the church, where a white marble slab is set up to the memory of this great man. As I remarked in the life of Cimabue, a contemporary commentator of Dante said: "Giotto was, and is the chief among the painters in that same city of Florence, as his works in Rome, Naples, Avignon, Florence, Padua, and many other parts of the world testify."

Giotto's pupils were Taddeo Gaddi, his godson as I have already said, and Puccio Capanna, a Florentine, who painted for the Dominican church of S. Cataldo at Rimini a most perfect fresco representing a ship apparently about to sink, while the men are throwing their goods into the water. Puccio has here portrayed himself in the midst of the sailors. After Giotto's death, the same artist painted a number of things in the church of S. Francesco at Assisi, and for the chapel of the Strozzi, beside the door on the river front of the church of Trinita he did in fresco a coronation of the Virgin with a choir of angels, in which he followed Giotto's style rather closely, while on the side walls are some very well executed scenes from the life of St Lucy. In the Badia of Florence he painted the chapel of S. Giovanni Evangelista of the family of the Covoni, which is next to the sacristy. At Pistoia he did frescoes in the principal chapel of S. Francesco, and the chapel of S. Ludovico, with scenes from the lives of the patron saints, which are very tolerable productions. In the middle of the church of S. Domenico in the same city is a crucifix with a Madonna and St John, executed with much softness, and at the feet an entire human skeleton, an unusual thing at that time, which shows that Puccio had made efforts to understand the principles of his art. This work contains his name, written after this fashion: *Puccio di Fiorenza me Fece*. In the same church, in the tympanum above the door of S. Maria Nuova are three half-length figures,—Our Lady, with the Child on her arm, St Peter on the one side and St Francis on the other, by the same artist. In the lower church of S. Francesco at Assisi he further painted in fresco some scenes from the passion of Jesus Christ, with considerable skill and much vigour, and in the chapel of S. Maria degli Angeli of that church he executed in fresco a Christ in glory, with the Virgin, who is interceding with Him for Christian people, a work of considerable merit, but much smoked by the lamps and candles which are always burning there in great quantity. In truth, so far as one can judge, although Puccio adopted the style and methods of his master Giotto, yet he did not make sufficient use of them in his works, although, as some assert, he did not live long, but sickened and died through working too much in fresco. His hand may also be recognised in the chapel of St Martin in the same church, in the history of the saint, done in fresco for the Cardinal Gentile. In the middle of a street called Portica may also be seen a Christ at the Column, and a picture of Our Lady between St Catherine and St Clare. His works are scattered about in many other places, such as Bologna, where there is a picture of the passion of Christ in the transept of the church, and scenes from the life of St Francis, besides other things which I omit for the sake of brevity. But at Assisi, where the majority of his works are, and where I believe he helped Giotto to paint, I found that they consider him to be a fellow-citizen, and there are some members of the family of the Capanni in that city to this day. From this we may gather that he was born in Florence, since he himself wrote that he was a pupil of Giotto, but that he took his wife from Assisi, and had children there, whose descendants still inhabit the town. But this matter is of very slight importance, and it is enough to know that he was a skilful master. Another pupil of Giotto, and a very skilful painter was Ottaviano da Faenza, who painted many things in S. Giorgio at Ferrara, a convent of the monks of Monte Oliveto. In Faenza, where he lived and died, he painted in the tympanum above the door of S. Francesco, Our Lady and St Peter and St Paul, and many other things in his own country and at Bologna.

Another pupil was Pace di Faenza, who was often with his master, and helped him in many things. At Bologna there are some scenes in fresco by his hand on the outside front of S. Giovanni Decollato. This Pace was a clever artist, especially in painting small figures, as may be seen to-day in the church of S. Francesco at Forli, in a tree of the cross and in a panel in tempera containing the life of Christ, and four small subjects from the life of Our Lady, which are all very well executed. It is said that he executed in fresco for the chapel of St Anthony at Assisi, some scenes from the life of that saint for a duke of Spoleto, who is buried there with a son. These two princes had been killed while fighting in the suburbs of Assisi, as may be seen by a long inscription on the sarcophagus of their tomb. The old book of the company of painters records that one Francesco, called "of Master Giotto," was another pupil of the master, but I know nothing more about him.

Yet another pupil of Giotto was Guglielmo da Forlì, who, besides many other works, painted the chapel of the high altar for S. Domenico at Forlì, his native place. Other pupils were Pietro Laureati, Simone Memmi of Siena, Stefano of Florence, and Pietro Cavallini of Rome. But as I intend to deal fully with these in their lives, I shall content myself here with simply saying that they were pupils of Giotto. That the master drew extremely well for his day may be seen on a number of parchments containing some water colours, pen and ink drawings, chiaroscuros with the lights in white, by his hand, in our book of designs, which are truly marvellous when compared with those of the masters who preceded him, and afford a good example of his style.

As has been said, Giotto was a very witty and pleasant person, very ready in speech, many of his sayings being still fresh in the memory of his fellow-citizens. Besides the one related by M. Giovanni Boccaccio, several very good stories are told by Franco Sacchetti in his "Three Hundred Tales." I give one in the author's own words, because it contains many expressions and phrases characteristic of the time. The rubric of this one runs: "Giotto, the great painter, is requested by a person of low birth to paint his buckler. Making a jest of the matter, he paints it so as to cover the applicant with confusion."

TALE LXIII.

Every one must have heard of Giotto, and how as a painter he surpassed all others. His fame came to the ears of a rude artizan, who, having to do service in some castle, wanted his buckler painted. Accordingly he presented himself abruptly at Giotto's workshop, with a man to carry the buckler behind him. He found Giotto in, and began: "God save thee, Master, I want to have my arms painted on this buckler." Giotto took stock of the man and his manners, but he said nothing except "When do you want it," and the man told him. "Leave it to me," said Giotto, and the man departed. When Giotto was alone he reflected: "What is the meaning of this? Has someone sent him here to play a trick on me? Be that as it may, no one has ever before brought me a buckler to paint. And the fellow who brought it is a simple creature, and asks me to paint his arms as if he was of the royal house of France. Decidedly I shall have to make him some new arms." Reflecting thus with himself he sat down before the buckler, and having designed what he thought proper, he called a pupil and told him to complete the painting of it, which he accordingly did. The painting represented a light helmet, a gorget, a pair of arm pieces, a pair of iron gauntlets, a pair of cuirasses, a pair of cuisses and gambadoes, a sword, a knife, and a lance. When the worthy man returned, who knew nothing of all this, he came up and said: "Master, is the buckler finished." "Oh yes," said Giotto, "go you and bring it here." When it arrived this gentleman by proxy looked hard at it and said to Giotto: "What rubbish have you painted here?" "Will you think it rubbish to pay for it?" said Giotto. "I won't pay you four deniers," said the man. "What did you ask me to paint?" asked Giotto. "My arms," replied the man. "Well," said Giotto, "are they not here, are any wanting?" "That is so," said the man. "A plague on you," said Giotto, "you must needs be very simple. If anyone asked you who you were you would be at a loss to tell him, and yet you come here and say, 'paint me my arms.' If you had been one of the Bardi, well and good, but what arms do you bear? Where do you come from? Who were your ancestors? Begin at least by coming into the world before you talk of arms as if you were the Dusnam of Bavaria. I have represented all your arms on the buckler, and if you have any more tell me and I will have them painted." "You have given me rough words," said the man, "and spoilt my buckler." He then departed to the justice, and procured a summons against Giotto. The latter appeared, and on his side issued a summons against the man for two florins, as the price of the painting. When the magistrates had heard the arguments, which were much better advanced on Giotto's side, they adjudged that the man should take away his buckler, and give six lire to Giotto, because he was in the right. Accordingly the rustic took his buckler, paid the money, and was allowed to go. Thus this man, who did not know his place, had it pointed out to him, and may this befall all such fellows who wish to have arms and found houses, and whose antecedents have often been picked up at the foundling hospitals!

It is said that while Giotto was still a boy, and with Cimabue, he once painted a fly on the nose of a figure which Cimabue had made, so naturally that when his master turned round to go on with his work, he more than once attempted to drive the fly away with his hand, believing it to be real, before he became aware of his mistake. I could tell many more of Giotto's practical jokes, and relate many of his sharp retorts, but I wish to confine myself to the things which concern the arts, and I must leave the rest to Franco and the others.

In conclusion, in order that Giotto should not be without a memorial, in addition to the works which came from his hand, and to the notices left by the writers of his day, since it was he who found once again the true method of painting, which had been lost many years before his time, it was decreed by public order that his bust in marble, executed by Benedetto da Maiano, an Excellent sculptor, should be placed in S. Maria del Fiore. This was due to the activity and zeal displayed by Lorenzo dei Medici, the Magnificent, the elder, who greatly admired Giotto's talents. The following verses by that divine man, Messer Angelo Poliziano, were inscribed on the monument, so that all men who excelled in any profession whatever, might hope to earn such a memorial, which Giotto, for his part, had most richly deserved and earned:

> Ille ego sum, per quem pictura extincta revixit,
> Cui quam recta manus. tam fuit et facilis.
> Naturae deerat nostrae, quod defait arti:
> Plus licuit nulli pingere, nec melius.
> Miraris turrim egregiam sacro aere sonantem?
> Haec quoque de modulo crevit ad astra meo.
> Denique sum Jottus, quid opus fuit illa referre?
> Hoc nomen longi carminis instar erit.

And in order that those who come after may see by Giotto's own designs the nature of the excellence of this great man, there are some magnificent specimens in my book, which I have collected with great care as well as with much trouble and expense.

AGOSTINO AND AGNOLO, SCULPTORS AND ARCHITECTS OF SIENA.

Among the others who worked in the school of the sculptors Giovanni and Niccola Pisani were Agostino and Agnolo, sculptors of Siena, whose lives we are now writing, and who achieved great success according to the standard of the time. I have discovered that their father and mother were both Sienese, and their antecedents were architects, for the Fontebranda was completed by them in the year 1190, under the government of the three Consuls, and in the following year they founded the Custom House and other buildings of Siena, under the same consulship. Indeed it is often seen that where the seeds of talent have existed for a long time they often germinate and put forth shoots so that they afterwards produce greater and better fruit than the first plants had done. Thus Agostino and Agnolo added many improvements to the style of Giovanni and Niccola Pisani, and enriched art with better designs and inventions, as their works clearly show. It is said that when Giovanni Pisano returned to Pisa from Naples in the year 1284, he stopped at Siena to design and found the façade of the Duomo, where the three principal doors are, so that it should be entirely adorned with marble. It was then that Agostino, who was not more than fifteen years of age at the time, associated with him in order to study sculpture, of which he had learned the first principles, being no less attracted by that art than by architecture. Under Giovanni's instruction and by means of unremitting study he surpassed all his fellow-pupils in design, grace and style, so that everyone remarked that he was his master's right eye. And because it is natural to desire for those whom one loves beyond all other gifts of nature, mind or fortune, that quality of worth which alone renders men great and noble in this life and blessed in the next, Agostino took advantage of Giovanni's presence to secure the same advantages for his younger brother Agnolo; nor was if very difficult to do so, for the practice already enjoyed by Agnolo with Agostino and the other sculptors, and the honour and benefits which he perceived could be gained from this art, had so inflamed him with a desire to take up the study of sculpture, that he had already made a few things in secret before the idea had occurred to Agostino. The elder brother was engaged with Giovanni in making the marble reliefs for the high altar of the Vescovado of Arezzo, which has been mentioned above, and he succeeded in securing the co-operation of Agnolo in that work, who did so well, that when it was completed, it was found that he had surpassed Agostino in excellence. When this became known to Giovanni, he employed both brothers in many other works undertaken by him subsequently in Pistoia, Pisa, and other places. And because Agostino practised architecture as well as sculpture, it was not long before he designed a palace in Malborghetto for the Nine who then ruled in Siena, that is to say, in the year 1308. The execution of this work won the brothers such a reputation in their native place, that, when they returned to Siena after the death of Giovanni, they were both appointed architects of the State, so that in the year 1317 the north front of the Duomo was made under their direction, and in 1321 the building of the wall of the porta Romana, then known as the porta S. Martino, was begun from their plans in its present style, being finished in 1326. They restored the Tufi Gate, originally called the Gate of S. Agata all Arco, and in the same year the church and convent of S. Francesco were begun from their design, in the presence of the cardinal of Gaeta, the papal legate. Not long afterwards Agostino and Agnolo were invited by means of some of the Tolomei who were staying in exile at Orvieto, to make some sculptures for the work of S. Maria in that city. Going thither they made in sculpture some prophets which are now on the façade, and are the finest and best proportioned parts of that celebrated work. Now in the year 1326 it chanced that Giotto was summoned to Naples by means of Charles, Duke of Calabria, who was then staying in Florence, to do some things in S. Chiara and other places there for King Robert, as has been related in that master's life. On his way to Naples Giotto stopped at Orvieto to see the work which had been executed there and which was still being carried on by so many men, wishing to examine everything minutely. But the prophets of Agostino and Agnolo of Siena pleased him more than all the other sculptures, from which circumstance it arose that Giotto not only commended them, but counted them among the number of his friends, to their great delight, and further recommended them to Piero Saccone of Pietramala, as the best sculptors of the day, and the best fitted to make the tomb of Guido, the lord and bishop of Arezzo, a matter referred to in the life of Giotto. Thus the fact that Giotto had seen the work of many sculptors at Orvieto and had considered that of Agostino and Agnolo of Siena to be the best, gave rise to their being commissioned to make this tomb after his designs and in accordance with the model which he had sent to Piero Saccone. They finished the tomb in the space of four years, conducting the work with great care, and they set it up in the chapel of the Sacrament in the church of the Vescovado of Arezzo. Above the sarcophagus, which rests on brackets carved in a really admirable manner, is stretched the form of the bishop, in marble, while at the side are some angels drawing curtains, done with considerable skill. Twelve square panels contain scenes of the life and acts of the bishop in an infinite number of small figures carved in half-relief. I do not think it too much trouble to relate the subjects of these scenes, so that it may appear with what labour they were executed, and how these sculptors endeavoured to discover the good style by study.

The first shows how the bishop, aided by the Ghibelline party of Milan, who sent him 400 masons and money, entirely rebuilt the wall of Arezzo, lengthening it more than it had previously been so that it took the shape of a galley. The second is the taking of Lucignano di Valdichiana; the third, that of Chiusi; the fourth, that of Fronzoli, a strong castle of that time above Poppi, held by the sons of the count of Battifolle. The fifth contains the final surrender to the bishop of the castle of Rondine, after it had been besieged by the Aretines for many months. The sixth is the capture of the castle del Bucine in Valdarno. The seventh contains the storming of the Rocca di Caprese, which belonged to the Count of Romena, after it had been besieged for several months. In the eighth the bishop is dismantling the castle of Laterino, and causing the hill which rises above it to be cut in form of a cross, so that it should not be possible to make another fortress there. The ninth represents the destruction and burning of Monte Sansavino and the driving out of all the inhabitants. The eleventh contains the bishop's coronation, with a number of richly dressed soldiers, both horse and foot, and of other people. The twelfth and last represents the bishop being carried by his men from Montenero, where he fell sick, to Massa, and thence, after his death, to Arezzo. In many places about the tomb are the Ghibelline insignia and the bishop's arms, which are six-squared stones or on a field *azure*, following the same arrangements as the six balls in the arms of the Medici. These arms of the bishop's house were described by friar Guittone, knight and poet of Arezzo, when he wrote of the site of the castle of Pietramala, whence the family derived its origin, in the lines:

> Dove si scontra il Giglion con la Chiassa
> Ivi furon i miei antecessori,
> Che in campo azzurro d'or portan sei sassa.

Agnolo and Agostino displayed more art, invention, and diligence in this work than had ever been employed on anything before their time. And indeed they deserve the highest praise, having introduced into it so many figures, such a variety of landscapes, places, towns, horses, men, and other things, that it is a veritable marvel. And although the tomb has been almost entirely destroyed by the French of the Duke of Anjou, who sacked the greater part of the city in revenge for some injuries received by them from their enemies, yet it is still clear that it was executed with the most excellent judgment by Agostino and Agnolo, who carved on it in rather large letters: *Hoc opus fecit magister Augustinus et magister Angelus de Senis.* In 1329 they did a marble bas-relief for the church of S. Francesco at Bologna, which is in a very fair manner, and besides the carved ornamentation, which is very fine, they introduced figures a braccia and a half high, of Christ crowning Our Lady, with three similar figures on either side, St Francis, St James, St Domenic, St Anthony of Padua, St Petronio, and St John the Evangelist, and under each of these figures is carved in bas-relief a scene from the life of the saint above. All these scenes contain a great number of half-length figures, which make a rich and beautiful ornamentation after the manner of those times. It is very apparent that Agostino and Agnolo threw an immense amount of labour into this work, and that they applied all their care and knowledge to make it worthy of praise, as it truly was, and even now when it is half destroyed, it is possible to read their names and the date, by means of which and of a knowledge of the time when they began it, one may see that they spent eight whole years upon it, although it is true that at the same time they made many other small things in different places for various persons.

Now while they were at work at Bologna, that city gave itself freely to the Church, through the mediation of the papal legate, and the Pope in return promised that he and his court would go to live at Bologna, but that for his security he wished to build a castle or fortress there. This was granted by the Bolognese, and the castle was quickly built under the direction and from the design of Agostino and Agnolo; but it had a very short life, for when the Bolognese discovered that all the promises made by the Pope were vain, they dismantled and destroyed it much more quickly than it had been made.

It is said that while these two sculptors were staying at Bologna, the Po impetuously burst its banks, doing incredible damage to the territories of Mantua and Ferrara, causing the death of more than ten thousand persons, and wasting the country for miles around. Being clever and worthy men, the assistance of Agostino and Agnolo was requested, and they succeeded in finding means of reducing that terrible river to its bed, and of confining it there with ditches and other effective remedies. This brought them much praise and benefit, for besides the fame which they acquired thereby, their services were acknowledged by the lords of Mantua and by the house of Este with most liberal rewards.

When they next returned to Siena in the year 1338, the new church of S. Maria, near the old Duomo, towards the piazza Manetti, was made under their direction from their design, and not long after, the Sienese, who were greatly pleased with all the works which they executed for them, decided to seize this excellent opportunity of carrying into effect a plan which they had long discussed, but till then without any result, namely, the erection of a public fountain on the principal piazza opposite the palace of the Signoria. The charge of this undertaking was entrusted to Agostino and Agnolo, and although it was a matter of great difficulty they brought water to the fountain by pipes made of lead and earth, and the first jet of water was thrown up on 1st June 1343, to the great delight and contentment of all the city, which on this account was under a great obligation to the talent of these two citizens. At the same time the hall of the greater council was made in the Palazzo del Pubblico, and the same artists directed and designed the building of the tower of that palace, which they completed in the year 1344, hanging two great bells on it, one of which came from Grosseto, while the other was made at Siena. In the course of time Agnolo arrived at Assisi, where he made a chapel in the lower church of S. Francesco, and a marble tomb for a brother of Napoleone Orsini, a cardinal and a Franciscan friar, who had died in that place. Agostino, who had remained at Siena in the service of the State, died while he was engaged upon the designs for the ornamentation of the piazza fountain, mentioned above, and was buried in the Duomo with honour. I have not been able to discover how or when Agnolo died, so that I can say nothing about it, nor do I know of any other works of importance by his hand, and so this is the end of their lives. It would, however, be an error, as I am following a Chronological order, not to make mention of some, who, although they have not done things which would justify a narration of their whole life, have nevertheless in some measure added things of utility and beauty to art and to the world. Therefore in connection with the mention made above of the Vescovado and Pieve of Arezzo, let me here relate that Pietro and Paolo, goldsmiths of Arezzo, who learned design from Agnolo and Agostino of Siena, were the first who executed great works of any excellence with the chisel; for they made for the head priest of the Pieve of Arezzo a silver head of life-size, in which was put the head of St Donato, bishop and protector of that city, a work which was certainly praiseworthy, if only because they introduced into it some figures in enamel, which were, as I have said, among the first things executed with the chisel.

About the same time, or shortly before, the art of the Calimara at Florence, entrusted to Master Cione, an excellent goldsmith, the greater part, if not the whole, of the silver altar of S. Giovanni Batista, which contains many scenes from the life of that saint, engraved in a very creditable manner on a silver plate. This work, on account of its dimensions, and the novelty of its execution, was considered marvellous by everyone who saw it. The same Master Cione, in 1330, when the body of St Zenobius was found under the vaults of St Reparata, placed in a silver head of life-size, the piece of the head of that saint which is still preserved therein, and is carried in procession. This head was considered a most beautiful thing at the time, and brought much reputation to the artist, who died soon after, a wealthy man, and held in high esteem.

Master Cione left many pupils, and among others, Forzore di Spinello of Arezzo, who did all manner of engraving excellently, but was especially good in making scenes in enamel on silver, such as may be seen in the Vescovado at Arezzo, for which he made a mitre with a beautiful border of enamel, and a fine pastoral staff in silver. He also executed many things in silver for the Cardinal Galeotto da Pietramala, who bequeathed them to the friars of la Vernia, where he wished to be buried, and where, besides the wall, which the Count Orlando, lord of Chiusi, a small castle below la Vernia, had caused to be set up, he built the church and many rooms in the convent, and all this without leaving any notice or other memorial of himself in any part of that place. Another pupil of Master Cione was Lionardo di Ser Giovanni of Florence, who executed a number of works with the chisel and with solder, with a better design than those who preceded him, especially the altar and silver bas-reliefs of S. Jacopo at Pistoia, where, beside a large number of subjects, the half-length figure of St James, more than a braccia high, is much admired. It is in full relief, and finished with such elaboration, that it seems to have been cast rather than engraved. The figure is placed in the midst of the scenes of the altar table, about which runs a legend in letters of enamel:

> Ad honorem Dei et S. Jacobi Apostoli, hoc opus factum fuit tempore
> Domini Franc. Pagni dictae operae operarii sub anno 1371 per me
> Leonardum Ser Jo. de Floren. aurific.

Now to return to Agostino and Agnolo, they had many pupils who produced many works after them in architecture and sculpture in Lombardy and other places in Italy. Among them was Jacopo Lanfrani of Venice, who founded S. Francesco of Imola, and executed the sculptures for the principal door, where he carved his name and the date, 1343; for the church of S. Domenico at Bologna the same Master Jacopo made a marble tomb for Gio. Andrea Calduino, doctor of law and secretary of Pope Clement VI., and another very well executed also in marble and in the same church for Taddeo Peppoli, protector of the people and of justice at Bologna. In the same year, that is to say in 1347, after the completion of this tomb, or shortly before, Master Jacopo returned to his native Venice and there founded the church of S. Antonio, which was originally of wood, at the request of a Florentine abbot of the ancient family of the Abati, M. Andrea Dandolo, being doge at the time. This church was completed in the year 1349.

Then again Jacobello and Pietro Paolo, Venetians, who were pupils of Agostino and Agnolo, erected in S. Domenico at Bologna a marble tomb for M. Giovanni da Lignano, doctor of laws, in the year 1383. All these and many other sculptors continued for a long space of time to employ the same manner, so that they filled all Italy with examples of it. It is further believed that the native of Pesaro, who besides many other things did the door of the church of S. Domenico in his native town, with the three marble figures of God the Father, St John the Baptist and St Mark, was a pupil of Agostino and Agnolo, and the style of the work gives colour to the supposition. This work was completed in the year 1385. But since it would take much too long to enter into particulars of the works made in this style by many masters of the time, I will let what I have said, in this general way, suffice, chiefly because they have not exercised a great influence upon our arts. Yet I thought it good to mention these men, because even if they do not deserve a long notice, yet they are not so insignificant as to be altogether passed over in silence.

STEFANO, PAINTER OF FLORENCE, AND UGOLINO OF SIENA.

Stefano, painter of Florence and pupil of Giotto, was so excellent that not only did he surpass all the artists who had studied the arts before him, but he so far surpassed his master himself that he was deservedly considered the best of the painters up to that time, as his works clearly prove. He painted the Madonna in fresco for the Campo Santo at Pisa, and it is somewhat superior in design and colouring to the work of Giotto. In the cloister of S. Spirito at Florence he painted three arches in fresco, in the first of which, containing the Transfiguration with Moses and Elias, he represented the three disciples in fine and striking attitudes. He has formed a fine conception of the dazzling splendour which astonished them, their clothes being in disorder, and falling in new folds, a thing first seen in this picture, as he tried to base his work upon the nude figures, an idea which had not occurred to anyone before, no not even to Giotto himself. Under that arch, in which he made a Christ releasing a demoniac, he drew an edifice in perspective, perfectly, in a style then little known, displaying improved form and more science. He further executed it in the modern manner with great judgment, and displayed such art and such invention and proportion in the columns, doors, windows and cornices, and such different methods from the other masters that it seemed as if he had begun to see some glimpses of the light of the good and perfect manner of the moderns. Among other ingenious things he contrived a very difficult flight of steps, which are shown both in painting and in relief, and possess such design, variety, and invention, and are so useful and convenient that Lorenzo de' Medici, the Magnificent, the elder, made use of the design for the steps outside the palace of Poggio a Caiano, now the principal villa of the Most Illustrious Duke. In the other arch is a representation of Christ saving St Peter from the fury of the waters, so well done that one seems to hear the voice of Peter saying: *Domine, salva nos, perimus*. This work is considered much finer than the other, because, besides the grace of the draperies, there is a sweetness in the bearing of the heads, a fear of the fortunes of the sea, while the terror of the apostles at various motions and appearances of the water, are represented in very suitable attitudes and with great beauty. And although time has partly destroyed the labour expended by Stefano on this work, one may still discern confusedly that the apostles are defending themselves with spirit from the fury of the winds and waves. This work, which has been highly praised by the moderns, must certainly have appeared a miracle in all Tuscany at the time when it was produced, Stefano then painted in the first cloister of S. Maria Novella a St Thomas Aquinas, next a door, where he also made a crucifix which has since been much damaged by other painters in restoring it. He also left unfinished a chapel in the church, which he began, now much damaged by time. In it may be seen the fall of the angels through the pride of Lucifer, in divers forms. Here it is noteworthy that the foreshortening of the arms, busts, and legs of the figures is much better done than ever before, and this shows us that Stefano began to recognise and had partially overcome the difficulties which stand in the way of the highest excellence, the mastery of which by his successors, by means of unremitting study, has rendered their works so remarkable. For this cause artists have well named him the ape of nature.

Some time after Stefano was invited to Milan where he began many things for Matteo Visconti, but was not able to complete them, because having fallen sick owing to the change of air, he was compelled to return to Florence. There he regained his strength and executed in fresco in the chapel of the Asini in S. Croce, the story of the martyrdom of St Mark by being drawn asunder, with many figures which possess merit. As a pupil of Giotto he was then invited to Rome where he did in fresco for the principal chapel of St Peter's, which contains the altar of that saint, some scenes from the life of Christ between the windows of the large apse, with such care that he approaches very closely to the modern style and surpasses his master Giotto in design and other things. After this he executed in fresco, at Araceli, on a pillar beside the principal chapel on the left, a St Louis, which is much admired because it possesses a vivacity which had not been apparent in any works up to that time, not even in those of Giotto. Indeed Stefano had great facility in design, as may be seen in a drawing by his hand in our book, in which the transfiguration is represented which he made for the cloister of S. Spirito, and indeed in my opinion he designed much better than Giotto. He next went to Assisi and in the apse of the principal chapel of the lower church, where the choir is, he began a representation in fresco of the Heavenly Glory; and although he did not finish it, what he did perform shows that he used the utmost diligence. In this work he began a series of saints with such beautiful variety in the faces of the youths, the men of middle age and the old men, that nothing better could be desired, and those blessed spirits exhibit so sweet and so united a style that it appears all but impossible that they could have been done by Stefano at that time. He however did execute them, although no more than the heads of the figures are finished. Above them is a choir of angels rejoicing in various attitudes, appropriately carrying theological symbols in their hands. All are turned towards a crucified Christ who is in the midst of the work immediately above a St Francis, who is surrounded by a multitude of saints. Besides this he made some angels as a border for the work, each of them holding one of those churches of which St John the Evangelist writes in the Apocalypse. These angels are represented with such grace that I am amazed to find a man of that age capable of producing them. Stefano began this work with the intention of thoroughly completing it, and he would have succeeded had he not been forced to leave it imperfect and to return to Florence on some important affairs of his own. During this stay at Florence and in order to lose no time, he painted for the Granfigliazzi lung' Arno, between their houses and the ponte alle Carraia in a small tabernacle on one side, Our Lady seated sewing, to whom a clothed child who is seated, is offering a bird, done with such care that although it is small it merits no less praise than the more ambitious efforts of the master.

On the completion of this work and the settling of his affairs, Stefano was summoned to Pistoia by the lords there, and was set by them to paint the chapel of St James in the year 1346. In the vault he did a God the Father with some apostles, and on the side walls the life of the saint, notably the scene where his mother, the wife of Zebedee, asks Jesus Christ to permit that her two sons shall sit, one on His right hand and the other on His left in the kingdom of His Father. Near this is a fine presentation of the beheading of the saint. It is thought that Maso, called Giottino, of whom I shall speak afterwards, was the son of this Stefano, and although, on account of his name, many believe him to be the son of Giotto, I consider it all but certain that he was rather the son of Stefano, both because of certain documents which I have seen, and also because of some notices written in good faith by Lorenzo Ghiberti and by Domenico del Grillandaio. However, this may be, and to return to Stefano, to him is due the credit of the greatest improvement in painting since the days of Giotto; because, besides being more varied in his inventions, he showed more unity in colouring and more shading than all the others, and above all, in diligence he had no rival. And although the foreshortenings which he made exhibit, as I have said, a bad manner owing to the difficulties of execution, yet as the first investigator of these difficulties he deserves a much higher place than those who follow after the path has been made plain for them. Thus a great debt is due to Stefano, because he who presses on through the darkness and shows the way, heartens the others, enabling them to overcome the difficulties of the way, so that in time they arrive at the desired haven. In Perugia also, in the church of S. Domenico, Stefano began in fresco the chapel of St Catherine which is still unfinished.

At the same time there lived a Sienese painter, called Ugolino, of considerable repute, and a great friend of Stefano. He did many pictures and chapels in all parts of Italy. But he kept in great part to the Byzantine style, to which he had become attached by habit, and always preferred, from a caprice of his own, to follow the manner of Cimabue rather than that of Giotto, which was held in such esteem. His works consist of a picture for the high altar of S. Croce, on a gold ground, and another picture which stood for many years on the high altar of S. Maria Novella, and which is now in the chapter-house, where every year the Spanish nation celebrates with a solemn feast the day of St James and its other offices and burial services. Besides these he did many other things in a good style, but without in the least departing from the manner of his master. It was he who painted on a pillar of bricks in the loggia, which Lapo had built on the piazza of Orsanmichele, that Madonna which, not many years after, worked so many miracles that the loggia was for a great time full of images, and to this day is held in the highest veneration. Finally, in the chapel of M. Ridolfo de' Bardi, in S. Croce, where Giotto painted the life of St Francis, he did a crucifix in tempera with the Magdalene and St John weeping, and two friars on either side. Ugolino died at an advanced age in the year 1349, and was honourably buried at Siena, his native place.

But to return to Stefano, who, they say, was also a good architect, and what has been said above makes this likely; he died, it is said, at the beginning of the Jubilee of 1350, at the age of forty-nine, and was buried at S. Spirito in the tomb of his ancestors with this epitaph:

> Stephano Florentino pictori, faciundis imaginibus ac colorandis figuris nulli unquam inferiori; Affines moestiss. pos. vix. an. XXXXIX.

PIETRO LAURATI, PAINTER OF SIENA.

Pietro Laurati, an excellent painter of Siena, proved by his life how great may be the contentment of men of undoubted talent, who realise that their works are valued, both in their native land and outside it, and who see themselves in request by all men; for in the course of his life he was employed and caressed by all Tuscany. The first works which brought him into notice were the scenes which he painted in fresco in la Scala, a hospital of Siena, in which he imitated the style of Giotto so successfully that these paintings became known throughout Tuscany and gave rise to the well-founded belief that he would become a better master than Cimabue, Giotto, and the others, as he actually did. In these scenes he represented the Virgin mounting the steps of the Temple, accompanied by Joachim and Anna, and received by the priest; then her marriage, both remarkable for good ornamentation, well-draped figures with simple folds of the clothes, and a majesty in the carnage of the heads, while the disposition of the figures is in the finest style. During the progress of this work, which introduced the good style of painting to Siena, being the first gleam of light for the many fine spirits who have flourished in that land in every age, Pietro was summoned to Monte Oliveto di Chiusuri, where he painted a picture in tempera which is now placed in the paradiso under the church. He next painted a tabernacle at Florence, opposite the left door of the church of S. Spirito, on the side where a butcher's shop now stands, which merits the highest praise from every attentive artist, on account of the grace of the heads and the smoothness which it exhibits. Proceeding from Florence to Pisa, he did for the Campo Santo on the wall next the principal door, all the life of the Holy Fathers, with such striking reality and in such fine attitudes, that they rival Giotto. For this work he won the highest praise, having expressed in some heads, in drawing and colour, all the vivacity of which the manner of the time was capable. From Pisa he passed to Pistoia, and in S. Francesco did a picture of Our Lady in tempera, surrounded by some angels, very well arranged, the predella beneath containing some scenes with small figures, presented with a vigour and life remarkable for those times. This work satisfied him as much as it delighted others, and accordingly he put his name to it in these words: *Petrus Laurati de Senis*. Afterwards, in the year 1355, Pietro was summoned to Arezzo by M. Guglielmo, head priest, and by Margarito Boschi and the other wardens of the Pieve of Arezzo. This church had been brought to an advanced stage in a better style and manner than had been practised in Tuscany up to that time, being ornamented with squared stones and carvings by the hand of Margaritone, as has been said. There Pietro painted in fresco the tribune and all the great apse of the chapel of the high altar, representing twelve scenes from the life of Our Lady, with life-size figures, from the chasing of Joachim out of the Temple, to the birth of Jesus Christ. In these works in fresco one meets with the ideas, lineaments, carriage of the heads, and attitudes of the figures characteristic of Giotto, his master. And although the whole of this work is beautiful, yet the paintings in the vault of the apse are certainly much better than the rest, because, in the place where he represented the ascent of Our Lady to heaven, besides making the apostles four braccia high each, in which he showed his greatness of mind, being the first artist who attempted to aggrandise his style, he gave such a beautiful turn to the heads and such grace to the vestments that more could not have been desired in those days. In like manner he painted in the vaulting a choir of angels flying in the air about a Madonna. As they gracefully dance they appear to be singing, with a joy truly angelic and divine; whilst they are playing various instruments their eyes are fixed and intent on another choir of angels, sustained by a cloud of almond shape bearing the Madonna to heaven arranged in beautiful attitudes and surrounded by rainbows. This work, which was deservedly popular, procured him a commission to paint in tempera the picture of the high altar of that Pieve, where in five panels of life-size figures, represented to the knees, he made Our Lady with the Child on her arm, with St John the Baptist and St Matthew on one side of her, and on the other the Evangelist and St Donate. In the predella are many small figures, as well as in the frame of the picture above, all really fine and executed in the best style. I have entirely restored this altar at my own expense and with my own hands, so that this picture has been placed above the altar of St Christopher, at the bottom of the church. I may take this opportunity, without appearing to be impertinent, of saying in this place that I have myself restored this ancient collegiate church, moved by Christian piety and by the affection which I bear to the venerable building, because it was my first instructress in my early childhood. This I did also because it appeared to me to be as it were abandoned, and it may now be said to have been called back to life from the dead. Besides increasing the light, for it was very dark, by enlarging the original windows and making new ones, I also took away the choir, which used to occupy a great part of the church, and put it behind the high altar, to the great satisfaction of the canons there. The new altar stands alone, and has on the table before it a Christ calling Peter and Andrew from their nets, and on the side next the choir is another picture of St George killing the serpent. On the sides are four panels, each of which contains two saints of life-size. Above and below in the predella are numerous other figures, which are omitted for the sake of brevity. The ornamentation of the altar is thirteen braccia high, and the predella two braccia. The interior is hollow and is approached by a staircase through a small iron door, very well arranged. Many valuable relics are preserved there, which may be seen from the outside through two iron gratings in the front. Among others is the head of St Donato, bishop and protector of Arezzo. In a chest of various materials, three braccia high, which I have caused to be newly made, are the bones of four saints. The predella of the altar, which entirely surrounds it, has in front of it the tabernacle or *ciborium* of the Sacrament, in carved wood, all gilt, about three braccia high, and it may be seen from the choir side as well as from the front. As I have spared neither pains nor expense, since I considered myself bound to do my best to honour God, I may venture to affirm that, so far as my ability would allow, this work lacks nothing in the way of ornament, whether of gold, carving, painting, marble, trevertine, porphyry, or other stones.

Now to return to Pietro Laurati. When he had completed the picture mentioned above, he did many things for St Peter's at Rome, which were afterwards destroyed in building the new church. He also executed some works at Cortona and at Arezzo, besides those already mentioned, and some others in the church of S. Fiore e Lucilla, a monastery of black monks, notably a representation in a chapel of St Thomas putting his hand into the wound in Christ's side.

A pupil of Pietro was Bartolommeo Bologhini of Siena, who executed many pictures at Siena and other places in Italy. There is one by his hand at Florence, on the altar of the chapel of St Silvester in S. Croce. The paintings of this man were executed about the year 1350. In my book, which I have so often referred to, may be seen a drawing by Pietro, representing a shoemaker sewing in a simple but most natural manner with an admirable expression. It affords a good example of Pietro's peculiar style. His portrait by the hand of Bartolommeo Bologhini was in a picture at Siena, where not many years ago I copied it, in the manner seen above.

ANDREA PISANO, SCULPTOR AND ARCHITECT.

While the art of painting has flourished, sculptors have never been lacking who could produce excellent work. To the attentive mind, the works of every age bear testimony to this fact, for the two arts are really sisters, born at the same time and nourished and animated by the same spirit. This is seen in Andrea Pisano, who practised sculpture in the time of Giotto, and made so much improvement in that art, both by practice and study, that he was considered the best exponent of the profession who had until then appeared in Tuscany, especially in casting bronze. For this reason his works were so honoured and prized by those who knew him, and especially by the Florentines, that he was able without a pang to change his country, relations, property, and friends. It was a great advantage to him that the masters who had preceded him in sculpture had experienced so much difficulty in the art that their works were rough and common, so that those who saw his productions, judged him a miracle by comparison. That these first works were rude may be credited, as has been said elsewhere, upon an examination of some which are over the principal door of S. Paolo at Florence, and some stone ones in the church of Ognissanti, which are so executed as to move to laughter those who regard them, rather than to excite in them any admiration or pleasure. It is certain that it was much more easy to recover the art of sculpture when the statues had been lost, as a man is a round figure by nature, and is so represented by that art, whereas in painting, on the other hand, it is not so easy to find the right shapes and the best manner of portraying them, which are essential to the majesty, beauty, grace, and ornament of a picture. In one circumstance fortune was favourable to Andrea, because, as has been said elsewhere, by means of the numerous victories won by the Pisans at sea, many antiquities and sarcophagi were brought to Pisa, which are still about the Duomo and Campo Santo. These gave him great assistance and much light, advantages which could not be enjoyed by Giotto, because the ancient paintings which have been preserved are not so numerous as the sculptures. And although statues have frequently been destroyed by fire, devastation, and the fury of war, or buried or transported to various places, yet it is easy for a connoisseur to recognise the productions of all the different countries by their various styles. For example, the Egyptian is slender, with long figures; the Greek is artificial, and much care is displayed on the nude, while the heads nearly always have the same turn; and the ancient Tuscan is careful in the treatment of hair and somewhat rude. As regards the Romans, and I call Roman for the most part those things which were brought to Rome after Greece was subjugated, as all that was good and beautiful in the world was carried thither; this Roman work, I say, is so beautiful in expression, attitudes, movements both in nude figures and in draperies, that the Romans may be said to have extracted the beautiful from all the other provinces and gathered it into a single style, making it the best and the most divine of all the arts.

At the time of Andrea all these good methods and arts were lost, and the only style in use was that which had been brought to Tuscany by the Goths and the rude Greeks. Thus he noted the new style of Giotto and such few antiquities as were known to him, and somewhat refined a great part of the grossness of that wretched manner by his own judgment, so that he began to work in better style, and endow his works with far more beauty than had hitherto been seen. When his intelligence, skill, and dexterity had become known he was assisted by many of his compatriots, and while he was still a young man, he was commissioned to make some small figures in marble for S. Maria a Ponte. These brought him such a good name that he was most earnestly desired to come to work at Florence by those in charge of the building of S. Maria del Fiore, as after the façade of the three doors had been begun, there was a lack of masters to execute the subjects which Giotto had designed for the beginning of that structure. Accordingly Andrea went to Florence in order to undertake that work, and because at that time the Florentines were desirous of making themselves agreeable and friendly to Pope Boniface VIII., who was then chief pontiff of the church of God, they wished Andrea, before everything else, to make his statue in marble. Andrea therefore set to work, and did not rest until he had finished the Pope's figure placed between St Peter and St Paul, the three figures being set up on the façade of S. Maria del Fiore, where they still are. Afterwards Andrea made some figures of prophets for the middle door of that church, in some tabernacles or niches. These showed that he had made great improvements in the art, and that in excellence and design he surpassed all those who had laboured for that structure up to that time. Hence it was decided that all works of importance should be entrusted to him and not to others. Soon after he was commissioned to make four statues of the principal doctors of the church—St Jerome, St Ambrose, St Augustine, and St Gregory. When these were finished they brought him favour and renown with the craftsmen and throughout the city, and he was commissioned to make two other figures in marble of the same size. These were St Stephen and St Laurence, which are on the front of S. Maria del Fiore at the outside angle. By Andrea's hand also is the marble Madonna, three and a half braccia high with the child at her neck, which is over the altar of the little church and company of the Misericordia on the piazza of S. Giovanni at Florence. This was much praised in those times, especially as on either side of the Madonna he put an angel two and a half braccia high. A setting of very finely carved wood has been made for this in our own day by Maestro Antonio called "Il Carota," with a predella beneath, full of most beautiful figures coloured in oil by Ridolfo, son of Domenico Grillandai. In like manner the half-length Madonna in marble which is over the side-door of the

Misericordia, on the façade of the Cialdonai, is by Andrea's hand, and was highly praised, because in it he had imitated the good antique manner, contrary to his habit, which was always different from it, as shown by some designs of his which are in our book, and in which he represents all the scenes from the Apocalypse. Now Andrea had studied architecture in his youth, and an opportunity occurred for his employment in this art by the commune of Florence, for as Arnolfo was dead and Giotto absent, he was entrusted with the preparation of plans for the castle of Scarperia, which is in Mugello at the foot of the Alps. Some say, though I will not vouch for the truth of it, that Andrea stayed a year at Venice, and there executed some small marble figures which are on the façade of S. Marco, and that in the time of M. Piero Gradenigo, doge of that republic, he designed the Arsenal. But as I know nothing of this beyond the bare mention of it which occurs in some writers, I must leave the matter to the judgment of my readers. From Venice he returned to Florence, where the city, fearing the coming of the emperor, with Andrea's co-operation, hastily added eight braccia to part of the wall between S. Gallo and the Prato Gate, and in other places he made bastions, palisades and works in earth and wood. Now some three years before, he had shown his skill in casting bronze in a much admired cross which he had sent to the Pope at Avignon, by means of his close friend Giotto; accordingly he was commissioned to make in bronze one of the doors of the church of S. Giovanni, for which Giotto had already made a very fine design. This, as I say, was given to him to finish, because he was considered the most talented, skilful, and judicious master of all those who had worked until then, not only in Tuscany, but throughout Italy. He set to work, resolved to spare neither time, pains, nor diligence upon the completion of a task of such importance. Fate was propitious to him in his casting, at a time when men were ignorant of the secrets known today, so that in the space of twenty-two years he brought the door to its present stage of perfection; and what is more, at the same time he made not only the tabernacle of the high altar of S. Giovanni, with an angel on either side which were considered most beautiful, but also the small marble figures about the base of the door of the campanile of S. Maria del Fiore, after Giotto's design, and about that campanile, in certain mandorle, the seven planets, the seven virtues, and the seven works of mercy in small figures in half-relief, which were then much admired. At the same time he made the three figures of four braccia high, which were placed in niches in that campanile, on the side towards the place where the Pupilli now are, that is towards the south, figures which were considered at the time to be of considerable merit. But to return to my starting-point, I say that the bronze door contains scenes in bas-relief from the life of St John the Baptist, from his birth to his death, most happily conceived and executed with great care. And although many are of opinion that these stories do not exhibit that fine design nor that high art which should be put into figures, yet Andrea merits the highest praise, because he was the first who undertook to complete a work which rendered it possible for those who came after him to produce what is beautiful, difficult and good in the other two doors, and in the exterior ornaments now to be seen. This work was set in the middle door of the church, and remained there until Lorenzo Ghiberti made the present one, when it was removed and set up opposite the Misericordia, where it is at the present time. I must not omit to say that in making this door Andrea was assisted by his son Nino, who afterwards became a much better master than his father had been, and that it was finished in the year 1339—that is to say, not only polished and cleaned, but gilt at the fire. It is thought that the metal was cast by some Venetian masters very skilful in founding; and a record of this is in the library of the art of the Calimara, guardians of the work of S. Giovanni. Whilst the door was being made, Andrea not only made the altars aforesaid, but many others, and in particular the model of the church of S. Giovanni at Pistoia, which was founded in the year 1337. In this same year, on the 25th day of January, was found the body of St Atto, bishop of that city, in excavating the foundations of the church. The body had been buried in that place for 137 years. The architecture of that temple, which is round, was meritorious for the time. Also by the hand of Andrea is a marble tomb in the principal church of Pistoia, the body of the sarcophagus of which is full of small figures, with some larger ones above. In this tomb rests the body of M. Cino d'Angibolgi, doctor of laws, and a very famous man of letters in his day, as M. Francesco Petrarca testifies in the sonnet:

"Piangette donne, e con voi pianga Amore;"

and in the fourth chapter of the *Trionfo d'Amore*, where he says:

"Ecco Cin da Pistoia; Guitton d'Arezzo,
Che di non esser primo per ch' ira aggia."

This marble tomb of Andrea's contains the portrait of M. Cino, who is represented as teaching a number of his scholars, who are about him, with such a fine attitude and style that it must have been considered a marvellous thing in those days, although it would not be valued now.

Walter, Duke of Athens and tyrant of Florence, also employed Andrea to enlarge the piazza, and to fortify his palace by barring the bottom of all the windows on the first floor, where the hall of the Two Hundred now is, with very strong square iron bars. The same duke also added, opposite S. Piero Scheraggio, the rough stone walls which are beside the palace to augment it, and in the thickness of the wall he made a secret staircase, to mount and descend unperceived. At the bottom face of the wall he made a great door, which now serves for the Customs, and over this he set his arms, the whole after the designs and with the advice of Andrea. Although the arms were defaced by the magistracy of the twelve, who took pains to obliterate every memorial of that duke, yet on the square shield there remained the form of the lion rampant with two tails, as any attentive observer may see. For the same duke Andrea made many towers about the city, and not only began the fine gate of S. Friano, leaving it in its present form, but also made the walls of the portals and all the gates of the city, and the smaller gates for the convenience of the people. And, because the duke purposed to make a fortress on the hill of S. Giorgio, Andrea prepared a model for it, which was never used, as the work was not begun, the duke being driven out in the year 1343. The duke's plan to convert the palace into a strong castle was in great measure effected, for a considerable addition was made to the original building, as may be seen to-day, the circuit comprising the houses of the Filipetri, the tower and houses of the Amidei, and Mancini, and those of the Bellaberti. And because, after this great undertaking was begun, all the materials required for it and for the great walls and barbicans were not ready, he kept back the building of the Ponte Vecchio, which was being hurried forward as a necessary thing, and made use of the dressed stones and timber designed for this without any consideration. Although Taddeo Gaddi was probably not inferior to Andrea Pisano as an architect, the duke would not employ him on these works because he was a Florentine, but made use of Andrea. The same Duke Walter wished to pull down S. Cicilia, in order to obtain a view of the Strada Romana and the Mercato Nuovo from his palace, and would also have destroyed S. Piero Scheraggio for his convenience, but the Pope would not grant him licence. At length, as has been said above, he was driven out by the fury of the people.

For his honoured labours of so many years Andrea not only deserved the highest rewards, but also civil honours. Accordingly he was made a Florentine citizen by the Signoria, offices and magistracies in the city were given to him, and his works were valued during his life and after his death, as no one was found to surpass him in workmanship until the advent of Niccolo of Arezzo, Jacopo della Quercia of Siena, Donatello, Filippo di Ser Brunellesco, and Lorenzo Ghiberti, whose sculptures and other works were such that people recognised in what error they had been living up till then, as these men had again discovered the true excellence which had been hidden for so great a number of years. The works of Andrea were executed about the year of grace 1340.

The pupils of Andrea were numerous, and, among others, Tommaso, architect and sculptor, of Pisa, who finished the chapel of the Campo Santo, and brought the campanile of the Duomo to completion—that is to say, the last part, where the bells are. This Tommaso was Andrea's son, if we may believe an inscription on the high altar of S. Francesco at Pisa, on which a Madonna and other saints are carved by him in half relief, with his name and that of his father beneath. Andrea left a son Nino, who devoted himself to sculpture, his first work being in S. Maria Novella at Florence, where he finished a marble Madonna, begun by his father, which is inside the door, near the chapel of the Minerbetti. Going afterwards to Pisa, he made for the Spina a half-length marble Madonna suckling the infant Jesus Christ, clothed in delicate draperies. In the year 1522 a marble ornament for this Madonna was made for M. Jacopo Corbini, who had a much larger and finer one made for another full-length marble Madonna of Nino, representing with great grace the mother offering a rose to the child, who takes it in childish fashion, and so prettily, that one may say that Nino had made some steps to subduing the roughness of the stone, and endowing it with the attributes of living flesh. The figure is between a St John and a St Peter in marble, the head of the latter being a portrait of Andrea. Nino also made two marble statues for an altar of S. Caterina at Pisa—that is to say, the Madonna and an angel in an Annunciation, executed, like his other works, with such care that they may be considered as the best productions of those times. On the base beneath this Madonna Nino carved the following words: "On the first day of February 1370;" and beneath the angel: "Nino, son of Andrea Pisano, made these figures."

He produced yet other works in that city and at Naples which it is not necessary to mention here. Andrea died at the age of seventy-five, in the year 1345, and was buried by Nino in S. Maria del Fiore with the following epitaph:

"Ingenti Andreas jacet hie Pisanus in urna,
Marmore qui potuit spirantes ducere vultus
Et simulacra Deum mediis imponere templis
Ex acre, ex auro, candenti et pulcro elephanto."

BUONAMICO BUFFALMACCO, PAINTER OF FLORENCE.

Buonamico di Cristofano, called Buffalmacco, painter of Florence, who was a pupil of Andrea Tafi, celebrated for his jests by M. Giovanni Boccaccio in his "Decameron," is well known to have been the close companion of Bruno and Calandrino, painters, and themselves facetious and pleasant men. He possessed a very fair judgment in the art of painting, as may be seen by his works, which are scattered throughout Tuscany. Franco Sacchetti relates in his "Three Hundred Tales" (to begin with the deeds of this artist while he was still young) that, while Buffalmacco was a boy with Andrea, it was his master's custom, when the nights were long, to rise to work before dawn and to call the boys. This thing displeased Buonamico, who enjoyed a good sleep, and he tried to devise a plan that should induce Andrea to leave off calling them to work so much before daylight. He soon found one, for in an ill-swept loft he happened to find thirty great beetles or cockroaches. With some thin needles and corks he fixed a small candle on the back of each beetle, and when the hour came for Andrea to rise he lighted the candles and put the beetles one by one through a hole leading into Andrea's room. When the master awoke, just about the hour when he was accustomed to call Buffalmacco, and saw these lights he began to tremble with fear, and to recommend himself to God, repeating his prayers and psalms. At length he put his head under the clothes and did not call Buffalmacco that night, but remained trembling in that posture until the day. The following morning when he arose he asked Buonamico if he, like himself, had seen more than a thousand devils. Buonamico said "No," because he had kept his eyes shut, and had wondered why he had not been called. "What!" said Tafi; "I had something else to think of besides painting, and I am resolved to go and live in another house." The following night, although Buonamico only put three beetles into Tafi's chamber, yet the poor man did not sleep a jot, owing to his fear of the past night and to those devils which he saw. No sooner was day come than he left the house, declaring he would never return to it, and it was long before they were able to induce him to change his mind. But Buonamico brought him the priest of the parish, who consoled him as best he could. When Tafi and Buonamico were talking over the matter afterwards, the latter said: "I have always heard tell that the devils are the greatest enemies of God, and consequently they must also be the chief adversaries of painters, because, besides the fact that we always make them very ugly, We do nothing else but represent saints on walls and tables, in order to render men more devout or better in despite of the devils. For this cause the devils are enraged with us, and as they have more power at night than during the day, they come and play these pranks, and will do worse if this practice of early rising is not entirely abandoned." With these words, and many others, Buffalmacco succeeded in settling the matter, as the priest supported his arguments, so that Tafi left off his early rising and the devils ceased to go through the house at night with lights. But not many months afterwards, when Tafi, induced by desire of gain, and crushing every fear, began once more to rise and work at night and to call Buffalmacco, the beetles also began to make their rounds, so that the master was compelled by fear to give it up entirely, being strongly advised to this by the priest.

When this thing became known through the city, it for a while prevented other painters as well as Tafi from rising to work at night. When, shortly afterwards, Buffalmacco himself became a fairly good master he left Tafi, as the same Franco relates, and began to work by himself, and he never lacked employment. Accordingly he took a house to serve equally as a workshop and a dwelling-house, next door to a worker of wool in easy circumstances, who, being a raw simpleton, was called Goosehead. This man's wife rose early every night, when Buffalmacco, who had worked up to that time, was going to rest, and setting herself at her spinning wheel, which she unfortunately placed over against Buffalmacco's bed, she spent all the night in spinning thread. Buonamico was unable to sleep a moment, and began to devise a means whereby to rid himself of this nuisance. It was not long before he perceived that, behind the brick wall which separated him from Goosehead, was the fire of his objectionable neighbour, and by means of a crack he could see everything that she did at the fire. Accordingly he devised a new trick, and provided himself with a long tube. When he found that the wife of Goosehead was not at the fire, he every now and again put through that hole in the wall into his neighbour's pot as much salt as he wished. When Goosehead returned either to dine or to sup he could, as a rule, neither eat nor drink or taste either soup or meat, as everything was made bitter by too much salt. For a little while he had patience, and only spoke of it or grumbled; but when he found that words did not suffice, he frequently gave blows to the poor woman, who was in despair, because she thought she had been more than cautious in salting the dish. As her husband beat her from time to time, she tried to excuse herself, which only increased the anger of Goosehead, so that he began to strike her again, and as she cried out at the top of her voice, the noise penetrated the whole neighbourhood, and drew thither Buffalmacco among others. When he heard of what Goosehead accused his wife and how she excused herself, he said to Goosehead: "Worthy friend, you should be reasonable; you complain that your morning and evening dishes are too salt, but I only wonder that your wife makes them so well as she does. I cannot understand how she is able to keep going all day, considering that she is sitting up the whole night over her spinning, and does not, I believe, sleep an hour. Let her give up rising at midnight, and you will see, when she has enough sleep, her brain will not wander, and she will not fall into such serious mistakes." Then he turned to the other neighbours, and succeeded so well in convincing them that he had found the true explanation that they all told Goosehead that Buonamico was right, and that he should follow this advice. Goosehead, believing what he was told, ordered his wife not to rise so soon, and the dishes were afterwards reasonably salted, except sometimes when the goodwife had risen early, because then Buffalmacco had recourse to his remedy, a fact which induced Goosehead to cause his wife to give up early rising altogether.

One of the earliest works Buffalmacco did was the decoration of the church of the nunnery of Faenza at Florence, where the citadel of Prato now is. Here he represented scenes from the life of Christ, among other things, everything in which is in good style, and he also did there the massacre of the Innocents by Herod's order. Here he displays with considerable vigour the expressions of the murderers as well as of the other figures, because some nurses and mothers, who are snatching the children from the hands of the murderers, are using their hands, nails, teeth, and every bodily agent to help them as much as possible, showing that their minds are not less full of rage and fury than of grief. As the monastery is destroyed to-day, nothing more of this work is to be seen than a coloured drawing in our book of designs, which contains the sketch for this by Buonamico's hand. In executing this work for the nuns of Faenza, Buffalmacco, who was as eccentric in his dress as his behaviour, did not always happen to wear the hood and mantle customary in those times, and the nuns who sometimes looked at him through the screen which he had caused to be made, began to say to the custodian that they objected to seeing him always in his doublet. After he had reassured them, they remained quiescent for a while. At length, as they always saw him attired after the same fashion, they thought he must be the boy to mix the colours and accordingly they induced the abbess to tell him that they should like to see the master himself at work and not this other one always. Buonamico, who always loved his joke, told them that so soon as the master arrived he would let them know, although he was sensible of the small amount of confidence which they placed in him. Then he took a table and put another on the top of it, setting a water jug on this, over the handle of which he put a hood and then covered the rest of the pitcher in a civilian's mantle, fastening it firmly about the tables. After this he put a brush in the spout from which the water flows, and there left it. When the nuns returned to see the work through an opening where he had torn the canvas, they saw the supposed master in his attire. They believed that he was working there to the utmost of his power, and would do much better than the mere boy had done, so they were several days thinking of nothing else. At last they were anxious to see what beautiful things the master had made. Fifteen days had passed since Buonamico had set foot in the place, and one night they went to see the paintings, thinking that the master could no longer be there. They were covered with confusion and blushes when one bolder than the rest discovered the nature of the solemn master, who had not done a stroke in the fortnight. When they learned that Buonamico had treated them according to their deserts, and that the works which he had made were excellent, they recalled him and he returned with much laughter and joking to take up the work, making them see that there is a difference between men and dummies, and that works must not always be judged by the clothes of those who produce them. After a few days he finished one subject there, with which they were very delighted since it appeared to them to be satisfactory in all its parts, except that the figures in the flesh colouring seemed to them to be rather too pale. When Buonamico heard this and learning that the abbess had the best vernaccia in Florence, which served for the sacrifice of the mass, he told them that in order to remedy such a defect, nothing would be serviceable except to temper the colours with a good vernaccia, for if the cheeks and other flesh parts of the figures were touched with this, they would become red and very freshly coloured. When the good sisters heard this they believed it completely and afterwards kept him supplied with the best vernaccia so long as the work lasted, while he on his part made merry and thenceforward with his ordinary colours rendered his figures more fresh and brilliant.

On the completion of this work Buffalmacco painted in the abbey of Settimo some scenes from the life of St James in the chapel dedicated to that saint which is in the cloister, on the vault of which he did the four Patriarchs and the four Evangelists, among whom the attitude of Luke is noteworthy for the natural way in which he is blowing his pen to make the ink flow. In the subjects for the walls, which are five, the figures are represented in fine attitudes and everything is carried out with originality and judgment. In order to make his flesh colouring easier to paint Buonamico used a ground of *pavonazzo di sale*, as is seen in this work, which in the course of time has caused a saltness by which the white and other colours are corroded and consumed so that it is no marvel that the work is damaged and destroyed, while many that were made long before have been excellently preserved. I formerly considered that the injury was caused by the damp, but afterwards by an examination of his other works I have proved by experience that it is not the damp, but this peculiar practice of Buffalmacco which has caused them to be so damaged that it is not possible to see the design or anything else, and where the flesh colour should be there remains nothing but the *pavonazzo*. This method of working should not be practised by anyone who desires a long life for his paintings.

After the two pictures mentioned above, Buonamico did two others in tempera for the monks of the Certosa at Florence, one of which is in the place where the singing books for the choir rest, and the other is below in the old chapels. In the Badia at Florence he painted in fresco the chapel of the Gondi and Bastari, beside the principal chapel, which was afterwards granted to the family of the Boscoli, and still retains these paintings of Buffalmacco. Here he did the Passion of Christ, with fine and original expressions, showing in Christ, when He washes the disciples' feet, the greatest humility and benignity, and cruelty and fierceness in the Jews who lead Him to Herod. But he displayed especial originality and facility in a Pilate whom he painted in prison and in Judas, hung to a tree, from which we may readily believe what is related of this pleasant painter, that when he wished to be diligent and take pains, which rarely happened, he was not inferior to any other artist of his time. That this is true is proved by his works in fresco in Ognissanti, where the cemetery now is, produced with such diligence and with such precautions that the water which has rained upon them for many years has not injured them or caused any harm except by preventing a recognition of their excellence. They are so well preserved because they were done simply upon fresh lime. On the walls are the Nativity of Jesus Christ and the Adoration of the Magi, that is to say, over the tomb of the Aliotti. After these works Buonamico went to Bologna, where he painted in fresco on the vaults of the chapel of the Bolognini in S. Petronio, but did not finish them, for some reason unknown to me. It is said that in the year 1302 he was summoned to Assisi, and in the chapel of St Catherine in the church of S. Francesco he painted the history of the former saint's life in fresco, works which are very well preserved, and containing some figures well worthy of praise. When he had completed the chapel and was on his way through Arezzo, the bishop Guido, who had heard that Buonamico was a pleasant man and a painter of talent, wished him to stay in the city and paint for him the chapel in the Vescovado containing the Baptism of Christ. Buonamico put his hand to the work and had already done a considerable part of it when a very strange adventure happened to him, related by Franco Sacchetti in his "Three Hundred Tales." The bishop possessed a baboon, the most mischievous and malignant creature that ever was seen. This animal was one day standing on his perch and watching Buonamico work, having lost thought of everything else, and never taking his eyes off him as he mixed the colours, managed the tools, broke the eggs to make the tempera, or did any other thing, no matter what. One Saturday evening Buonamico left the work and this baboon; on Sunday morning, although he had a great log of wood attached to his legs, which the bishop made him carry so that he should not leap everywhere, notwithstanding this heavy weight, leapt on to the scaffolding where Buonamico used to stand to work, and there took up the phials and emptied them one by one, made the mixtures, broke as many eggs as were there, and began to daub all the figures with the brush, never resting until he had repainted everything himself. That done he made a fresh mixture of all the colours which were left over, although they happened to be few, and then descended from the scaffolding and departed. When Buonamico came back to his work on Monday morning and saw his figures spoiled, his phials emptied and everything upside down, he was filled with amazement and confusion. After turning the matter over in his mind for some time he concluded that some Aretine had done this from envy or for some other reason. Accordingly he went to the bishop and told him what had happened and what he suspected, at which the bishop was much troubled, yet he encouraged Buonamico to go on with the work, and to repaint the part which had been spoiled. He further pledged himself to give the artist six armed men of his infantry, who should stand with falchions to watch, when he was not working, and to cut to pieces without mercy anyone who should come. Accordingly the figures were repainted a second time, and one day while the soldiers were on the watch they heard a curious rolling noise in the church, and soon after the baboon appeared, jumped upon the seat, made the mixtures in an instant, and set to work upon the saints of Buonamico. The guard then called the master, and showed him the criminal, and when they saw him standing with them and watching the animal work, they burst into laughter, and Buonamico himself, though grieved at the damage, could not help laughing in the midst of his sorrow. At length he dismissed the soldiers who had been on guard with their falchions, and went to the bishop and said to him: "My lord, you like my manner of painting, but your baboon prefers another." He then related the matter, adding: "It was not necessary for you to send away for painters since you had a master in the house, although perhaps he did not know how to mix his colours properly. Now that he knows, let him work by himself, for I am of no further use here, and as his worth is now recognised, I shall be contented with no other wages for my work except permission to return to Florence." Although much displeased, the bishop could not refrain from laughing when he heard this, especially when he considered that a beast had made a jest of the most jest-loving man in the world. After they had laughed and talked over this new adventure, the bishop prevailed so far, that Buonamico set himself a third time to do the work, and he finished it. The baboon, as a punishment and penance for his fault, was shut up in a large cage of wood, and kept there while Buonamico worked, until the painting was quite finished. It is not possible to imagine the antics which the great beast played in that cage with his mouth, his body and his hands, at seeing others work while he was not able to imitate them. When the decoration of the chapel was completed the bishop asked, for a jest or for some other reason, that Buffalmacco should paint him on a wall of his palace an eagle on the back of a lion which it had killed. The cunning painter promised to do as the bishop desired, and made a large partition of boards, saying that he did not wish anyone to see such a thing being painted. This done, and while being shut up all alone inside, he painted the contrary to what the bishop wished, a lion crushing an eagle. When the work was completed, he asked licence from the bishop to go to Florence to procure some colours which he needed. Accordingly, having locked up his picture, he went to Florence intending never to return. The bishop after waiting some time and seeing that the painter did not return, caused the painting to be opened, and found that Buonamico was wiser than himself. Furious at the trick which had been played upon him he threatened to take the artist's life. When Buonamico heard this, he sent to tell him to do his worst, wherefore the bishop menaced him with a malediction. But at length he reflected that the artist had only been jesting, and that he should take the matter as a jest, whereupon he pardoned Buonamico the insult, and acknowledged his pains most liberally. What is more, he induced him to come again to Arezzo not long after, and caused him to paint many things in the old Duomo, which have been thrown down to-day, treating him always as his friend and most faithful servant. The same artist also painted in Arezzo the apse of the principal chapel of S. Giustino. Some write that when Buonamico was in Florence he was often in the workshop of Maso del Saggio with his friends and companions. He was also present with many others in arranging the regatta which the men of the borgo S. Friano in Arno celebrate on the calends of May, and that when the ponte alla Carraia, which was then of wood, broke down because it was too crowded with people, who had run thither to see the spectacle, he did not perish then like many others, because when the bridge fell right on a machine, representing Hell in a barque on the Arno, he had gone to buy some things that were wanted for the feast.

Not long after these things Buonamico was invited to Pisa, and painted a series of subjects from the Old Testament, from the Creation of Man to the building of the Tower of Nimrod, for the abbey of S. Paolo a ripa d'Arno, which then belonged to the monks of Vallombrosa, on the whole of the crossing of that church, on three sides, from the roof to the ground. This work, which is now almost entirely destroyed, is remarkable for the vigour of the figures, the skill and beauty of the colouring and artist's faculty of expressing his ideas, although he was not very good in design. On the wall of this crossing opposite that which contains the side door, there are some scenes of the life of St Anastasia, where some women, painted in a graceful manner, exhibit certain antique habits and gestures, very prettily and well. No less fine are some figures in a barque, arranged in well designed attitudes, among them being the portrait of Pope Alexander IV., which it is said Buonamico had from his master Tafi, who had represented that pontiff in mosaic in St Peter's. Similarly in the last subject which represents the martyrdom of the saint, and of others, Buonamico finely expresses in the faces the fear of death, the grief and dread of those who are standing by to see her tormented and put to death, while she stands bound to a tree, and above the fire. Bruno di Giovanni, a painter, assisted Buonamico in this work. He is called painter in the old book of the company. This Bruno, also celebrated as a joke-loving man by Boccaccio, finished the said scenes for the walls, and painted the altar of St Ursula for the same church, with her company of virgins, inserting in one hand of the saint a standard with the arms of Pisa, which are a white cross on a red ground, while she places the other on a woman who is rising between two mountains, and touches the sea with one foot and places her hands together in an act of entreaty. This woman represents Pisa, her head being circled with a gold crown, while she wears a garment full of circles and eagles, and being in much trouble at sea she petitions the saint. But because Bruno complained when he executed those figures that they were not life-like as those of Buonamico were, the latter in jest, to teach him to make figures, which if not life-like, should at least converse, made him put some words issuing from the mouth of the woman who is entreating the saint, and also the saint's reply to her, a device which Buonamico had seen in the works executed by Cimabue in the same church. This thing pleased Bruno and other foolish men of the time, just as to-day it pleases certain clumsy fellows, who have thus employed vulgar devices worthy of themselves. It is certainly curious that in this way advice intended simply as a jest has been generally followed, so much so that a great part of the Campo Santo done by masters of repute is full of this clumsiness.

The works of Buonamico having greatly pleased the Pisans, those in charge of the fabric of the Campo Santo commissioned him to do four scenes in fresco from the beginning of the world until the building of Noah's ark, surrounding them with an ornamentation, in which he drew his own portrait from life, that is to say, in a border in the middle and at the corners of which are some heads, among which, as I have said, is his own. He wears a hood, just like the one that may be seen above. This work contains a God who holds in his arms the heavens and the elements, and all the apparatus of the universe, so that Buonamico, explaining his scene with verses, like the paintings of the age, wrote at the foot in capital letters with his own hand the following sonnet, as may be seen, which for its antiquity and simplicity of diction peculiar to the time, has seemed to me to be worth insertion in this place, so that if it does not perchance give much pleasure, though I think it will, yet it is a matter which will perhaps bear testimony to the amount of the knowledge of the men of that age:

> "Voi che avvisate questa dipintura
> Di Dio pietoso sommo creatore,
> Lo qual fe' tutte cose con amore
> Pesate, numerate ed in misura.
> In nove gradi angelica natura
> In ello empirio ciel pien di splendore,
> Colui che non si muove et è motore,
> Ciascuna cosa fecie buona e pura.
> Levate gli occhi del vostro intelletto
> Considerate quanto è ordinato
> Lo mondo universale; e con affetto
> Lodate lui che l' ha si ben creato:
> Pensate di passare a tal diletto
> Tra gli angeli, dove e ciascun beato.
> Per questo mondo si vede la gloria,
> Lo basso, e il mezzo, e l'alto in questa storia."

It was indeed bold of Buonamico to set himself to make a God the Father five braccia high, the hierarchy, the heavens, the angels, the zodiac, and all the things above to the sky of the moon, and then the element of fire, the air, the earth, and finally the centre. For the two lower corners he did a St Augustine and a St Thomas Aquinas. At the top of this Campo Santo, where the marble tomb of the Corte now is, Buonamico painted the Passion of Christ, with a great number of figures on foot and on horse, all in varied and beautiful attitudes, and in conformity with the story. He also did the Resurrection and the Apparition of Christ to the apostles very satisfactorily. When he had completed these labours, and had at the same time spent everything that he had gained at Pisa, which was not a little, he returned to Florence as poor as he had left it, and there he did many pictures and works in fresco, which it is not necessary to describe further. When his close friend Bruno, with whom he had returned from Pisa after squandering everything, was employed to do some works in S. Maria Novella, because he had not much skill in design or invention, Buonamico designed for him all that he afterwards did for a wall of that church opposite the pulpit, filling the space between column and column. This was the story of St Maurice and his companions, who were beheaded for the faith of Jesus Christ. Bruno executed this work for Guido Campese, then constable of the Florentines. The artist took his portrait before his death, in the year 1320, and afterwards put it in this work, as an armed man, as was customary in those days, and behind him he made an array of warriors, all armed in the antique style, forming a fine spectacle, while Guido himself kneels before Our Lady, who has the child Jesus in her arms while St Domenic and St Agnes, who are on either side of her, intercede for him. Although this painting is not remarkable for its design and invention, yet it is worthy of some amount of praise, chiefly on account of the variety of clothing, and of the barbed and other armour of the time. I myself made use of it in some scenes which I did for Duke Cosimo, in which it was necessary to represent an armed man in the antique style and other similar things of that age. This thing greatly pleased His Most Illustrious Excellency and others who have seen it. From this it may be seen what an advantage it is to draw materials from inventions and works made by these ancients, for although they are not perfect, yet it is useful to know in what manner they can be made of service, since they opened the way to the marvels which have since been produced. Whilst Bruno was engaged upon these works, a rustic desired him to do a St Christopher, and they made an agreement at Florence, the terms being that the price should be eight florins, and the figure should be twelve braccia high. Accordingly Buonamico went to the church where he was to do the St Christopher, and found that as its length and breadth did not exceed nine braccia he could not manage to get the figure in, so he determined, in order to fulfil the agreement, to make the figure lying down, but as even then it would not entirely come in, he was compelled to turn it from the knees downwards on to another wall. When the work was completed the rustic refused to pay for it, exclaiming that he had been cheated. The matter thus came before the official of the Grascia, who judged that Buonamico was justified by the terms of the contract.

At S. Giovanni in l'Arcore there was a very fine Passion of Jesus Christ by Buonamico's hand, and among other much admired things it contained a Judas hanging from a tree, done with much judgment and in good style. There was also an old man blowing his nose very naturally, and the Maries are represented with such a sad air in weeping that they merit high praise for a time when men had not acquired the facility of expressing the emotions of the soul with the brush. In the same wall is a St Ivo of Brittany with many widows and orphans at his feet—a good figure—and two angels in the air who crown him, executed in the sweetest style. This building, together with the paintings, was thrown down in the year of the war of 1529. Again Buonamico painted many things in the Vescovado of Cortona for M. Aldebrando, bishop of that city, especially the chapel and the picture of the high altar; but as during the restoration of the palace and church everything was thrown down, it is not worth while to say more about them. In S. Francesco and in S. Margherita of the same city, there are still some pictures by the hand of Buonamico. From Cortona he went once more to Assisi, where in the lower church of S. Francesco he painted in fresco all the chapel of the Cardinal Egidio Alvaro of Spain, and because he was successful he was liberally recognised by the cardinal. Finally, after Buonamico had done many pictures in every part of la Marca, he stayed at Perugia on his way back to Florence, and there painted the chapel of the Buontempi in fresco in the church of S. Domenico, representing scenes from the life of St Catherine, virgin and martyr. In the old church of S. Domenico he painted also in fresco on the wall the scene where St Catherine, daughter of King Costa, disputes with, convinces, and converts certain philosophers to the faith of Christ.

As this scene is the finest that Buonamico ever produced, it may be said with truth that he has surpassed himself, and moved by this, as Franco Sacchetti writes, the Perugians directed that he should paint on the piazza St Ercolano, bishop and protector of that city. Accordingly when the terms had been settled a screen of boards and wicker work was made in the place where he was to paint, so that the master should not be seen at work, and this done he set himself to the task. But before ten days had passed everyone who passed asked when the picture would be finished, as if such things were cast in moulds. This disgusted Buonamico, who was angered by such importunity, and when the work was finished he resolved to be quietly avenged on the people for their impatience. An idea came to him, and before he uncovered his work he showed it to the people, who were delighted. But when the Perugians wanted to remove the screen, Buonamico said that they must let it remain for two days longer, because he wished to retouch some things *a secco*, and this was done. Buonamico then climbed up to where he had made a great diadem of gold for the saint, done in relief with the lime, as was customary in those days, and replaced it by a crown or garland of fish. That done, permission to depart being granted to him, he went away to Florence. When two days had passed, the Perugians not seeing the painter about, as he was accustomed to be, enquired what had become of him, and learned that he had returned to Florence. Accordingly they at once went to uncover the work, and found their St Ercolano solemnly crowned with fishes. They immediately informed their magistrates, and horsemen were sent off in haste to find Buonamico. But all was in vain, since he had returned with great speed to Florence. They, therefore, agreed to get one of their own painters to remove the crown of fishes and to repaint the saint's diadem, saying all the evil things imaginable of Buonamico and of the other Florentines. Thus Buonamico returned to Florence, caring little for what the Perugians said, and began to do many works which I shall not mention for fear of being too tedious. I will only remark that having painted a Madonna and child at Calcinaia, the man who had commissioned him to paint it, gave him promises instead of gold. Buonamico, who had not reckoned upon being used and cheated in this way, determined to be even with him. Accordingly he went one morning to Calcinaia and converted the child which he had painted in the Virgin's arms into a little bear, with simple tints, without glue or tempera, but made with water only. When the countryman saw this not long after, he was in despair, and went to find Buonamico, begging him to be so good as to remove the bear and repaint a child as at first, because he was ready to satisfy him. Buonamico did this with pleasure, for a wet sponge sufficed to set everything right, and he was paid for his first and second labours without further delay. As I should occupy too much space if I wished to describe all the jests and paintings of Buonamico Buffalmacco, especially these perpetrated in the workshop of Maso del Saggio, which was a resort of citizens and of all the pleasant and jest-loving men in Florence, I shall conclude this notice of him. He died at the age of seventy-eight, and he was of the company of the Misericordia, because he was very poor, and had spent more than he had earned, that being his temperament, and in his misfortunes he went to S. Maria Nuova, a hospital of Florence. He was buried in the year 1340, like the other poor in the Ossa, the name of a cloister or cemetery of the hospital. His works were valued during his lifetime, and they have since been considered meritorious for productions of that age.

AMBRUOGIO LORENZETTI, PAINTER OF SIENA.

Great as the debt owed by artists of genius to Nature undoubtedly is, our debt to them is far greater, seeing that they labour to fill our cities with noble and useful buildings and with beautiful paintings, while they usually win fame and riches for themselves. This was the case with Ambruogio Lorenzetti, painter of Siena, whose powers of invention were fine and prolific, and who excelled in the arrangement and disposition of the figures in his subjects. Evidence of this may be seen at the Friars Minors at Siena in a very gracefully painted scene by him in the cloister. Here he represented the manner in which a youth becomes a friar, and how he and some others go to the Soldan, and are there beaten and sentenced to the gallows, hung to a tree, and finally beheaded, during the progress of a fearful tempest. In this painting he has very admirably and skilfully depicted the disturbance of the and the fury of the rain and wind, by the efforts of the figures. From these modern masters have learned originally how to treat such a scene, for which reason the artist deserves the highest commendation. Ambruogio was a skilful colourist in fresco, and he exhibited great address and dexterity in his treatment of colours in tempera, as may still be seen in the pictures which he completed at Siena in the hospital called Mona Agnesa, in which he painted and finished a scene with new and beautiful composition. On the front of the great hospital he did in fresco the Nativity of Our Lady, and when she goes among the virgins to the temple. For the friars of St Augustine in that city he did the chapterhouse, on the vault of which are represented the Apostles holding scrolls containing that part of the Credo which each of them made. At the foot of each is a small scene representing the meaning of the writing above. On the principal wall are three scenes of the life of St Catherine the Martyr, representing her dispute with the tyrant in the temple, and in the middle is the Passion of Christ with the thieves on the Cross and the Maries below, supporting the Virgin, who has fallen down. These things were finished by Ambruogio with considerable grace, and in a good style. He also depicted in the great hall of the palace of the Signoria at Siena the war of Asinalunga, the peace following, and the events which then took place, comprising a map, perfect for the time. In the same palace he did eight scenes in *terra verde* very smoothly. It is said that he also sent to Volterra a picture in tempera, which was much admired in that city; and at Massa, in conjunction with others, he did a chapel in fresco and a picture in tempera, showing the excellence of his judgment and talent in the art of painting. At Orvieto he painted in fresco the principal chapel of St Mary. After these works he betook himself to Florence, and in S. Procolo did a picture and the life of St Nicholas on small figures in a chapel, to please some of his friends, who were anxious to see a specimen of his work. He completed this painting in so short a time, and with such skill, that he greatly increased his name and reputation. This work, in the predella of which he made his own portrait, procured him an invitation to Cortona, by command of the Bishop degli Ubertini, then lord of that city, where he worked in the church of S. Margherita, which had shortly before been erected on the summit of the mountain for the friars of St Francis. Some of this, particularly parts of the vaulting and walls, is so well done, that even now when they are almost destroyed by time, it is clear that the figures had very good expressions, and show that he deserved the commendation which he received. On the completion of this work Ambruogio returned to Siena, where he passed the remainder of his days, honoured not only because he was an excellent master in painting, but also because in his youth he had devoted himself to letters, which were a sweet and useful companion to painting, and such an ornament to all his life, that they rendered him no less amiable and pleasing than the profession of painting had done. Thus he not only conversed with men of letters and of worth, but was also employed on the affairs of his republic with much honour and profit. The manners of Ambruogio were in every respect meritorious, and rather those of a gentleman and a philosopher than of an artist. Moreover, and this tests the prudence of men more severely, he was always ready to accept what the world and time brought him, so that he supported with an equable mind the good and the evil which Fortune sent him. In truth it is impossible to overestimate what art gains by good society, gentle manners, and modesty, joined with other excellent traits, especially when these emanate from the intellect and from superior minds. Thus everyone should render himself no less pleasing by his character than by the excellence of his art. At the end of his life Ambruogio executed a much admired picture for Monte Oliveto of Chiusuri. Soon after, at the age of eighty-three, he passed in a happy and Christian manner to the better life. His works were executed about 1340.

As has been said, the portrait of Ambruogio by his own hand may be seen in S. Procolo in the predella of his picture, where he is wearing a hood on his head. His skill as a designer may be seen in our book, which contains some things by his hand of considerable merit.

PIETRO CAVALLINI, PAINTER OF ROME.

At a time when Rome had been deprived for many centuries, not only of good letters and of the glory of arms, but also of all the sciences and fine arts, there was born in that city, by God's will, one Pietro Cavallini, at the very time when Giotto, who may be said to have restored life to painting, had attained to the chief place among the painters of Italy. Pietro, who had been a pupil of Giotto, and had done some mosaics with him in St Peter's, was the first after him who illuminated that art, and who first showed signs that he was not an unworthy pupil of so great a master, when he painted over the door of the sacristy at Araceli, some scenes which are now destroyed by time, and in S. Maria di Trastevere very many coloured things in fresco for the whole church. Afterwards he worked in mosaic in the principal chapel, and did the front of the church, proving that he was capable of working in mosaic without Giotto's assistance, as he had already succeeded in doing in painting. In the church of S. Grisogono he also did many scenes in fresco and endeavoured to make himself known as the best pupil of Giotto and as a good artist. In the Trastevere also he painted almost the whole of the church of S. Cecilia in fresco, and many things in the church of S. Francesco appresso Ripa. He then executed in mosaic the front of S. Paolo, outside Rome, and in the middle nave did many scenes from the Old Testament. In executing some things in fresco for the chapter-house of the first cloister, he displayed such diligence that he was considered by men of judgment to be a most excellent master, and was for the same reason so much favoured by the prelates, that they employed him to do the wall space between the windows inside St Peter's. Among these things he did the four Evangelists, of extraordinary size as compared with the figures of the time usually seen, executed very finely in fresco; also a St Peter and a St Paul, and in the nave a good number of figures, in which, because the Byzantine style greatly pleased him, he always used it in conjunction with that of Giotto. We see by this work that he spared no effort to give his figures the utmost possible relief. But the best work produced by him in that city was in the church of Araceli sul Campidoglio mentioned above, where he painted in fresco on the vaulting of the principal apse, Our Lady with the child in her arms, surrounded by a circle of suns; beneath her is the Emperor Octavian, adorning the Christ who is pointed out to him by the Tiburtine sybil. The figures in this work, as has been said elsewhere, are much better preserved than the others, because dust cannot attack the vaulting so seriously as the walls. After these things Pietro came to Tuscany in order to see the works of the other pupils of his master Giotto, and those of the master himself. Upon this occasion he painted in S. Marco at Florence many figures which are not visible to-day, the church having been whitewashed with the exception of an Annunciation which is beside the principal door of the church, and which is covered over. In S. Basilio, by the aide of the Macine, there is another Annunciation in fresco on the wall, so similar to the one which he had previously made for S. Marco, and to another which is at Florence that there are those who believe, not without some amount of reason, that all of them are by the hand of this Pietro; certainly it is impossible that they could more closely resemble each other. Among the figures which he made for S. Marco of Florence was the portrait of Pope Urban V., with the heads of St Peter and St Paul. From this portrait Fra Giovanni da Fiesole copied the one which is in a picture in S. Domenico, also at Fiesole. This is a fortunate circumstance because the portrait which was in S. Marco was covered with whitewash as I have said, together with many other figures in fresco in that church, when the convent was taken from the monks who were there originally and given to the Friars Preachers, everything being whitewashed with little judgment and discretion. On his way back to Rome Pietro passed through Assisi in order not only to see the buildings and notable works done then by his master and by some of his fellow-pupils, but to leave something of his own there. In the transept on the sacristy side of the lower church of S. Francesco he painted in fresco a Crucifixion of Jesus Christ with armed men on horseback, in varied fashions, with a great variety of extraordinary costumes characteristic of divers foreign nations. In the air he made some angels floating on their wings in various attitudes; all are weeping, some pressing their hands to their breasts, some crossing them, and some beating their hands, showing the extremity of their grief at the death of the Son of God, and all melt into the air, from the middle downwards, or from the middle upwards. In this work which is well executed in fresh and vivacious colouring, the joints of the lime are so well made that it looks as if it had all been done in a single day: in it I have found the arms of Walter, Duke of Athens, but as it contains no date or other writing, I cannot affirm that it was executed by command of that prince. But besides the fact that everyone considers it to be by Pietro's hand, the style alone is a sufficient indication, while it seems most probable that the work was made by Pietro at the duke's command seeing that the painter flourished at the time when the duke was in Italy. Be that as it may, the painting is certainly admirable for an antique production, and its style, besides the common report, proclaims it as being by Pietro's hand. In the church of S. Marco at Orvieto, which contains the most holy relic of the Corporale, Pietro executed in fresco some scenes of the life of Christ and of His body, with much diligence. It is said that he did this for M. Benedetto, son of M. Buonconte Monaldeschi, at that time lord and tyrant of the city. Some further affirm that Pietro made some sculptures with success, because he excelled in whatever he set himself to do, and that the Crucifix which is in the great church of S. Paolo outside Rome is by him. This is said to be the same one that spoke to St Brigida in the year 1370, and we are bound to believe it. By the same hand were some other things in that style which were thrown down when the old church of St Peter's was destroyed to make the new one.

Pietro was very diligent in all his efforts and endeavoured steadily to do himself honour and to acquire fame in art. Not only was he a good Christian, but very devoted and kind to the poor, and beloved for his goodness, not only in his native city of Rome, but by every one who knew him or his works. In his extreme old age he devoted himself so thoroughly to religion, leading an exemplary life, that he was considered almost a saint. Thus there is no cause for marvel if his crucifix spoke to the saint, as is said, nor that a Madonna, by his hand, has worked and still works miracles. I do not propose to speak of this work, although it is famous throughout Italy, and although it is all but certain that it is by Pietro's hand by the style of the painting, but Pietro's admirable life and piety to God are worthy of imitation by all men. Let no one believe by this that it is impossible to attain to honoured rank without good conduct, and without the fear and grace of God, for constant experience proves the contrary. Giovanni of Pistoia was a pupil of Pietro, and did some things of no great importance in his native place. Pietro died at length in Rome, at the age of eighty-five, of a malady in his side caused by working at a wall, by the damp and by standing continually at that exercise. His paintings were executed about 1364. He was buried in S. Paolo outside Rome, with honour, and with this epitaph:

"Quantum Romans Petrus decus addidit urbi
Pictura, tantum, dat decus ipse polo."

SIMONE MARTINI AND LIPPO MEMMI, PAINTERS OF SIENA.

Happy indeed may we call those men who are inclined by nature to those arts which may bring them not only honour and great profit, but what is more, fame, and an all but immortal name. How much more happy then are those who, from their cradle, besides such an inclination, exhibit gentleness and civil manners, which render them very acceptable to all men. But the most happy of all, I speak of artists, are those who, besides having a natural inclination to the good, and whose manners are noble by nature and training, live in the time of some famous writer, by whose works they sometimes receive a reward of eternal honour and fame in return for some small portrait or other courtesy of an artistic kind. This reward should be specially desired and sought after by painters, since their works, being on a surface and a field of colour, cannot hope for that eternity that bronze and marble give to sculpture, and which the strength of building materials afford to the architect. It was thus a very fortunate matter for Simone that he lived in the time of M. Francesco Petrarca, and happened to meet this amorous poet at the court of Avignon, anxious to have the portrait of Madonna Laura by his hand; because when he had received one as beautiful as he desired, he celebrated Simone in two sonnets, one of which begins:

> "Per mirar Policleto a prova fiso
> Con gli altri, che ebber fama di quell' arte;"

and the other:

"Quando giunse a Simon l'alto concetto
Ch'a mio nome gli pose in man lo stile."

In truth these sonnets and the mention of the artist in one of his intimate letters in the fifth book, beginning *Non sum nescius*, have given more fame to the poor life of Simone than all his own works have done or ever will do, for a day will come when they will be no more, whereas the writings of such a man as Petrarch endure for all time.

Simone Memmi of Siena then was an excellent painter, remarkable in his own day and much esteemed at the Pope's court, because, after the death of his master Giotto, whom he had followed to Rome when he did the *Navicella* in mosaic, and other things, he had imitated his master's style in making a Virgin Mary in the porch of St Peter's, and a St Peter and a St Paul in that place near where the bronze pine apple is, in a wall between the arches of the portico, on the outside. For this style he was praised, especially as he had introduced into the work a portrait of a sacristan of St Peter's lighting some lamps, and has made his figures very vigorous. This led to Simone being summoned very urgently to the Pope's court at Avignon, where he executed so many pictures in fresco and on panels that his works realised the fame which had preceded him thither. Returning to Siena in great credit and high in favour, he was employed by the Signoria to paint in fresco a Virgin Mary, with many figures about her in a chamber in their palace. He completed this with every perfection, to his great glory and advantage. In order to show that he was no less skilful in painting on panels than in fresco, he executed a panel in that palace, for which reason he was afterwards commissioned to do two in the Duomo and a Madonna with the child in her arms in a most beautiful attitude, above the door of the opera of that building. In this picture some angels which are holding up a standard in the air, are flying and looking down on saints below them, who are surrounding Our Lady, forming a very beautiful and decorative composition. That done, Simone was invited to Florence by the general of St Augustine and did the chapter-house in S.

Spirito, showing remarkable invention and judgment in the figures and horses, as may be believed on seeing the story of the Passion of Christ, remarkable alike for the ingenuity, discretion, and exquisite grace displayed by the artist. The thieves on the cross are seen in the act of expiring, the soul of the good one being carried with rejoicing to heaven by angels, while that of the guilty one is roughly dragged down by devils to hell. Simone has also shown originality and judgment in the disposition and bitter weeping of some angels about the cross. But most remarkable of all is the way in which the spirits cleave the air with their shoulders, because they maintain the movement of their flight while turning in a circle. This work would supply much clearer evidence of Simone's excellence if, in addition to the ravages of time, it had not been further damaged in the year 1560, through the fathers who, not being able to use the chapter-house on account of the damp, and throwing down the little that remained of the paintings of this man, in replacing a worm-eaten floor by vaulting. About the same time Simone painted in tempera on a panel Our Lady and a St Luke with other saints, which is to-day in the chapel of the Gondi in S. Maria Novella, signed with his name. Simone afterwards did three sides of the chapter-house of S. Maria Novella very successfully. On the first, that over the entrance door, he did the life of St Domenic; on the next one towards the church he represented the religious and order of that saint fighting against the heretics, who are represented by wolves attacking some sheep, these being defended by a number of dogs, spotted white and black, the wolves being repulsed and slain. There are also some heretics who have been convinced in the disputes and are tearing up their books, and, having repented, they confess, and their souls pass to the gate of Paradise, in which are many small figures doing various things. In heaven is seen the glory of the saints and Jesus Christ. In the world below the pleasures and delights are represented by human figures, especially some ladies, seated among whom is Petrarch's Laura drawn from life, clothed in green, with a small flame of fire between her breast and her throat. There also is the Church of

Christ, guarding which are the Pope, the Emperor, the King, Cardinals, Bishops, and all the Christian Princes, among them, beside a knight of Rhodes, M. Francesco Petrarch, also drawn from life, which Simone did in order to keep green the memory of the man who had made him immortal. For the Church Universal he made the church of S. Maria del Fiore, not as it stands to-day, but as he had taken it from the model and design left by the architect Arnolfo in the Opera, as a guide to those who were to continue the building after his death. As I have said elsewhere, no memory of these models would have been preserved, owing to the negligence of the wardens of S. Maria del Fiore, had not Simone painted them in this work. On the third side, that of the altar, he did the Passion of Christ, who is going up from Jerusalem with the cross on His shoulder, and proceeds to Mount Calvary, followed by a throng of people, where He is seen raised on the cross between the thieves, together with the other incidents of that story. I shall not attempt to describe the presence of a good number of horses, the throwing of lots by the servants of the court for the raiment of Christ, the release of the Holy Fathers from limbo, and all the other clever inventions which would be most excellent in a modern master and are remarkable in an ancient one. Here he occupies the entire wall and carefully makes the different scenes, one above the other, not dividing the separate subjects from one another by ornaments, as the ancients used to do, and according to the practice of many moderns, who put the earth above the air four or five times. This has been done in the principal chapel of the same church, and in the Campo Santo at Pisa, where Simone painted many things in fresco, and was compelled against his will to make such divisions, as the other painters who had worked there, such as Giotto and Buonamico his master, had begun the scenes in this bad style. Accordingly he continued that style in the Campo Santo, and made in fresco a Madonna above the principal door on the inside. She is borne to heaven by a choir of angels, who sing and play so realistically that they exhibit all the various expressions which musicians are accustomed to show when playing or singing, such as bending the ear to the sound, opening the mouth in various ways, raising the eyes to heaven, puffing the cheeks, swelling the throat, and in short all the movements which are made in music. Under this Assumption, in three pictures, he did the life of St Ranieri of Pisa. In the first is the youth playing the psalter, to the music of which some little children are dancing,—very beautiful for the arrangement of the folds, the ornamentation of the clothes, and the head-dresses of those times. The same Ranieri is next seen rescued from such lasciviousness by St Albert the hermit. He stands weeping with his face down, and his eyes red with tears, full of repentance for his sin, while God in the air, surrounded by a heavenly light, makes as if to pardon him. The second picture represents Ranieri distributing his property among God's poor, then mounting into a barque he has about him a throng of poor and maimed, of women and children, anxiously pressing forward to petition and to thank him. In the same picture is when the saint after receiving the pilgrim's dress in the church, stands before Our Lady, who is surrounded by many angels, and shows him that he shall rest, in her bosom at Pisa. The heads of all these figures are vigorous with a fine bearing. The third picture represents the saint's return after seven years from beyond the sea, where he had spent three terms of forty days in the Holy Land, and how while standing in the choir and hearing the divine offices where a number of boys are singing, he is tempted by the devil, who is seen to be repelled by the firm purpose guiding Ranieri not to offend God, assisted by a figure made by Simone to represent Constancy, who drives away the ancient adversary represented with fine originality not only as terrified, but holding his hands to his head in his flight, with his head buried as far as possible in his shoulders, and saying, according to the words issuing from his mouth: "I can do no more." The last scene in the same picture is when Ranieri kneeling on Mount Tabor sees Christ miraculously in the air with Moses and Elias. All the parts of this work and other things which concern it show that Simone was very ingenious, and understood the good method of composing figures lightly in the style of the time. When these scenes were finished he made two pictures in tempera in the same city, assisted by Lippo Memmi his brother, who had also helped him to paint the chapter-house of S. Maria Novella and other works. Although Lippo did not possess Simone's genius, yet he followed his style so far as he was able, and did many things in fresco, in conjunction with his brother in S. Croce at Florence, the picture of the high altar of the Friars Preachers in S. Catarina at Pisa, and in S. Paolo on the River Arno, and besides many beautiful scenes in fresco, he did the picture in tempera now over the high altar, comprising Our Lady, St Peter, St Paul, St John the Baptist, and other saints, to which work Lippo put his name. After these things he did by himself a picture in tempera for the friars of St Augustine in S. Gimigniano, and acquired such fame thereby, that he was obliged to send to Arezzo to the Bishop Guido de' Tarlati a picture with three half-length figures, which is now in the chapel of St Gregory in the Vescovado. While Simone was working at Florence, a cousin of his who was a clever architect, Neroccio by name, succeeded in the year 1332 in sounding the great bell of the commune of Florence, which no one had been able to accomplish for the space of seventeen years, except by the efforts of twelve men. This man, however, balanced it so that it could be moved by two persons, and when once in motion one person alone could ring it, although it weighed more than sixteen thousand pounds; accordingly, in addition to the honour, he received three hundred gold florins as his reward, a considerable sum for that time. But to return to our two masters of Siena. Besides the things already mentioned, Lippo executed from Simone's design a picture in tempera, which was taken to Pistoia and put over the high altar of the church of S. Francesco, where it was considered very fine. When Simone and Lippo at length returned to their native Siena, the former began a large coloured work over the great gate of Camollia. Here he represented the coronation of Our Lady with a quantity of figures, but the work remained incomplete, as he fell very sick, and succumbing to the disease he passed from this life in the year 1345, to the great sorrow of the whole city, and of Lippo his brother, who gave him honoured burial in S. Francesco. Lippo afterwards finished many pictures which Simone had left imperfect. Among these were a Passion of Jesus Christ at Ancona, over the high altar of S. Niccola, in which Lippo finished what Simone had begun, imitating what he had done in the chapter-house of S. Spirito at Florence, and which Simone had entirely completed. This work is worthy of a longer life than it appears likely to enjoy, for it contains many finely posed horses and soldiers, actively engaged in various matters, wondering whether or no they have crucified the Son of God. At Assisi he also finished some figures which Simone had begun in the lower church of S. Francesco, at the altar of St Elizabeth, which is at the entrance of the door leading into the chapel, representing Our Lady, a St Louis, King of France, and other saints, eight figures in all, from the knees upwards, but good and very well coloured. Besides this Simone had begun in the principal refectory of that monastery, at the top of the wall, many small scenes and a crucifix with a Tree of the Cross. This remained unfinished, and is drawn, as may be seen to-day, in red with the brush on the rough wall. This method was favoured by the old masters in order to work in fresco with greater rapidity, for after they had sectioned out all their work on the rough wall, they drew it with the brush, following a small design which served as a guide, increasing this to the proper size, and this done they at once set to work. That many other works were painted in the same manner as this is seen in those cases where the work has peeled off, the design in red remaining on the rough wall. But to return to Lippo. He drew very fairly, as may be seen in our book, in a hermit with his legs crossed. He survived Simone twelve years, doing many things for all parts of Italy, but especially two pictures in S. Croce at Florence. As the style of the two brothers is somewhat similar, their works may be distinguished thus: Simone wrote at the bottom of his: *Simonis Memmi Senensis opus*; Lippo omitted his surname and careless of his Latinity wrote: *Opus Memmi de Seals me fecit*. On the wall of the chapter-house of S. Maria Novella, besides the portraits of Petrarch and Laura mentioned above by Simone's hand, are those of Cimabue, Lapo the architect, Arnolfo his son, and Simone himself, the Pope being a portrait of Benedict XI. of Treviso, a friar preacher, whose figure had been given to Simone by his master Giotto, when the latter returned from the Pope's court at Avignon. In the same place, next to the Pope, he portrayed the Cardinal Niccola da Prato, who had at that time come to Florence as the Pope's legate, as Giov. Villani relates in his "History." Over Simone's tomb was set the following epitaph: *"Simoni Memmio pictorum omnium omnis aetatis celeberrimo, Vixit ann. ix. metis ii. d. iii."* As may be seen in our book, Simone did not excel greatly in design, but was naturally full of invention and was very fond of drawing from life. In this he was considered the best master of his time, so that the lord Pandolfo Malatesta sent him to Avignon to make the portrait of M. Francesco Petrarch, at whose request he afterwards made the much admired portrait of Madonna Laura.

TADDEO GADDI, PAINTER OF FLORENCE.

It is a truly useful and admirable task to reward talent largely at every opportunity, because great abilities which would otherwise lie dormant, are excited by this stimulus and endeavour with all industry, not only to learn, but to excel, to raise themselves to a useful and honourable rank, from which flow honour to their country, glory to themselves, and riches and nobility to their descendants, who, being brought up on such principles, often become very rich and noble, as did the descendants of Taddeo Gaddi the painter, by means of his works. This Taddeo di Gaddo Gaddi of Florence, after the death of Gaddo, had been the pupil of his godfather Giotto for twenty-four years, as Cennino di Drea Ceninni, painter of Colle di Valdelsa writes. On the death of Giotto he became the first painter of the day, by reason of his judgment and genius, surpassing his fellow-pupils. His first works, executed with a facility due to natural ability rather than to acquired skill, were in the church of S. Croce at Florence in the chapel of the sacristy, where, in conjunction with his fellow-pupils of the dead Giotto, he did some fine scenes from the life of St Mary Magdalene, the figures and draperies being very remarkable, the costumes being those then worn. In the chapel of the Baroncelli and Bandini, where Giotto had already done a picture in tempera, Taddeo did some scenes from the life of the Virgin in fresco on the wall, which were considered very beautiful. Over the door of the same sacristy he painted the scene of Christ disputing with the doctors in the temple, which was afterwards destroyed when Cosimo de' Medici the elder built the noviciate, the chapel and the vestibule of the sacristy, in order to put a stone cornice above that door. In the same church he painted in fresco the chapel of the Bellacci and that of St Andrew, next to one of the three done by Giotto, in which he represented Christ calling Andrew and Peter from their nets, and the crucifixion of the latter apostle with such truth that it was much admired and praised when it was completed, and is still held in esteem at the present day. Over the side door and under the tomb of Carlo Marsupini of Arezzo, he made a dead Christ with Mary, in fresco, which was much admired. Below the screen of the church, on the left hand above the crucifix of Donato, he painted in fresco a miracle of St Francis, where he raises a boy killed by a fall from a terrace, with an apparition in the air. In this scene he drew the portraits of his master Giotto, the poet Dante, Guido Cavalcanti, and some say of himself. In different places in the same church he made a number of figures, which are recognised by artists from their style. For the company of the Temple he painted the tabernacle which is at the corner of the via del Crocifisso, containing a fine deposition from the cross. In the cloister of S. Spirito he did two scenes in the arches next the chapter-house, in one of which he represented Judas selling Christ, and in the other the Last Supper with the Apostles. In the same convent over the door of the refectory he painted a crucifix and some saints, which distinguish him, among the others who worked there, as a true imitator of the style of Giotto, whom he always held in the highest veneration. In S. Stefano of the Ponte Vecchio he painted the picture and predella of the high altar with great care, and in the oratory of S. Michele in Orto he very skilfully represented in a picture a dead Christ, wept over by Mary, and deposited in the sepulchre by Nicodemus with great devotion. In the church of the Servites he painted the chapel of St Nicholas, belonging to the Palagio family, with stories of that saint, where, in his painting of a barque, he has clearly shown with the greatest judgment and grace, that he had a thorough knowledge of a tempestuous sea and of the fury of Fortune. In this work St Nicholas appears in the air, while the mariners are emptying the ship and throwing out the merchandise, and frees them from their danger. This work gave great satisfaction and was much admired, so that Taddeo was commissioned to paint the chapel of the high altar of that church. Here he did in fresco some stories of Our

Lady, and in tempera on a panel, Our Lady with many saints, a very vigorous representation. Similarly, on the predella of this picture he did some stories of Our Lady in small figures, into the details of which it is not necessary to enter, because everything was destroyed in the year 1467 when Ludovico, Marquis of Mantua, made in that place the tribune which is there now, from the design of Leon Battista Alberti, and the choir of the friars, causing the picture to be taken to the chapter-house of that convent, in the refectory of which he made above the wooden backs, the Last Supper of Jesus Christ with the Apostles, and above that a crucifix with many saints. When Taddeo had completed this work he was invited to Pisa where he painted the principal chapel of S. Francesco in fresco, very well coloured, for Gherardo and Bonaccorso Gambacorti, with many figures and stories of the saint, and of St Andrew and St Nicholas. On the vaulting and the wall is Pope Honorius confirming the rule, and a representation of Taddeo from life, in profile, with a hood folded over his head. At the bottom of this scene are these words:

Magister Taddeus Gaddus de Florentia pinxit hanc hittoriam Sancti Francisci et Sancti Andreæ et Sancti Nicolai anno Domini MCCCXLII. de mense Augusti.

In the cloister of the same convent he further made a Madonna in fresco, with the child at her neck, very well coloured. In the middle of the church, on the left hand on entering, is seated a St Louis the bishop, to whom St Gherardo da Villamagna, who was a friar of the order, is recommending one fra Bartolommeo, then superior of the convent. The figures of this work, being drawn from life, exhibit the utmost vivacity and grace, in that simple style which was in some respects better than Giotto's, particularly in the expression of intercession, joy, grief, and other feelings, the good representation of which always constitutes the highest claim of the painter to honour. Taddeo then returned to Florence and continued for the commune the work of Orsan-michele, refounding the pillars of the Loggia, using dressed and hewn stones in place of the original bricks, but without making any change in the design left by Arnolfo, who provided that a palace with two vaults should be made above the Loggia for the preservation of the provisions of grain made by the people and commune of Florence. For the completion of this work the Art of the Porta S. Maria, to whom the charge of the structure had been entrusted, ordained the payment of the gabelle of the piazza and of the grain market, and some other changes of very small importance. But an ordinance of far more importance was that each of the arts of Florence should make a pilaster for itself, placing on a niche in it the patron saint of each, and that every year the consuls of the arts should go to make offerings on their saints' feast days and keep their standard and insignia there all that day, but that the alms so collected should be made to the Virgin for the needy poor.

In the year 1333 a great flood had carried away the parapets of the Ponte Rubaconte, thrown down the castle of Altafronte, left nothing of the Ponte Vecchio except the two middle piles, entirely destroyed the Ponte S. Trinita, a single shattered pile alone standing, and half the Ponte alla Carraia, breaking down the flood-gates of Ognissanti. For this cause the rulers of the city took counsel together, because they did not wish that those who dwelt beyond the Arno should again suffer this inconvenience of having to cross by barques. Accordingly they called in Taddeo Gaddi, because his master Giotto had gone to Milan, and instructed him to make the model and design of the Ponte Vecchio, directing him to render it as strong and as beautiful as it could possibly be. To this end he spared neither pains nor expense, building it with such strong piers and such fine arches, all of hewn stone, that it now sustains twenty-two shops on either side, making forty-four in all, to the great benefit of the commune, who that year expended upon it eight hundred florins of rent. The length of the span from one side to the other is 32 braccia, the middle way is 16, and the shops on either side 8 braccia. For this work, which cost sixty thousand gold florins, Taddeo not only deserved the praise accorded by his contemporaries, but he merits our commendation to-day to an even greater degree, for, not to speak of many other floods, the bridge did not move in the year 1537, on 13th September, when the Ponte a Santa Trinita, two arches of the Carraia, and a great part of the Rubaconte all fell, and more damage was done. Certainly no man of judgment can refrain from amazement, or at least wonder, when he considers how firmly the Ponte Vecchio resisted the impetus of the water, the timber, and other debris, without yielding. At the same time Taddeo laid the foundations of the Ponte a Santa Trinita, which was finished with less success in the year 1346 at a cost of twenty thousand gold florins. I say with less success, because, unlike the Ponte Vecchio, it was ruined by the flood of 1557. It was also under Taddeo's direction that the wall on the side of S. Gregorio was made at the same time, with driven piles, two piers of the bridge being taken to enlarge the ground on the side of the piazza de' Mozzi, and to set up the mills which are still there.

Whilst all these things were being done under Taddeo's direction and from his plans, he did not allow them to stop his painting, and did the tribunal of the old Mercanzia, where, with poetical imagination, he represented the tribunal of six men, that being the number of the chief of that magistracy, who are watching Truth taking out Falsehood's tongue, the former clothed in velvet over her naked skin, the latter in black: underneath are these lines:

"La pura Verita per ubbidire
Alla santa Giustizia che non tarda
Cava la lingua alla falsa bugiarda."

Lower down are the following lines:

"Taddeo dipinse questo bel rigestro
Discepol fu di Giotto il buon maestro."

In Arezzo some works in fresco were allotted to him, which he carried out with the greatest perfection with the aid of his pupil Giovanni da

Milano. One of these, representing the Passion of Jesus Christ, may still be seen in the oratory of the Holy Spirit, in front of the high altar. It contains many horses, and the thieves on the cross, and is considered a very beautiful thing on account of his conception of the nailing to the cross, where there are some figures which vividly express the rage of the Jews, some drawing Him by the legs with a rope, others bringing the sponge, and others in various attitudes, such as Longinus, who pierces His side with the spear, and the three soldiers who are playing for His garments, their faces depicting hope and fear in throwing the dice. The first of these men stands in a constrained attitude awaiting his turn, and is so eager to draw that he apparently does not notice the discomfort; the second is loading the dice-box, and frowns as he looks at the dice, his mouth and eyes open as if from suspicion of fraud, showing clearly to an observant beholder his eagerness to win; the third, who is about to throw the dice, spreads out on the ground with trembling arm the garments, where he shows with a smile that he intends to throw them. On the sides of the church also may be seen some stories of St John the Evangelist, which are executed with such wonderful style and design that they cannot fail to excite astonishment. In the chapel of St Sebastian, next the sacristy in S. Agostino, he did the life of that martyr and the dispute of Christ with the doctors, so well executed and finished that the beauty and variety displayed, as well as the grace of their colouring, are marvellous.

In Casentino, in the church of the Sasso del Vernia, he painted in the chapel the scene where S. Francis receives the stigmata. Here Taddeo was assisted in matters of minor importance by Jacopo di Casentino, who thus became his pupil. When this was completed Taddeo returned with Giovanni of Milan to Florence, where in the city and without they made a number of panels and pictures of importance. In the process of time Taddeo acquired so much money that, by steadily saving, he founded the wealth and nobility of his family, being always considered a wise and courteous man. In S. Maria Novella he painted the chapter-house which was allotted to him by the prior of the place, who supplied him with the idea. It is known that, because the work was a great one, and as the chapter-house of S. Spirito was uncovered at the same time as the bridges were building, to the great glory of Simone Memmi who painted it, the prior wished to secure Simone to do half of the work; accordingly he consulted Taddeo, who was very willing to agree to this, since Simone had been a fellow-pupil of Giotto with him, and they had always remained close friends and companions. O truly noble souls to love one another fraternally without emulation, ambition, or envy, so that each rejoiced at the advancement and honour of his friend as if it had been his own. The work was accordingly divided, three sides being allotted to Simone, as I have said in his life, and the left side and the whole of the vaulting to Taddeo, who divided his work into four divisions or quarters, according to the disposition of the vaulting. In the first he made the Resurrection of Christ, in which he apparently endeavours to cause the glorified body to emit light, which is reflected on a city and on some mountain rocks; but he abandoned this device in the figures and in the rest of the composition, possibly because he was not confident of his ability to carry it out, owing to the difficulties which presented themselves. In the second compartment he made Jesus Christ delivering Peter from drowning, when the apostles, who are managing the boat, are certainly very fine, and especially a man who is fishing with a line on the sea-shore (a thing first attempted by Giotto in the mosaic of the *Navicella* in St Peter's), represented with vigorous and life-like expression. In the third he painted the Ascension of Christ, while the fourth represents the Descent of the Holy Spirit, remarkable for the fine attitudes of the Jews, who are endeavouring to enter the door. On the wall beneath are the seven sciences, with their names, and appropriate figures below each. Grammar habited like a woman is teaching a boy; beneath her sits the writer Donato. Next to Grammar sits Rhetoric, at whose feet is a figure with its two hands resting on books, while it draws a third hand from beneath a mantle and holds it to its mouth. Logic has a serpent in her hand, and is veiled, with

Zeno Eleate at her feet reading. Arithmetic holds the table of the Abacus, and under her sits Abraham, its inventor. Music has musical instruments, with Tubal Cain beneath, beating with two hammers upon an anvil, with his ears listening to the sound. Geometry has the quadrant and sextant, with Euclid beneath. Astrology has the sphere of the heavens in her hands, and Atlas under her feet. On the other side sit the seven theological sciences, each one having beneath it a person of an appropriate condition, pope, emperor, king, cardinal, duke, bishop, marquis, etc., the pope being a portrait of Clement V. In the middle, and occupying a higher place, is St Thomas Aquinas, who was master of all these sciences, and certain heretics under his feet, Arius, Sabellius, and Averroes. About him are Moses, Paul, John the Evangelist, and some other figures with the four cardinal virtues, and the three theological ones, in addition to an infinite number of other ideas set forth by Taddeo with no small design and grace, so that this may be considered the best devised and the most finely preserved of all his works. In the same S. Maria Novello, over the transept he did a St Jerome dressed as a cardinal. He held that saint in reverence, choosing him as the protector of his house, and after Taddeo's death his son Agnolo made a tomb for his descendants covered with a marble slab adorned with the arms of the Gaddi under this picture. For these descendants the cardinal Jerome, aided by their merits and the goodness of Taddeo, has obtained from God most distinguished places in the church, such as clerkships of the chamber, bishoprics, cardinalates, provostships, and most honourable knighthoods. The descendants of Taddeo have uniformly valued and encouraged men of genius in painting and sculpture, assisting them to the utmost of their power. At length when Taddeo had reached the age of fifty years, he was seized with a severe fever and passed from this life in the year 1350, leaving Agnolo his son and Giovanni to carry on the painting, recommending them to Jacopo di Casentino for their material well being, and to Giovanni da Milano for instruction in art. This Giovanni, besides many other things, made a picture, after Taddeo's death, which was placed in S. Croce at the altar of St Gherardo da Villamagna, fourteen years after he had been left without his master, and also the high altar picture of Ognissanti, where the Umiliati friars are stationed, a much admired work; and in Assisi he made for the tribune of the high altar a crucifix, Our Lady, and St Clare, and on the side wall stories of Our Lady. He subsequently went to Milan, where he did many works in tempera and in fresco, and at length died there.

Now Taddeo always adopted Giotto's style, but did not greatly improve it, except in the colouring, which he made fresher and more vivid. Giotto had made such efforts to overcome other difficulties of this art, that although he considered colouring also, yet it was not granted to him to master this completely. Taddeo, on the other hand, profiting by his master's labours, had an easier task, and was able to add something of his own in improving the colouring.

Taddeo was buried by Agnolo and Giovanni his sons in S. Croce, in the first cloister, and in the tomb which he had made for Gaddo his father. He was much honoured in the verses of the learned of the time as a man who had deserved much for his character, and because he had, besides his pictures, successfully completed many structures very useful to his city. In addition to the works already mentioned, he had with care and diligence completed the campanile of S. Maria del Fiore from the design of his master Giotto. This campanile was so constructed that it would be impossible to join stones with more care, or to make a tower which should be finer in the matter of ornament, expense, and design. The epitaph made for Taddeo was as follows:

> Hoc uno dici poterat Florentia felix
> Vivente: at certa est non potuisse mori.

Taddeo's method of designing was very broad and bold, as may be seen in our book, which contains a drawing by his hand of the scene which he did in the chapel of St Andrew in S. Croce, at Florence.

ANDREA DI CIONE ORCAGNA, PAINTER, SCULPTOR, AND ARCHITECT OF FLORENCE.

It frequently happens that when a man of genius excels in one thing, he is easily able to learn another, especially such as are similar to his first profession, and which proceed, as it were, from the same source. An example of this is Orcagna of Florence, who was painter, sculptor, architect, and poet, as will be said below. He was born in Florence, and while quite a child began to practise sculpture under Andrea Pisano, and so continued for many years. When he afterwards became desirous of enriching his invention for the purpose of composing beautiful scenes, he carefully studied design, aided as he was by nature, who wished to make him a universal genius, and as one thing leads to another, he practised painting in colours in tempera and fresco, and succeeded so well with the aid of Bernardo Orcagna his brother, that Bernardo himself procured his assistance to do the life of Our Lady in the principal chapel of S. Maria Novella, which then belonged to the family of the Ricci. This work was considered very beautiful, although, owing to the neglect of those who afterwards had charge of it, it was destroyed by water through the breaking of the roof not many years after, and consequently it is restored in its present manner, as will be said in the proper place. Suffice it to say, that Domenico Grillandai, who repainted it, made considerable use of the inventions of Orcagna which were there. In the same church, and in conjunction with his brother Bernardo, Andrea did in fresco the chapel of the Strozzi, which is near the door of the sacristy and the belfry. In this chapel, which is approached by some stone steps, he painted on one wall the glory of Paradise, with all the saints in the various habits and head-dresses of the time. On the other wall he did Hell, with the holes, centres, and other things described by Dante, of whom Andrea was a diligent student. In the church of the Servites, in the same city he painted in fresco, also in conjunction with Bernardo, the chapel of the family of the Cresci, and in S. Pier Maggiore in a picture of considerable size, the Coronation of the Virgin, and another picture in S. Romeo near the side door.

He and his brother Bernardo also painted in fresco together the façade of S. Apollinare, with such diligence that the colours are bright and beautiful and marvellously preserved to this day in that exposed place. The governors of Pisa, moved by the renown of these works of Orcagna, which were much admired, sent for him to do a part of the wall in the Campo Santo of that city, as Giotto and Buffalmacco had previously done. Accordingly he put his hand to the work, and painted a Last Judgment, with some fancies of his own, on the wall towards the Duomo, next to the Passion of Christ made by Buffalmacco. In the first scene he represented all ranks of temporal lords enjoying the pleasures of this world, seating them in a flowery meadow under the shadow of many orange trees, forming a most agreeable wood. Above the branches are some cupids, who are flying round and over a number of young women, evidently portraits of noble women and ladies of the day, though they are not recognisable after this lapse of time. The cupids are preparing to transfix the hearts of the ladies, near whom are young men and lords listening to playing and singing and watching the amorous dancing of men and maidens, delighting in the sweetness of their loves. Among these lords Orcagna drew Castruccio, the lord of Lucca, a youth of the most striking aspect, with a blue hood bound about his head and a sparrowhawk on his hand. Near him are other lords of the time, whose identity is not known. In fine, in this first part he represented in a most gracious manner all the delights of the world in accordance with the demands of the place and the requirements of art. On the other side of the same scene he represented, on a high mountain, the life of those who, being moved by penitence for their sins and by the desire of salvation, have escaped from the world to this mountain, which is thus full of holy hermits serving the Lord, and doing various things with very realistic expressions. Some are reading and praying, and are all intent on contemplation; while others are working to earn their living, and are exercising themselves in various activities. Here is a hermit milking a goat in the most vigorous and realistic manner. Below this is St Macario showing to three kings, who are riding to hunt with their ladies and suite, the corpses of three kings, partly consumed in a tomb, emblematic of human misery, and which are regarded with attention by the living kings in fine and varied attitudes, expressive of wonder, and they seem to be reflecting that they themselves must shortly become such. One of these kings is the portrait of Uguccione della Faggiuola of Arezzo, in a figure represented as holding his nose with his hand in order not to smell the odour of the dead kings. In the middle of this scene is Death, flying through the air and clothed in black, while he raises his scythe to take the life of many who are on the earth, of every state and condition, poor, rich, lame, whole, young, old, men, women, and, in short, a multitude of every age and sex. And because Orcagna knew that the invention of Buffalmacco had pleased the Pisans, by which Bruno caused his figures in S. Paolo a ripa d'Arno to speak, making letters issue from their mouths, he has filled all these works of his with such writings, of which the greater number, being destroyed by time, cannot be deciphered. He makes some lame old men say—

> Da che prosperitade ci ha lasciati.
> O morte medecina d'ogni pena
> Deh vieni a darne omai l'ultima cena,

with other words which cannot be made out, and similar lines composed in the old style by Orcagna himself, as I have discovered, for he was addicted to poetry, and wrote some sonnets. About these bodies are some devils, who take their souls out of their mouths and carry them to gulfs full of fire upon the top of a very high mountain. On the other hand, there are some angels who, in like manner, take the souls of the dead, who happen to have been good, out of their mouths, and carry them flying to Paradise. In this scene is a large scroll, held by two angels, containing the following words:

> Ischermo di savere e di richezza,
> Di nobilitate ancora e di prodezza,
> Vale neente ai colpi di costei,

with some other words which cannot easily be understood. Underneath in the ornamentation of these scenes are nine angels who hold some words written in the border of the painting, in the vulgar tongue and in Latin, put there because they would spoil the scene if placed higher, and to omit them altogether did not appear fitting to the author, who considered this method very fine, and perhaps it was to the taste of that age. The greater part of these are omitted here in order not to tire the reader with impertinent matter of little interest, and moreover the greater number of the scrolls are obliterated, while the remainder are in a very imperfect condition. After this Orcagna made the Last Judgment. He placed Jesus Christ on high above the clouds in the midst of his twelve Apostles to judge the quick and the dead, exhibiting on the one side, with great art and vigour, the despair of the damned, as they are driven weeping to Hell by furious demons; and on the other side the joy and rejoicing of the elect, who are transported to the right hand side of the blessed by a troop of Angels led by the Archangel Michael. It is truly lamentable that for lack of writers, the names and identity of few or none of these can be ascertained out of such a multitude of magistrates, knights and other lords, who are evidently drawn from life, although the pope there is said to be Innocent IV. the friend of Manfred.

After this work and some sculptures in marble executed to his great glory in the Madonna, which is on the side of the Ponte Vecchio, Andrea left his brother Bernardo to work by himself in the Campo Santo at a Hell made according to Dante's description, which was afterwards much damaged in 1530, and restored by Solazzino, a painter of our own day. Meanwhile Andrea returned to Florence, where he painted in fresco in the middle of the Church of S. Croce on a very large wall on the right hand, the same things which he had done in the Campo Santo at Pisa, in three similar pictures, but omitting the scene in which St Macario is showing human wretchedness to the three kings, and the life of the hermits who are serving God on the mountain. But he did all the rest of that work, displaying better design and more diligence than at Pisa, but retaining almost the same methods in the inventions, style, scrolls and the rest, without changing anything except the portraits from life; because in this work he introduced the portraits of some of his dearest friends into his Paradise, while he condemned his enemies to hell. Among the elect may be seen the portrait in profile of Pope Clement VI. with the tiara on his head, who reduced the Jubilee from a hundred to fifty years, was a friend of the Florentines, and possessed some of their paintings which he valued highly. Here also is Maestro Dino del Garbo, then a most excellent physician, clothed after the manner of the doctors of that day with a red cap on his head lined with miniver, while an angel holds him by the hand. There are also many other portraits which have not been identified. Among the damned he drew the Guardi, sergeant of the Commune of Florence, dragged by the devil with a hook. He may be recognised by three red lilies on his white hat, such as were worn by the sergeants and other like officials. Andrea did this because the sergeant had upon one occasion distrained his goods. He also drew there the notary and the judge who were against him in that cause. Next to Guardi is Cecco d'Ascoli, a famous wizard of the time, and slightly above him, and in the middle is a hypocritical friar, who is furtively trying to mingle with the good, while an angel discovers him and thrusts him among the damned. Besides Bernardo, Andrea had another brother called Jacopo, who devoted himself, but with little success, to sculpture. For this brother Andrea had sometimes made designs in relief in clay, and this led him to wish to do some things in marble to see if he remembered that art, which he had studied at Pisa, as has been said. Accordingly he applied himself earnestly to that pursuit, and attained to such a measure of success that he afterwards made use of it with credit, as will be said. He next devoted all his energies to the study of architecture, thinking that he might have occasion to make use of it. Nor was he mistaken, for in the year 1355 the Commune of Florence bought some private houses near the palace to enlarge that building and increase the piazza, and also to make a place where citizens could withdraw in time of rain, and in winter to do under cover the things which were done in the uncovered arcade when bad weather did not interfere. They procured a number of designs for the construction of a large and magnificent loggia near the palace for this purpose as well as for a mint for coining money. Among these designs prepared by the best masters of the city, that of Orcagna was universally approved and accepted as being larger, finer and more magnificent than the others, and the large loggia of the piazza was begun under his direction by order of the Signoria and Commune, upon foundations laid in the time of the Duke of Athens, and was carried forward with much diligence in squared stones excellently laid. The arches of the vaults were constructed in a manner new for that time, not being pointed as had previously been customary, but in half circles after a new pattern, with much grace and beauty, and the building was completed under Andrea's direction in a short time. If it had occurred to him to erect it next to S. Romolo and to turn its back towards the north, which he perhaps omitted to do in order that it should be convenient for the door of the palace, it would have been a most useful construction for all the city, as it is a most beautiful piece of work, whereas it is impossible to remain there in winter owing to the strong wind. In the decoration of this loggia Orcagna made seven marble figures in half relief between the arches of the façade representing the seven virtues, theological and cardinal. These are so fine, that taken in conjunction with the whole work they prove their author to have been an excellent sculptor as well as a distinguished painter and architect. Besides this he was in all his deeds a pleasant, well-bred and amiable man so that his fellow was never seen. And since he never abandoned the study of one of his three professions when he took up another, he painted a picture in tempera with many small figures while the loggia was building, and a predella of small figures for that chapel of the Strozzi where his brother Bernardo had already done some things in fresco. On this picture he wrote his name thus: *Anno Domini MCCCLVII Andreas Cionis de Florentia me pinxit*, being of opinion that it would exhibit his powers to better advantage than his works in fresco could. When this was finished he did some paintings on a panel which were sent to the pope to Avignon, in the cathedral church of which they still remain. Shortly afterwards, the men of the company of Orsanmichele, having collected a quantity of money of alms and goods given to the Madonna there on account of the mortality of 1348, they decided that they would make about her a chapel or tabernacle richly adorned not only with marble carved in every manner and with other stones of price, but also with mosaic and ornaments of bronze, the best that could be desired, so that in workmanship and material it should surpass every other work produced up to that day. The execution of this was entrusted to Orcagna as being the foremost man of the age. He made a number of designs, one of which was chosen by the directors of the work as being the best of all. Accordingly the task was allotted to him and everything was committed to his judgment and counsel. He and his brother undertook to do all the figures, giving the rest to various masters from other countries. On the completion of the work, he caused it to be built up and joined together very carefully without lime, the joints, being of lead and copper so that the shining and polished marbles should not be blemished. This proved so successful and has been of such use and honour to those who came after him, that it appears to an observer that the chapel is hollowed out of a single piece of marble, so excellently are parts welded together, thanks to this device of Orcagna. Although in the German style its grace and proportions are such that it holds the first place among the things of the time, owing chiefly to the excellent composition of its great and small figures and of the angels and prophets in half-relief about the Madonna. The casting of the carefully polished bronze ornaments which surround it is marvellous, for they encircle the whole work, enclose it and bind it together, so that this part is as remarkable for its strength as the other parts are for their beauty. But he devoted the highest powers of his genius to the scene in half-relief on the back of the tabernacle, representing in figures of a braccia and a half, the twelve apostles looking up at the Madonna ascending to heaven in a mandorla, surrounded by angels. He represented himself in marble as one of the apostles, an old man, clean shaven, a hood wound round his head, with a flat round face as shown in his portrait above, which it taken from this. On the base he wrote these words in the marble: *Andreas Cionis pictor florentinus oratorii archimagister extitit hujus, MCCCLIX*. It appears that the erection of the loggia and of the marble tabernacle, with all the workmanship involved cost 96,000 gold florins, which were very well expended, because in architecture, in sculpture and other ornaments they are comparable in beauty with any other work of the time, without exception, and so excellent as to assure to the name of Andrea Orcagna immortality and greatness. In signing his paintings he used to write Andrea di Clone, sculptor, and on his sculptures, Andrea di Cione, painter, wishing his sculpture to recommend his painting and his painting his sculpture. Florence is full of his paintings, some of which may be recognised by the name, such as those in S. Romeo, and some by his style, like that in the chapter-house of the monastery of the Angeli. Some which he left imperfect were finished by his brother Bernardo, who survived him, though not for many years. Andrea, as I have said, amused himself in making verses and other poems, and when he was an old man he wrote some sonnets to Burchiello, then a youth. At length at the age of sixty he completed the course of his life in 1389, and was borne with honour to burial from his house in the via Vecchia de' Corazzai.

In the days of the Orcagna there were many who were skilful in sculpture and architecture, whose names are unknown, but their works show that they are worthy of high praise and commendation. An example of such work is the Monastery of the Certosa of Florence, erected at the cost of the noble family of the Acciaiuoli, and particularly of M. Niccola, Grand Seneschal of the King of Naples, containing Niccola's tomb with his effigy in stone, and those of his father and a sister, both of whose portraits in the marble were made from life in the year 1366. There also and by the same hand may be seen the tomb of M. Lorenzo, Niccola's son, who died at Naples, arid was brought to Florence and buried there with most honourable obsequies. Similarly the tomb of the Cardinal S. Croce of the same family, which is before the high altar in a choir then newly built, contains his portrait in a marble stone very well executed in the year 1390.

The pupils of Andrea in painting were Bernardo Nello di Giovanni Falconi of Pisa, who did a number of pictures for the Duomo of Pisa, and Tommaso di Marco of Florence, who, besides many other things, painted a picture in the year 1392, which is in S. Antonio at Pisa on the screen of the church. After Andrea's death, his brother Jacopo, who, as has been said, professed sculpture and architecture, was employed in the year 1328 in building the tower and gate of S. Pietro Gattolini, and it is said that the four gilded stone lions at the four corners of the principal palace of Florence are by his hand. This work incurred no little censure, because it was placed there without reason, and was perhaps a greater weight than was safe. Many would have preferred the lions to have been made of copper gilded over and hollow inside, and then set up in the same place, when they would have been much less heavy and more durable. It is said that the horse in relief in S. Maria del Fiore at Florence is by the same hand. It is gilded, and stands over the door leading to the oratory of S. Zanobi. It is believed to be a monument to Pietro Farnese, captain of the Florentines, but as I know nothing more of the matter I cannot assert this positively. At the same time Andrea's nephew Mariotto made a Paradise in fresco for S. Michel Bisdomini in the via de' Servi at Florence, over the altar, and another picture with many figures for Mona Cecilia de' Boscoli, which is in the same church near the door. But of all Orcagna's pupils none excelled Francesco Traini, who executed for a lord of the house of Coscia, buried at Pisa in the chapel of St Dominic in the church of S. Caterina, a St Dominic on a panel on a gold ground, with six scenes from his life surrounding him, very vigorous and life-like and excellently coloured. In the chapel of St Thomas Aquinas in the same church he made a picture in tempera, with delightful invention, and which is much admired. He introduced a figure of St Thomas seated, from life; I say from life because the friars of the place brought a portrait of him from the abbey of Fossanuova, where he had died in 1323. St Thomas is seated in the air with some books in his hand, illuminating with their rays and splendour the Christian people; kneeling below him are a large number of doctors and clerks of every condition, bishops, cardinals and popes, including the portrait of Pope Urban VI. Under the saint's feet are Sabellius, Arius, Averroes, and other heretics and philosophers with their books all torn. On either side of St Thomas are Plato, showing the Timæus, and Aristotle pointing to his Ethics. Above is Jesus Christ, also in the air, with the four Evangelists about him. He is blessing St Thomas, and apparently sending the Holy Spirit upon him, filling him therewith and with His grace. On the completion of this work Francesco Traini acquired great name and fame, for he had far surpassed his master Andrea in colouring, in unity, and in invention. Andrea was very careful in his designs, as may be seen in our book.

TOMMASO CALLED GIOTTINO, PAINTER OF FLORENCE.

When there is emulation among the arts which are based on design and when artists work in competition with each other there is no doubt that men's abilities, being stimulated by constant study, discover new things every day to satisfy the varied tastes of man. Thus in painting, some introduce obscure and eccentric things into their work and by a mastery of the difficulties display the brightness of their talent in the midst of darkness. Others employ themselves on soft and delicate things conceiving that these should be more pleasing to the eye of the beholder; so that they pleasantly attract the greater number of men. Others again paint smoothly, softening the colours and confining the lights and shades of the figures to their places, for which they merit the highest praise, displaying their intention with wonderful skill. This smooth style is always apparent in the works of Tommaso di Stefano, called Giottino, who was born in the year 1324, and after he had learned the elements of painting from his father, he resolved while still a youth, that he would most carefully imitate Giotto's style rather than that of Stefano. He succeeded so well in this that he won thereby in addition to the style, which was much finer than his master's, the nickname of Giottino, which he always retained. Hence many, misled by his manner and name, believed him to be Giotto's son, but they fell into a very great error, for it is certain, or rather highly probable (since no one can affirm such things absolutely), that he was the son of Stefano, painter of Florence. Tommaso was so diligent in painting and so fond of it, that although not many of his works have been found, yet those which are extant are good and in excellent style. For the draperies, hair, beards, and other details are executed and composed with such grace and care that they prove him to have possessed a far better idea of unity in art than was to be found in the works of Giotto, master of Stefano his father. In his youth Giottino painted in S. Stefano at the Ponte Vecchio at Florence, a chapel by the side door, and although it has suffered a great deal from the damp, yet enough remains to prove the skill and genius of the craftsman. He next did SS. Cosmo and Damian beside the mills in the Frati Ermini, of which but little can now be seen owing to the ravages of time. He did a chapel in fresco in the old S. Spirito of that city, which was afterwards destroyed at the burning of that church. Over the principal door of the same church he painted in fresco the Descent of the Holy Spirit, and on the piazza of the church, leading to the side of the Cuculia, next the convent, he did the tabernacle which may still be seen there, with Our Lady and other saints about her, who in their heads and other parts approach very closely to the modern style, because Tommaso endeavoured to vary and change the flesh tints and to combine a graceful and judicious treatment of the figures with variety in the colouring and in the draperies. In the chapel of St Silvester at S. Croce he did the history of Constantine with great care, with many fine ideas in the gestures of the figures. His next work was to be placed behind a marble ornament made for the tomb of M. Bettino de' Bardi, a man of eminent military rank of the time. He represented him from life, in armour, rising on his knees from the tomb, summoned by the Last Trump sounded by two angels who accompany a Christ in the clouds, very well done. At the entrance to S. Pancrazio, on the right hand side, he did a Christ carrying the cross, and some saints near, markedly in Giotto's style. In S. Gallo, a convent outside the gate of that name, and which was destroyed at the siege, he painted a Pieta in fresco in a cloister, a copy of which is in S. Pancrazio mentioned above, on a pilaster beside the principal chapel. He painted SS. Cosmo and Damian in fresco in S. Maria Novella at the chapel of St Lorenzo de' Giuochi, at the entry of the church by the right hand door, on the front wall. In Ognissanti he did a St Christopher and a St George, which were ruined by bad weather and were restored by some ignorant painters. An uninjured work of Tommaso in the same church is in the tympanum over the sacristy door, which contains a Madonna in fresco, with the child in her arms; it is a good thing as he took pains with it.

By means of these works Giottino acquired so much renown, imitating his master, as I have said, both in design and in inventions, that the spirit of Giotto himself was said to be in him, owing to the freshness of his colouring and to his skill in design. Now, on 2nd July 1343, when the Duke of Athens was hunted from Florence, and had by oath renounced the government and rendered the Florentines their liberty, Giottino was constrained by the Twelve Reformers of the State, and especially by the prayers of M. Agnolo Acciaiuoli, then a very distinguished citizen, who had great influence over him, to paint on the tower of the Podesta Palace the duke and his followers, M. Ceritieri Visdomini, M. Maladiasse, his Conservator and M. Ranieri da S. Gimignano, all with mitres of Justice on their heads, represented thus shamefully as a sign of contempt. About the duke's head he painted many beasts of prey and other sorts, indicative of his nature and quality; and one of these counsellors had in his hand the palace of the priors of the city, which he was offering to the duke, like a false traitor. Beneath everyone of them were the arms and insignia of their families, with inscriptions which can now only be read with difficulty owing to the ravages of time. This work, because it was well designed and very carefully executed, gave universal satisfaction, and the method of the artist pleased everyone. He next made a St Cosmo and a St Damian at the Campora, a place of the black monks outside the gate of S. Piero Gattolini. These were afterwards destroyed in whitewashing the church. On the bridge at Romiti in Valdarno he did the tabernacle which is built in the middle, painting it in fresco in a very fine style. It is recorded by many writers that Tommaso practised sculpture, and did a marble figure four braccia high for the campanile of S. Maria del Fiore at Florence, towards the place where the orphan asylum now stands.

At Rome again he successfully completed a scene in S. John Lateran in which he represented the pope in various dignities, but the painting is now much damaged and eaten by time. In the house of the Orsini he did a hall full of famous men, and a very fine St Louis on a pilaster at Araceli, on the right-hand side at the high altar. Above the pulpit in the lower church of S. Francesco at Assisi, that being the only place left undecorated, he painted a coronation of Our Lady, in an arch, surrounded by many angels, so graceful, with such beautiful faces, so soft and so delicate, exhibiting that union of colours customary in the artist, and which constitutes his peculiar excellence, that he may clearly be compared with any of his predecessors. About this arch he did some stories of St Nicholas. Similarly, in the middle of the church, in the monastery of S. Chiara, in the same city, he painted a scene in fresco of St Clare, upheld in the air by two angels, represented with much life, raising a dead child, whilst many beautiful women standing about are filled with amazement, all being dressed in very graceful costumes of the time. In the same city of Assisi, in an arch over the inside of the city door which leads to the Duomo, he did a Madonna and child with so much care that she seems alive, and a very fine St Francis, with other saints. These two works, although the scene with St Clare is unfinished, for Tommaso returned sick to Florence, are perfect and worthy of all praise.

It is said that Tommaso was a melancholy and solitary man, but very diligent and fond of his art. This is clearly shown in a picture of his in tempera in the church of S. Romeo at Florence, placed on the screen on the right-hand side, for nothing was ever better done on wood. It represents a dead Christ with Mary and Nicodemus, accompanied with other figures, who are weeping bitterly for the dead. Their gentleness and sweetness are remarkable as they twist their hands and beat themselves, showing in their faces the bitter sorrow that our sins should cost so dear. It is a marvellous thing, not that Tommaso could rise to this height of imagination, but that he could express his thought so well with his brush. Consequently this work deserves the highest praise, not so much because of the subject and conception as for the art in which he exhibited the heads of some who are weeping, for although the brows, eyes, nose and mouth are distorted by the emotion, yet this does not mar or destroy the beauty of his faces, which usually suffers much at the hands of those who represent weeping if they are not versed in the good methods of art. But it is no wonder that Giottino was so successful with this picture, because the object of all his labour was rather fame and glory than any other reward or desire of gain, which causes the masters of our own time to be less careful and good. Not only Tommaso did not endeavour to acquire great wealth, but he went without many of the comforts of life, living in poverty, seeking rather to please others than to live at ease; so managing badly and working hard, he died of phthisis at the age of thirty-two, and was buried by his relations outside S. Maria Novella at the gate of Martello, near the tomb of Bontura.

The pupils of Giottino, who left more fame than property, were Giovanni Tossicani of Arezzo, Michelino, Giovanni dal Ponte, and Lippo, who were meritorious masters of the art. Giovanni Tossicani excelled the others, and after Tommaso's death he executed many works in that same style, in all Tuscany, and particularly in the Pieve of Arezzo, where he did the chapel of St Maria Maddalena of the Tuccerelli, and in the Pieve of Empoli, where he did a St James on a pilaster. Again, he did some things in the Duomo at Pisa, which were afterwards removed to make way for modern works. His last work was executed in a chapel of the Vescovado of Arezzo, for the Countess Giovanna, wife of Tarlato di Pietramala, and represented an Annunciation, with St James and St Philip. As this work was on a wall, the back of which is exposed to the north, it was almost destroyed by the damp, when Master Agnolo di Lorenzo of Arezzo restored the Annunciation, and Giorgio Vasari, then a youth, restored the SS. James and Philip, to his great advantage, as he learnt a great deal which he had not been able to obtain from other masters, by observing Giovanni's methods, and from the shadows and colours of this work, damaged as it was. The following words of the epitaph to the Countess, who caused the work to be done, may still be read: Anno Domini 1335 de mense Augusti hanc capellam constitui fecit nobilis Domina comitissa Joanna de Sancta Flora uxor nobilis militis Domini Tarlati de Petramela ad honorem Beatæ Mariæ Virginis.

I make no mention of the works of the other pupils of Giottino, because they are quite ordinary and bear little resemblance to those of their master and of Giovanni Tossicani, their fellow-pupil. Tommaso drew very well, as appears by some sheets by his hand which are in our book, which are very carefully executed.

GIOVANNI DA PONTE, PAINTER OF FLORENCE.

Although the old proverb that a bon vivant never lacks means is untrue and unworthy of confidence, the contrary being the case, since a man who does not live within his means comes at last to live in want, and dies in misery; yet it sometimes happens that Fortune rather assists those who throw away without reserve than those who are orderly and careful in all things. When the favour of Fortune is wanting, Death frequently repairs the defect and remedies the consequences of men's thoughtlessness, for it comes at the very moment when they would begin to realise, with sorrow, how wretched a thing it is to have squandered everything when young to pass one's age on shortened means in poverty and toil. This would have been the fate of Giovanni da S. Stefano a Ponte of Florence, if, after he had devoured his patrimony as well as the gains which came into his hand, rather through good fortune than by his desserts, and some legacies which came to him from unexpected quarters, he had not reached the end of his life at the very time when he had exhausted his means. He was a pupil of Buonamico Buffalmacco, and imitated his master more in following worldly pleasures than in endeavouring to make himself a skilful painter. He was born in the year 1307, and was Buffalmacco's pupil in his youth. He executed his first works in fresco in the Pieve of Empoli in the chapel of St Laurence, painting many scenes from the life of that saint with such care, that so good a beginning was considered to promise much better things in the future. Accordingly he was invited in the year 1344 to Arezzo, where he did an Assumption in a chapel in S. Francesco. Being in some credit in that city, for lack of other artists, he next painted in the

Pieve the chapel of St Onofrio and that of St Anthony, ruined to-day by the damp. He left other paintings in S. Giustina and S. Matteo, which were pulled down with the churches when Duke Cosimo was fortifying the city. Almost on this very spot, near S. Giustina, at the foot of the abutment of an ancient bridge, at the point where the river enters the city, they there found a fine marble head of Appius Ciccus, and one of his son, with an ancient epitaph, which are now in the Duke's wardrobe. When Giovanni returned to Florence, at the time when the middle arch of the Ponte a S. Trinita was being completed, he decorated a chapel built on a pile, and dedicated to St Michael the Archangel, an ancient and beautiful building, doing many figures, both inside and out, and the whole of the principal front. This chapel was carried away, together with the bridge, in the flood of 1557. Some assert that he owed his name of Giovanni dal Ponte to these works. In Pisa, in the year 1335, he did some scenes in fresco behind the altar in the principal chapel of St Paolo a ripa d'Arno, which are now ruined by damp and time. Another work of his is the chapel of the Scali in S. Trinita at Florence, and another beside it, as well as one of the stories of St Paul beside the principal chapel, which contains the tomb of Maestro Paolo, the astrologer. In S. Stefano, at the Ponte Vecchio, he did a panel and other paintings in tempera and fresco for Florence and elsewhere, which won him considerable renown. He was beloved by his friends, but rather in his pleasures than in his labours, and he was a friend of men of letters, and especially of all those who were studying his own art in the hope of excelling in it; and although he had not troubled to acquire for himself what he desired for others, he never ceased to advise others to work diligently. At length, when he had lived fifty-nine years, he departed this life in a few days in consequence of a disorder of the chest. Had he lived a little longer, he would have suffered much inconvenience, as there remained hardly sufficient in his house to afford him decent burial in S. Stefano dal Ponte Vecchio. His works were executed about 1345.

Our book of designs of various ancient and modern masters contains a water-colour by Giovanni representing St George on horseback killing a serpent; also a skeleton, the two affording an excellent illustration of his method and his style in designing.

AGNOLO GADDI,
PAINTER OF FLORENCE.

The virtue and husbandry of Taddeo Gaddi afford an excellent illustration of the advantages and honours accruing from excellence in a noble art, for by his industry and labour he provided a considerable property, and left the affairs of his family so ordered that when he passed to the other life his sons Agnolo and Giovanni were enabled without difficulty to lay the foundations of the vast wealth and distinction of the house of Gaddi, which is now amongst the noblest in Florence and of high repute in all Christendom. Indeed it was no more than reasonable, after Gaddo, Taddeo, Agnolo and Giovanni had adorned with their art and talents so many considerable churches, that their descendants should be decorated with the highest ecclesiastical dignities by the Holy Roman Church and her Pontiffs. Taddeo, whose life we have already written, left two sons, Agnolo and Giovanni, among his many pupils, and he hoped that Agnolo in particular would attain to considerable excellence in painting. But although Agnolo when a youth promised to far surpass his father, he did not realise the good opinions which were then formed about him. Being born and brought up in ease, which is often a hindrance to application, he was more devoted to trading and commerce than to the art of painting. This is no new or strange circumstance, for avarice almost invariably proves a bar to those geniuses who would have attained the summit of their powers, had not the desire of gain stood in their way in their first and best years.

In his youth Andrea did a small scene for S. Jacopo tra fossi at Florence, in figures of little more than a braccia high, representing the Resurrection of Lazarus, who had been four days dead. Considering the corrupt state of the body, which had been in the tomb three days, he presented the grave clothes bound about him as soiled by the putrefaction of the flesh, and certain livid and yellowish marks in the flesh about the eyes, between quick and dead, very well considered. He also shows the astonishment of the disciples and other figures, who in varied and remarkable attitudes are holding their garments to their noses so as not to smell the stench of the corrupt body, and exhibit every shade of fear and terror at this marvellous event, as well as the joy and delight of Mary and Martha at seeing the dead body of their brother return to life. This work was deemed so excellent that there were many who thought that the talents of Andrea would prove superior to those of all the pupils of Taddeo and even to those of the master himself. But the event proved otherwise, for as in youth will conquers every difficulty in the effort after fame, so it often happens that the years bring with them a certain heedlessness which causes men to go backwards instead of forwards, as was the case with Agnolo. Owing to the high repute of his ability, the family of the Soderini, expecting a great deal, allotted to him the principal chapel of the Carmine, where he painted the whole of the life of Our Lady, but in a style so inferior to the Resurrection of Lazarus that anyone could perceive that he had little desire to devote all his energies to the study of painting. In the whole of this great work there is not more than a single good scene, namely, that in which Our Lady is in an apartment surrounded by a number of maidens, whose habits and headdresses vary according to the divers customs of the time, and who are engaged in various employments, some spinning, some sewing, some winding silk, and some weaving and doing other things, all very well conceived and executed by Agnolo.

Similarly in painting in fresco the principal chapel of the church of S. Croce for the noble family of the Alberti, he represented the incidents which took place on the finding of the Cross, executing the work with much skill, though it is somewhat lacking in design, the colouring alone being meritorious. He succeeded much better afterwards in some other paintings in fresco in the chapel of the Bardi, and in some stories of St Louis in the same church. He worked capriciously, sometimes with great care and sometimes with little. Thus in S. Spirito at Florence, where he did the inside of a door leading from the piazza to the convent, and above another door a Madonna and child, with St Augustine and St Nicholas, all in fresco—they are all so well done that they look as if they had been painted yesterday. The secret of working in mosaic had as it were descended to Agnolo by inheritance, and in his house he had the instruments and other apparatus used by his grandfather Gaddo; accordingly to para the time, and for one reason or another, he did some things in mosaic when he had the whim. Thus since many of the marble facings of the exterior of S. Giovanni were wasted by time, and as the damp had pierced through and done considerable injury to the mosaics previously executed there by Andrea Tafi, the Consuls of the Art of the Merchants proposed to restore the greater part of this marble covering, in order that no further damage should be done, and also to repair the mosaics. The commission for this was given to Agnolo, and in the year 1346 he caused the building to be covered with new marble, overlaying the joints to a distance of two fingers with great care, notching the half of each stone as far as the middle. He then cemented them together with a mixture of mastic and wax, and completed the whole with such care that from that time forward neither the vaulting nor the roof has ever suffered any harm from the water. His subsequent restoration of the mosaics led by his advice to the reconstruction from his well-devised plans of the whole of the cornice of the church above the marble, under the roof, in its present form, whereas it was originally much smaller and by no means remarkable. He also directed the construction of the vaulting for the hall of the Podesta palace, where an ordinary roof had formerly existed, so that in addition to the added beauty which it gave the room, it rendered it proof against damage by fire, which it had frequently suffered before. By his advice the present battlements were added to the palace, where nothing of the kind had previously existed.

While these works were proceeding, he did not entirely abandon painting, but executed in tempera a picture of Our Lady for the high altar of S. Pancrazio, with St John the Baptist, St John the Evangelist, the brothers St Nereus, Achilleus, and Prancrazius, and other saints hard by. But the best part of this work, and indeed the only part of it which is really good, is the predella filled with small figures, divided into eight scenes dealing with the Madonna and St Reparata. Subsequently in a picture for the high altar of S. Maria Novella at Florence, executed for Barone Capelli in 1348, he made a very fair group of angels about a Coronation of the Virgin. Shortly afterwards he painted in fresco a series of subjects from the life of the Virgin in the Pieve of Prato, which had been rebuilt under the direction of Giovanni Pisano in 1312, as has been said above, in the chapel where Our Lady's girdle was deposited, and he did a number of other works in other churches of that same country which is full of very considerable monasteries and convents. In Florence he next painted the arch over the gate of S. Romeo, and in Orto S. Michele did in tempera a Christ disputing with the doctors in the temple. At the same time for the enlargement of the piazza of the Signori a large number of buildings was pulled down, and notably the church of S. Romolo, which was rebuilt from Agnolo's plans. In the churches of this city many pictures by his hand may be seen, and a quantity of his works may be met with in the lordship. These he produced with great advantage to himself, although he worked rather for the sake of following in the steps of his ancestors than from any inclination of his own; for he had devoted all his attention to trading, which was of great service to him, as appeared when his sons, who did not wish to live by painting any longer, devoted themselves entirely to commerce, opening an establishment at Venice in conjunction with their father, who after a certain time abandoned painting altogether, only to take it up as an amusement and pastime. By dint of trading and practising his art, Agnolo had amassed considerable wealth when he came to die in the sixty-third year of his life, succumbing to a malignant fever which carried him off in a few days. His pupils were Maestro Antonio da Ferrara, who did many fine works in Urbino and at Citta di Castello, and Stefano da Verona, who painted with the greatest perfection in fresco, as may be seen in several places in his native Verona, and at Mantua, where his works are numerous. Among other things he excelled in beautifully rendering the expressions of the faces of children, women and old men, as his works show, which were all imitated and copied by that Piero da Perugia, miniature painter, who illuminated all the books in the library of Pope Pius in the Duomo of Siena, and who was a skilful colourist in fresco. Other pupils of Agnolo were Michaele da Milano and his own brother Giovanni, who in the cloister of S. Spirito, where the arches of Gaddo and Taddeo are, painted the dispute of Christ with the doctors in the temple, the Purification of the Virgin, the Temptation of Christ in the wilderness, and the baptism of John, but after having given rise to the highest expectations he died. Cennino di Drea Cennini da Colle of Valdelsa also learned painting from Andrea. He was very fond of his art and wrote a book describing the methods of working in fresco, in tempera, in glue and in gum, and also how to illuminate and all the ways of laying on gold. This book is in the possession of Giuliano, goldsmith of Siena, an excellent master and fond of that art. The first part of the book deals with the nature of colours, both minerals and earths, as he had learned it of Agnolo his master. As he did not perhaps succeed in painting with perfection, he was at least anxious to know the peculiarities of the colours, the temperas, the glues and of chalks, and what colours one ought to avoid mixing as injurious, and in short many other hints which I need not dilate upon, since all these matters, which he then considered very great secrets, are now universally known. But I must not omit to note that he makes no mention of some earth colours, such as dark terra rossa, cinnabar and some greens in glass, perhaps because they were not in use. In like manner umber, yellow-lake, the smalts in fresco and in oil, and some greens and yellows in glass which the painters of that age lacked, have since been discovered. The end of the treatise deals with mosaics, with the grinding of colours in oil to make red, blue, green and other kinds of grounds, and with mordants for the application of gold but not at that time for figures. Besides the works which he produced with his master in Florence, there is a Madonna with saints by his hand under the loggia of the hospital of Bonifazio Lupi, of such style and colouring that it has been very well preserved up to the present day.

In the first chapter of his book Cennino says these words in speaking of himself: "I, Cennino di Drea Cennini da Colle of Valdelsa, was instructed in this art for twelve years by Agnolo di Taddeo of Florence, my master, who learned the art of his father Taddeo, whose godfather was Giotto and who was Giotto's pupil for twenty-four years. This Giotto transmuted the art of painting from Greek into Latin, and modernised it, and it is certain that he gave more pleasure than any one else had ever done." These are Cennino's very words, by which it appears that as those who translate from Greek into Latin render a very great service to those who do not understand Greek, so Giotto, in transmuting the art of painting from a style which was understood by no one, except perhaps as being extremely rude, into a beautiful, facile, and smooth manner, known and understood by all people of taste who possess the slightest judgment, conferred a great benefit upon mankind.

All these pupils of Agnolo did him the greatest credit. He was buried by his sons, to whom he is said to have left the value of 50,000 florins or more, in S. Maria Novella, in the tomb which he had made for himself and his descendants, in the year 1387. The portrait of Agnolo by his own hand may be seen in the chapel of the Alberti in S. Croce in the scene in which the Emperor Heraclius is bearing the cross; he is painted in profile standing beside a door. He wears a small beard and has a red hood on his head, after the manner of the time. He was not a good draughtsman, according to the evidence of some sheets from his hand which are in our book.

BERNA,
PAINTER OF SIENA.

If the thread of life of those who take pains to excel in some noble profession was not frequently cut off by death in the best years, there is no doubt that many geniuses would attain the goal desired by them and by the world. But the short life of man and the bitterness of the various accidents which intervene on every hand sometimes deprive us too early of such men. An example of this was poor Berna of Siena, who died while quite young, although the nature of his works would lead one to believe that he had lived very long, for he left such excellent productions that it is probable, had he not died so soon, he would have become a most excellent and rare artist. Two of his works may be seen in Siena in two chapels of S. Agostino, being some small scenes of figures in fresco, and in the church on a wall which has recently been demolished to make chapels there, a scene of a young man led to punishment, of the highest imaginable excellence, the representation of pallor and of the fear of death being so realistic that it merits the warmest admiration. Beside the youth is a friar who is consoling him, with excellent gestures, and in fine the entire scene is executed with such vigour as to leave no doubt that Berna had penetrated deeply into the horror of that situation, full of bitter and cold fear, since he was able to represent it so well with the brush that the actual event passing before one's eyes could not move one more. In Cortona, besides many things scattered up and down the city, he painted the greater part of the vaulting and walls of the church of S. Margherita where the Zoccolanti friars now are. From Cortona he proceeded to Arezzo in the year 1369, at the very time when the Tarlati, formerly lords of Pietramela, had finished the convent and church of S. Agostino, under the direction of Moccio, sculptor and architect of Siena. In the aisles of this building where many citizens had erected chapels and tombs for their families, Berna painted in fresco in the chapel of St James, some scenes from the life of that saint. Among these the most remarkable is the story of the cozener Marino, who through love of gain had contracted his soul to the devil and then recommended his soul to St James, begging him to free him from his promise, whilst a devil shows him the deed and makes a great disturbance. Berna expresses the emotions of all these figures with great vigour, especially in the face of Marino, who is divided between his fear and his faith and confidence in St James, although he sees the marvellously ugly devil against him, employing all his eloquence to convince the saint. St James, after he has brought Marino to a thorough penitence for his sin, promises him immunity, delivers him and brings him back to God. According to Lorenzo Ghiberti, Berna reproduced this story in S. Spirito at Florence before it was burned, in a chapel of the Capponi dedicated to St Nicholas. After these works Berna painted a large crucifix in a chapel of the Vescovado of Arezzo for M. Guccio di Vanni Tarlati of Pietramela, with Our Lady at the foot of the cross, St John the Baptist, St Francis la a very sad attitude, and St Michael the archangel, with such care that he deserves no small praise, especially as it is so well preserved that it might have been made yesterday. At the foot of the cross, lower down, is the portrait of Guccio himself, in armour and kneeling. In the Pieve of the same city he did a number of stories of Our Lady for the chapel of the Paganelli, and there drew from life a portrait of St Ranieri, a holy man and prophet of that house, who is giving alms to a crowd of poor people surrounding him. Again in S. Bartolommeo he painted some scenes from the Old Testament and the story of the Magi, and in the church of S. Spirito he did some stories of St John the Evangelist, drawing his own portrait and those of many of his noble friends of the city in some figures there. When these labours were completed he returned to his native city and did many pictures on wood, both small and great. But he did not remain there long, because he was invited to Florence to decorate the chapel of St Nicholas in S. Spirito, as mentioned above, and which was greatly admired, as well as to do some other things which perished in the unfortunate fire at that church. In the Pieve of S. Gimignano di Valdelsa he did in fresco some scenes from the New Testament. When he was on the point of completing these things he fell to the ground from the scaffolding, suffering such severe injuries that he expired in two days, by which art suffered a greater loss than he, for he passed to a better sphere. The people of S. Gimignano gave him honourable burial in that Pieve, with stately obsequies, having the same regard for him when dead as they had entertained for him while alive, while for many months they were constantly affixing to the tomb epitaphs in the Latin and vulgar tongues, for the people of those parts take a natural pleasure in *belles lettres*. This then was the fitting reward of the honourable labours of Berna, that those whom he had honoured with his paintings should celebrate him with their pens. Giovanni da Asciano, who was a pupil of Berna, completed his work and did some pictures for the hospital of the Scala at Siena. In Florence also he did some things in the old houses of the Medici, by which he acquired a considerable reputation. The works of Berna of Siena were produced about 1381. Besides what we have already said, he was a fairly facile draughtsman and the first who began to draw animals well, as we see by some sheets by his hand in our book, covered with wild beasts of various parts, so that he merits the highest praise and that his name should be honoured among artists. Another pupil of his was Luca di Tome of Siena who painted many works in Siena and in all Tuscany, but especially the picture and chapel of the Dragomanni in S. Domenico at Arezzo. The chapel is in the German style and was very handsomely decorated by that picture and by the frescoes executed there by the skill and talent of Luda of Siena.

DUCCIO, PAINTER OF SIENA.

There is do doubt that those who invent anything noteworthy occupy the greatest share of the attention of historians, The reason for this is that original inventors are more noticed and excite more wonder, because new things always possess a greater charm than improvements subsequently introduced to perfect them. For if no one ever made a beginning, there would never be any advance or improvement, and the full achievement of marvellous beauty would never be attained. Accordingly Duccio, a much esteemed painter of Siena, is worthy to receive the praise of those who have followed him many years after, since in the pavement of the Duomo of Siena he initiated the treatment in marble of figures in chiaroscuro, in which modern artists have performed such wonders in these days. Duccio devoted himself to the imitation of the old style and very judiciously gave the correct forms to his figures, overcoming the difficulty presented by such an art. Imitating the paintings in chiaroscuro, he designed the first part of the pavement with his own hand; and painted a picture in the Duomo which was then put at the high altar and afterwards removed to make room for the tabernacle of the body of Christ which is now seen there. According to Lorenzo di Bartolo Ghiberti, this picture was a Coronation of Our Lady, very much in the Byzantine style, though mingled with much that is modern. It was painted on both sides, as the altar stood out by itself, and on the back Duccio had with great care painted all the principal incidents of the New Testament in some very fine small figures. I have endeavoured to discover the whereabouts of the picture at the present time, but although I have taken the utmost pains in the search, I have not succeeded in finding it or of learning what Francesco di Giorgio the sculptor did with it, when he restored the tabernacle in bronze as well as the marble ornaments there. At Siena Duccio did many pictures on a gold ground and an Annunciation for S. Trinita, Florence. He afterwards painted many things at Pisa, Lucca and Pistoia for different churches, which were all much admired and brought him much reputation and profit. The place of his death is not known, nor are we aware what relations, pupils or property he left. It is enough that he left to art the inheritance of his inventions in painting, marble and chiaroscuro, for which he is worthy of the highest commendation and praise. He may safely be enumerated among the benefactors who have increased the dignity and beauty of our craft, and those who pursue investigations into the difficulties of rare inventions, deserve a special place in our remembrance for this cause apart from their marvellous productions.

It is said at Siena that in 1348 Duccio designed the chapel which is on the piazza in front of the principal palace. It is also recorded that another native of Siena called Moccio, flourished at the same time. He was a fair sculptor and architect and did many works in every part of Tuscany, but chiefly at Arezzo in the Church of S. Domenico, where he made a marble tomb for of the Cerchi. This tomb supports and decorates the organ of that church, and if some object that it is not a work of high excellence, I reply that it must be considered a very fair production seeing that he made it in the year 1356 while quite a youth. He was employed on the work of S. Maria del Fiore as under architect and as sculptor, doing some things in marble for that structure. In Arezzo he rebuilt the Church of S. Agostino, which was small, in its present form, the expense being borne by heirs of Piero Saccone de' Tarlati, who had provided for this before his death at Bibbiena in the territory of Casentino. As Moccio constructed this church without vaulting, he imposed the burden of the roof on the arcading of the columns, running a considerable risk, for the enterprise was too bold. He also built the Church and Convent of S. Antonio, which were at the Faenza gate before the siege of Florence, and are now entirely in ruins. In sculpture he decorated the gate of S. Agostino at Ancona, with many figures and ornaments like those which are at the gate of S. Francesco in the same city. In this church of St Agostino he also made the tomb of Fra Zenone Vigilanti, bishop and general of the order of St Augustine, and finally the loggia of the merchants in that city, which has from time to time received, for one cause and another, many improvements in modern style, and ornamentation of various descriptions. All these things, although very much below the general level of excellence of to-day, received considerable praise then owing to the state of information of the time. But to return to Duccio, his works were executed about the year of grace 1350.

ANTONIO, PAINTER OF VENICE.

There are many men who, through being persecuted by the envy and oppressed by the tyranny of their fellow-citizens, have left their native place and have chosen for a home some spot where their worth has been recognised and rewarded, producing their works there and taking the greatest pains to excel, in order, in a sense, to be avenged on those by whom they have been outraged. In this way they frequently become great men, whereas had they remained quietly at home they might possibly have achieved little more than mediocrity in their art. Antonio of Venice, who went to Florence, in the train of Agnolo Gaddi, to learn painting, so far acquired the proper methods that not only was he esteemed and loved by the Florentines, but made much of for this talent and for his other good qualities. Then, becoming possessed by a desire to return to his native city and enjoy the fruits of his labours, he went back to Venice. There, having made himself known by many things done in fresco and tempera, he was commissioned by the Signoria to paint one of the walls of the Council Chamber, a work which he executed with such skill and majesty that its merits should have brought him honours and rewards; but the rivalry, or rather the envy, of the other artists, together with the preference accorded by some noblemen to other and alien painters, brought about a different result. Hence poor Antonio, feeling himself repelled and rebutted, thought it would be as well to go back to Florence, deciding that he would never again return to Venice, but would make Florence his home. Having reached that city, he painted in an arch in the cloister of S. Spirito the calling of Peter and Andrew from their nets, with Zebedee and his sons. Under the three arches of Stefano he painted the miracle of the loaves and fishes, exhibiting great diligence and love, as may be seen in the figure of Christ Himself, whose face and aspect betray His compassion for the crowd and the ardent charity which leads Him to distribute the bread. The same scene also shows very beautifully the affection of an apostle, who is very active in distributing the bread from a basket. The picture affords a good illustration of the value in art of always painting figures so that they appear to speak, for otherwise they are not prized. Antonio showed this on the façade in a small representation of the Fall of the Manna, executed with such skill and finished with such grace, that it may truly be called excellent. He next did some stories of St Stephen in the predella of the high altar of S. Stefano at the Ponte Vecchio, with so much loving care that even in illuminations it would not be possible to find more graceful or more delicate work. Again he painted the tympanum over the door of S. Antonio on the Ponte alla Carraia. This and the church were both pulled down in our own day by Monsignor Ricasoli, bishop of Pistoia, because they took away the view from his houses, and in any case even if he had not done so, we should have been deprived of the work, for, as I have said elsewhere, the flood of 1557 carried away two arches on this side, as well as that part of the bridge on which the little church of S. Antonio was situated. After these works Antonio was invited to Pisa by the wardens of the Campo Santo, and there continued the series dealing with the life of St Ranieri, a holy man of that city, which had been begun by Simone of Siena and under his direction. In the first part of Antonio's portion of the work is a representation of the embarkation of Ranieri to return to Pisa, with a goodly number of figures executed with diligence, including the portrait of Count Gaddo, who had died ten years before, and of Neri, his uncle, who had been lord of Pisa. Another notable figure in the group is that of a man possessed, with distorted, convulsive gestures, his eyes glistening, and his mouth grinning and showing his teeth, so remarkably like a person really possessed that nothing more true or life-like can be imagined. The next picture contains three really beautiful figures, lost in wonder at seeing St Ranieri reveal the devil in the form of a cat on a tub to a fat innkeeper, who looks like a boon companion, and who is commending himself fearfully to the saint; their attitudes are excellently disposed in the style of the draperies, the variety of poses of the heads, and in all other particulars. Hard by are the maidservants of the innkeeper, who could not possibly be represented with more grace as Antonio has made them with disengaged garments arranged after the manner of those worn by the servants at an inn, so that nothing better can be imagined. Nothing of this artist gives more pleasure than the wall containing another scene from the same series in which the canons of the Duomo of Pisa, in the fine robes of the time, very different from those in use to-day and very graceful, receive St Ranieri at table, all the figures being made with great care. The next of his scenes is the death of the saint, containing fine representations not only of the effect of weeping, but of the movements of certain angels who are carrying his soul to heaven surrounded by a brilliant light, done with fine originality. In the scene where the saint's body is being carried by the clergy to the Duomo one can but marvel at the representation of the priests singing, for in their gestures, carriage, and all their movements they exactly resemble a choir of singers. This scene is said to contain a portrait of the Bavarian. Antonio likewise painted with the greatest care the miracles wrought by Ranieri when he was being carried to burial, and those wrought in another place, after his body had been deposited in the Duomo, such as blind who receive their sight, withered men who recover the use of their limbs, demoniacs who are released, and other miracles represented with great vigour. But one of the most remarkable figures of all is a dropsical man, whose withered face, dry lips, and swollen body exhibit with as much realism as a living man could, the devouring thirst of those suffering from dropsy and the other symptoms of that disease. Another marvellous thing for the time in this work is a ship delivered by the saint after it had undergone various mishaps. It contains an excellent representation of the activity of the mariners, comprising everything that is usually done in such case. Some are casting into the greedy sea without a thought the valuable merchandise won with so much toil, some are running to preserve the ship which is splitting, and in short performing all the other duties of seamen which it would take too long to tell. Suffice it to say that all are executed with remarkable vigour, and in a fine style. In the same place beneath the lives of the holy fathers painted by Pietro Laurati of Siena, Antonio did the bodies of St Oliver and the Abbot Paphnuce, and many circumstances of their lives, represented on a marble sarcophagus, the figure being very well painted. In short, all the works of Antonio in the Campo Santo are such that they are universally considered, and with good cause, to be the best of the entire series of works produced there by many excellent masters over a considerable interval of time. In addition to the particulars already mentioned, Antonio did everything in fresco, and never retouched anything *a secco*. This is the reason why his colours have remained so fresh to the present day, and this should teach artists to recognise the injury that is done to pictures and works by retouching *a secco* things done in fresco with other colours, as is said in the theories, for it is an established fact that this retouching ages the painting, and the new colours which have no body of their own will not stand the test of time, being tempered with gum-tragacanth, egg, size, or some such thing which varnishes what is beneath it, and it does not permit the lapse of time and the air to purge what has been actually painted in fresco upon the soft stucco, as they would do had not other colours been superimposed after the drying. Upon the completion of this truly admirable work Antonio was worthily rewarded by the Pisans, who always entertained a great affection for him. He then returned to Florence, where he painted at Nuovoli outside the gate leading to Prato, in a tabernacle at Giovanni degli Agli, a dead Christ, with a quantity of figures, the story of the Magi and the Last Judgment, all very fine. Invited next to the Certosa, he painted for the Acciaiuoli, who built that place, the picture of the high altar, which survived to our own day, when it was consumed by fire through the carelessness of a sacristan of the monastery, who left the censer hung at the altar full of fire, which led to the picture being burnt. It was afterwards made entirely of marble by the monks, as it is now. In the same place this same master did a very fine Transfiguration in fresco on a cupboard in the chapel. Being much inclined by nature to the study of herbs, he devoted himself to the mastery of Dioscorides, taking pleasure in learning the properties and virtues of each plant, so that he ultimately abandoned painting and devoted himself to distilling simples with great assiduity. Having thus transformed himself from a painter into a physician, he pursued the latter profession for some time. At length he fell-sick of a disorder of the stomach, or, as some say, through treating the plague, and finished the course of his life at the age of seventy-four in the year 1384, when the plague was raging in Florence. His skill as a physician equalled his diligence as a painter, for he gained an extensive experience in medicine from those who had employed him in their need, and he left behind him a high reputation in both arts. Antonio was a very graceful designer with the pen, and so excellent in chiaroscuro that some sheets of his in our book, in which he did the arch of S. Spirito, are the best of the age. Gherardo Starnini of Florence was a pupil of Antonio, and closely imitated him, while another pupil of his, Paolo Uccello, brought him no small credit. The portrait of Antonio of Venice by his own hand is in the Campo Santo at Pisa.

JACOPO DI CASENTINO, PAINTER.

As the fame and renown of the paintings of Giotto and his pupils had been spread abroad for many years, many, who were desirous of obtaining fame and riches by means of the art of painting, began to be animated by the hope of glory, and by natural inclination, to make progress towards the improvement of the art, feeling confident that, with effort, they would be able to surpass in excellence Giotto, Taddeo, and the other painters. Among these was one Jacopo di Casentino, who was born, as we read, of the family of M. Cristoforo Landino of Pratovecchio, and was associated by the friar of Casentino, then superior at the Sasso del Vernia, with Taddeo Gaddi, while he was working in that convent, in order that he might learn design and colour. In a few years he so far succeeded, that, being taken to Florence in the company of Giovanni di Milano, in the service of their master, Taddeo, where they were doing many things, he was asked to paint in tempera the tabernacle of the Madonna of the Old Market, with the picture there, and also the one on the Via del Cocomoro side of the Piazza S. Niccolo. A few years ago both of these were restored by a very inferior master to Jacopo. For the Dyers, he did the one at S. Nofri, on the side of their garden wall, opposite S. Giuseppe. While the vaulting of Orsanmichele, upon its twelve pillars, was being completed, and covered with a low, rough roof, awaiting the completion of the building of the palace, which was to be the granary of the Commune, the painting of these vaults was entrusted to Jacopo di Casentino, as a very skilled artist. Here he painted some prophets and the patriarchs, with the heads of the tribes, sixteen figures in all, on an ultramarine ground, now much damaged, without other ornamentation. He next did the lower walls and pilasters with many miracles of Our Lady, and other things which may be recognised by their style. This done, he returned to Casentino, and after painting many works in Pratovecchio, Poppi, and other places of that valley, he proceeded to Arezzo, which then governed itself with a council of sixty of the richest and most honoured citizens, to whom all the affairs of the state were entrusted. Here, in the principal chapel of the Vescovado, he painted a story of St Martin, and a good number of pictures in the old Duomo, now pulled down, including a portrait of Pope Innocent VI. in the principal chapel. He next did the wall where the high altar is, and the chapel of St Maria della Neve, in the church of S. Bartolommeo, for the chapter of the canons of the Pieve, and for the old brotherhood of S. Giovanni de' Peducci he did a number of scenes from the life of that saint, which are now whitewashed over. He also did the chapel of St Christopher in the church of S. Domenico, introducing a portrait of the blessed Masuolo releasing from prison a merchant of the Fei family, who built the chapel. This saint was a contemporary of the artist, and a prophet who predicted many misfortunes for the Aretines. In the church of S. Agostino, Jacopo did some stories of St Laurence in fresco in the chapel and at the altar of the Nardi with marvellous style and skill. Since he also practised architecture, he was employed by the sixty chief citizens mentioned above to bring under the walls of Arezzo the water which comes from the slopes of Pori, 300 braccia from the city. In the time of the Romans this water had been originally brought to the theatre, traces of which still exist, and thence from its situation on the hill where the fortress now is, to the amphitheatre of the city in the plain, the buildings and conduits of this being afterwards entirely destroyed by the Goths. Thus after Jacopo had, as I have said, brought the water under the wall, he made the fountain, then known as the Fonte Guizianelli, but is now called by corruption Fonte Viniziana. It remained standing from 1354 until 1527, but no longer, because the plague of the following year, and the war which followed, deprived it of many of its advantages for the use of the gardens, particularly as Jacopo did not bring it inside, and for these reasons it is not standing to-day, as it should be.

Whilst Jacopo was engaged in bringing water to the city he did not abandon his painting, and in the palace which was in the old citadel, destroyed in our day, he did many scenes of the deeds of the Bishop Guide and of Piero Sacconi, who had done great and notable things for the city both in peace and war. He also did the story of St Matthew under the organ in the Pieve, and a considerable number of other works. By these paintings, which he did in every part of the city, he taught Spinello of Arezzo the first principles of that art which he himself had learned from Agnolo, and which Spinello afterwards taught to Bernardo Daddi, who worked in the city and adorned it with many fine paintings, which, united to his other excellent qualities, brought him much honour among his fellow-citizens, who employed him a great deal in magistracies and other public affairs. The paintings of Bernardo were numerous and highly valued, first in St Croce, the chapel of St Laurence and those of St Stephen of the Pulci and Berardi, and many other paintings in various other parts of that church. At length, after he had painted some pictures on the inside of the gates of the city of Florence, he died, full of years, and was buried honourably in S. Felicita in the year 1380.

To return to Jacopo. In the year 1350 was founded the company and brotherhood of the Painters. For the masters who then flourished, both those who practised the old Byzantine style and those who followed the new school of Cimabue, seeing that they were numerous, and that the art of design had been revived in Tuscany and in their own Florence, created this society under the name and protection of St Luke the Evangelist, to render praise and thanks to God in the sanctuary of that saint, to meet together from time to time, remembering the welfare of their souls as well as of the bodies of those who might be in need of assistance at various times. This is still the practice of many of the Arts in Florence, but it was much more common in former times. Their first sanctuary was the principal chapel of the hospital of S. Maria Nuova, which was granted them by the family of the Portinari. The first governors of the company were six in number, with the title of captains, and in addition there were two councillors and two chamberlains. This may be seen in the old book of the company begun then, the first chapter of which opens thus:

"These articles and regulations were agreed upon and drawn up by the good and discreet men of the art of the Painters of Florence, and in the time of Lapo Gucci, painter; Vanni Cinuzzi, painter; Corsino Buonaiuti, painter; Pasquino Cenni, painter; Segnia d'Antignano, painter. The councillors were Bernardo Daddi and Jacopo di Casentino, painters. Consiglio Gherardi and Domenico Pucci, painters, the chamberlains."

The company being thus formed by the consent of the captains and others, Jacopo di Casentino painted the picture of their chapel, representing St Luke drawing a picture of Our Lady, and in the predella, all the men of the company kneeling on one side and all the women on the other. From this beginning, whether they meet or no, the company has existed continuously from this time and has recently been remodelled, as is related in the new articles of the company approved by the Most Illustrious Lord, Duke Cosimo, the very benignant protector of these arts of design.

At length Jacopo, overwhelmed with years and toil, returned to Casentino and died there at Prato Vecchio, at the age of eighty. He was buried by his relations and friends in S. Agnolo, an abbey of the Camaldoline order, outside Prato Vecchio. Spinello introduced his portrait into a picture of the Magi in the old Duomo, and his style of draughtsmanship may be seen in our book.

SPINELLO,
PAINTER OF AREZZO.

Upon one of the occasions when the Ghibellines were driven from Florence and when they settled at Arezzo, Luca Spinelli had a son born to him there, to whom he gave the name of Spinello. This boy had so much natural inclination to be a painter, that almost without a master and while still quite a child he knew more than many who have practised under the best teachers, and what is more, he contracted a friendship with Jacopo di Casentino while the latter was working at Arezzo, and learned something from him, so much so indeed that before he was twenty years of age he was a far better master, young as he was, than Jacopo, who was already an old man. Spinello's early reputation as a good painter induced M. Dardano Acciaiuoli to employ him to decorate the church of S. Niccolo at the pope's halls, which he had just erected, behind S. Maria Novella in the Via dei Scala, and there buried a brother who was a bishop. Here Spinello painted scenes from the life of St Nicholas, bishop of Bari, in fresco, completing the work in 1334 after two years of unremitting labour. In it he exhibited equal excellence as a colourist and as a designer, so that the colours remained in excellent preservation up to our own day, and the excellence of the figures was well expressed, until a few years ago when they were in great part damaged by a fire which unfortunately broke out in the church at a time when it happened to be full of straw, brought there by some indiscreet persons who made use of the building as a barn for the storage of straw. The fame of the work induced M. Barone Capelli, citizen of Florence, to employ Spinello to paint in the principal chapel of S. Maria Maggiore, a number of stories of the Madonna in fresco, and some of St Anthony the abbot, and near them the consecration of that very ancient church by Pope Paschal II. Spinello did all this so well that it looks as if it had all been the work of a single day and not of many months, as was actually the case. Near the pope is the portrait of M. Barone from life, in the dress of the time, excellently done and with good judgment. On the completion of this, Spinello worked in the church of the Carmine in fresco, doing the chapel of St James and St John, apostles, where, among other things, he has given a very careful representation of the request made of Christ by the wife of Zebedee and mother of James, that her sons should sit the one on the right and the other on the left of the Father in the kingdom of Heaven. A little further over one sees Zebedee, James and John leaving their nets and following Christ, done with wonderful vigour and style. In another chapel of the same church, beside the principal one, Spinello also did in fresco some stories of the Madonna and the Apostles, their miraculous appearance to her before her death, her death and her being carried to Heaven by angels. As the scene was on a large scale, and the chapel being a very small one of not more than ten braccia in length and five in height, would not take it all, especially in the case of the Assumption of Our Lady, Spinello very judiciously continued the scene to the vaulting on one of the sides at the place where Christ and the angels are receiving her. In a chapel of S. Trinita, Spinello made a very fine Annunciation and for the high altar picture of the church of S. Apostolo he painted in tempera the Descent of the Holy Spirit upon the Apostles in tongues of fire. In S. Lucia de' Bardi he also painted a panel and did a larger one for the chapel of St John the Baptist, decorated by Giotto.

After these things, and on account of the great reputation which his labours in Florence had procured for him, Spinello was recalled to Arezzo by the sixty citizens who governed it, and was commissioned by the Commune to paint the story of the Magi in the old Duomo outside the city, and in the chapel of St Gismondo, a St Donate, who by means of a benediction causes a serpent to burst. Similarly he made some various figures on many pilasters of that Duomo, and on a wall he did a Magdalene in the house of Simon anointing Christ's feet, with other paintings which there is no need to mention, since that church is now entirely destroyed, though it was then full of tombs, the bones of saints and other notable things. But in order that the memory of it may at least remain, I will remark that it was built by the Aretines more than thirteen hundred years ago, at the time when they were first converted to the faith of Jesus Christ by St Donato, who afterwards became bishop of the city. It was dedicated to him, and richly adorned both within and without with very ancient spoils of antiquity. The ground plan of the church, which is discussed at length elsewhere, was divided on the outside into sixteen faces, and on the inside into eight, and all were full of the spoils of those times which had originally been dedicated to idols; in short, it was, at the time of its destruction, as beautiful as such a very ancient church could possibly be. After the numerous paintings which he had done in the Duomo, Spinello painted for the chapel of the Marsupini in S. Francesco, Pope Honorius confirming and approving the rule of that saint, the pope being a portrait of Innocent IV., he having by some means obtained the likeness. In the chapel of St Michael, the Archangel, in the same church in which the bells are rung, he painted many scenes relating to him; and rather lower down, in the chapel of M. Giuliano Baccio, he did an Annunciation, with other figures, which are much admired. The whole of the works in this church were done in fresco with great boldness and skill between the years 1334 and 1338. In the Pieve of the same city he afterwards painted the chapel of St Peter and St Paul, and below it that of St Michael the Archangel; for the fraternity of S. Maria della Misericordia he did the chapel of St James and St Philip; and over the principal door of the fraternity which is on the piazza, that is to say, in the tympanum, he painted a Pieta, with a St John, at the request of the rectors of the fraternity. The foundation of the brotherhood took place in this way. A certain number of good and honourable citizens began to go about asking alms for the poor who were ashamed to beg, and to succour them in all their necessities, in the year of the plague of 1348. The fraternity acquired a great reputation, acquired by means of the efforts of these good men, in helping the poor and infirm, burying the dead, and performing other kindred acts of charity, so that the bequests, donations and inheritances left to them became so considerable that they amounted to one-third of the entire wealth of Arezzo. The same happened in 1383, which was also a year of severe plague. Spinello then being of the company, often undertook to visit the infirm, bury the dead, and perform other like pious duties which the best citizens have always undertaken and still do in that city. In order to leave a memorial of this in his paintings, he painted for the company on the wall of the church of S. Laurentino and Pergentino, a Madonna with her mantle open in front, and beneath her the people of Arezzo, comprising portraits of many of the earliest members of the fraternity, drawn from life, with wallets round their necks and a wooden hammer in their hands, like those with which they knocked at the doors to ask alms. Similarly, in the company of the Annunciation he painted the large tabernacle which is outside the church, and part of a portico which is opposite it, and the picture of the company, which is an Annunciation, in tempera. The picture which is now in the church of the nuns of S. Giusto, where a little Christ, who is at His mother's neck, is espousing St Catherine, with six small scenes in little figures of the acts of that saint, is also a work of Spinello and much admired. Being afterwards invited to the famous abbey of Camaldoli in Casentino in the year 1361, he painted for the hermits of that place the picture of the high altar, which was taken away in the year 1539, when the entire church was rebuilt and Giorgio Vasari did a new picture, painting the principal chapel of the abbey all in fresco, the transept of the church in fresco and two pictures. Summoned thence to Florence by D. Jacopo d'Arezzo, Abbot of S. Miniato in Monte of the order of Monte Oliveto, Spinello painted the vaulting and four walls of the sacristy of that monastery, besides the picture of the altar, all in tempera, with many stories of the life of St Benedict, executed with much skill and a great vivacity in the colouring, learned by him by means of long practice and continual labour, with study and diligence, such as are necessary to every one who wishes to acquire an art perfectly. After these things the said abbot left Florence and received the direction of the monastery of S. Bernardo of the same order, in his native land, at the very time when it was almost entirely completed on the land granted by the Aretines, on the site of the Colosseum. Here the abbot induced Spinello to paint in fresco two chapels which are beside the principal chapel, and two others, one on either side of the door leading to the choir in the screen of the church. In one of the two, next the principal chapel, is an Annunciation in fresco, made with the greatest diligence, and on a wall beside it, is the Madonna ascending the steps of the Temple, accompanied by Joachim and Anna; in the other chapel is a Crucifix with the Madonna and St John weeping, and a St Bernard adoring on his knees. On the inner wall of the church where the altar of Our Lady stands, he painted the Virgin with the child at her neck, which was considered a very beautiful figure, and did many other things for the church, painting above the choir Our Lady, St Mary Magdalene and St Bernard, very vivaciously. In the Pieve of Arezzo in the Chapel of St Bartholomew, he did a number of scenes from the life of that saint, and on the opposite side of the church, in the chapel of St Matthew, under the organ, which was painted by his master Jacopo di Casentino, besides many stories of that saint, which are meritorious, he did the four Evangelists in some medallions, in an original style, for above the bust and human limbs he gave St John the head of an eagle, St Mark the head of a lion, St Luke that of an ox, while only St Matthew has a human face, that is to say an angel's. Outside Arezzo, he decorated the church of S. Stefano, built by the Aretines upon many columns of granite and marble, to honour and preserve the names of several martyrs who were put to death by Julian the Apostate. Here he did a number of figures and scenes with great diligence and such a style of colouring that they were in a wonderfully fresh state of preservation when they were destroyed not many years ago. But the really remarkable piece of work in that place, besides the stories of St Stephen, in figures larger than life size, is the sight of Joseph, in the story of the Magi, beside himself with joy at the coming of those kings, and keenly watching the kings as they are opening the vessels of their treasures and are offering them to him. In the same church is a Madonna offering a rose to the Christ child, which was and is considered a most beautiful figure, and so highly reverenced by the Aretines that when the church of S. Stefano was pulled down, without sparing either pains or expense, they cut it out of the wall, ingeniously removed it and carried it into the city, depositing it in a small church in order to honour it, as they do, with the same devotion which they bestowed upon it at first. There is no wonder that the work inspired such reverence, for it is a natural characteristic of Spinello to endow his figures with a certain simple grace, partaking of modesty and holiness, so that his saints and particularly his Virgins breathe an indefinable sanctity and divinity which inspire men with devotion. This may be seen also in a Madonna which is on the side of the Albergetti, in one on an outside wall of the Pieve in Seteria, and in another of the same kind on the side of the canal. By Spinello's hand also is the descent of the Holy Spirit on the Apostles, on the wall of the hospital of S. Spirito, which is very fine, as are the two scenes below representing St Cosmo and St Damian cutting a healthy leg off a dead Moor to attach it to a man whose broken limb they have removed. In like manner the *Noli me tangere* between these two works is very beautiful. In a chapel of the company of the Puracciuoli on the piazza of St Agostino he did a very finely coloured Annunciation, and in the cloister of that convent he painted a Madonna in fresco with St James and St Anthony and the portrait of an armed soldier kneeling there, with these words: *Hoc opus fecit fieri Clemens Pucci de Monte Catino, cujus corpus jacet hic, etc. Anno Domini 1367 die 15 mensis Maii.* The representations in the chapel of that church, of St Anthony and other saints are known by their style to be by Spinello's hand, and he afterwards painted the whole of a portico in the hospital of S. Marco, now the monastery of the nuns of St Croce as their original house, which was outside, was pulled down. The figure of St Gregory the Pope, among the many represented in this work, standing beside a Misericordia, is a portrait of Pope Gregory IX. The chapel of St Philip and St James at the entry into the church of S. Domenico in the same city, was done in fresco by Spinello in a fine and vigorous style, as was also a three-quarter length figure of St Anthony, painted on the wall of the church, which is so fine that it apes life. It is placed in the midst of four scenes from his life, and these and many other scenes of the life of St Anthony, also by Spinello's hand, are in the chapel of St Anthony, in the church of S. Giustino. On one side of the church of S. Lorenzo he painted some stories of the Madonna, and outside the church he painted her seated, doing the work very gracefully in fresco. In a small hospital opposite of the nuns of S. Spirito, near the gate on the road to Rome, the whole of the portico is painted by his hand with a representation of the dead Christ in the lap of the Maries, executed with so much skill and judgment that it proves him to have equalled Giotto in the matter of design and to have far surpassed him as a colourist. In the same place he has represented Christ seated, with a very ingenious theological signification, having placed the Trinity inside a Sun so that the same rays and the same glory issue from each of the three figures. But the same fate has befallen this work as has happened to many others, to the infinite loss of the lovers of this art, for it was thrown down to make way for the fortifications of the city. At the company of the Trinity may be seen a tabernacle outside the church, by Spinello very finely worked in fresco, comprising the Trinity, St Peter and SS. Cosmo and Damian dressed in the robes habitually worn by the physicians of the time. During the production of these works D. Jacopo d'Arezzo was appointed general of the congregation of Monte Oliveto, nineteen years after he had employed Spinello to do a number of things at Florence and at Arezzo, as has been said above. Being stationed according to the custom of the order, at Monte Oliveto the greater, of Chiusuri in the Siena district, as being the principal house of that body, he conceived a longing to have a beautiful picture made in that place. Accordingly he sent for

Spinello, remembering how well he had been served upon other occasions, and induced him to do the picture for the principal chapel. Here Spinello produced a large number of figures in tempera, both small and great, on a gold ground, with great judgment, and afterwards caused it to be framed in an ornament in half-relief by Simone Cini of Florence, while in some parts he put an additional ornament with stucco of a rather firm glue, which proved very successful. It was gilded all over by Gabriello Saracini, who wrote at the bottom the three names: Simone Cini of Florence did the carving, Gabriello Saracini the gilding, and Spinello di Luca of Arezzo the painting, in the year 1385.

On the completion of this work, Spinello returned to Arezzo having received numerous favours from the general and other monks, besides his payment. But he did not remain long there for the city was in disorder owing to the feuds of the Guelph and Ghibelline parties and was just then sacked. He removed with his family and his son Parri, who was learning painting, to Florence, where he had a goodly number of friends and relations. In that city, in order to pass the time, he painted an Annunciation in a tabernacle outside the gate at S. Piero Gattolini on the Roman road, where the way branches to Pozzolatico, a work which is now half destroyed, and other pictures in another tabernacle, where the ruin of Galluzzo is. Being afterwards invited to Pisa to finish in the Campo Santo beneath the life of St Ranieri the remainder of other subjects in a blank space, in order to unite them to the scenes painted by Giotto, Simone of Siena, and Antonio of Venice, he there executed in fresco six stories of St Petitus and St Epirus. The first represents the saint as a young man, presented by his mother to the Emperor Diocletian, and appointed general of the armies which were to march against the Christians. As he is riding with his troop Christ appears to him, and showing him a white cross commands the youth not to persecute Him. Another scene represents the angel of the Lord giving to the saint, while he is riding, the banner of the Faith, with a white cross on a red field, which has ever afterwards constituted the arms of the Pisans, because St

Epirus had besought God to give him a sign to wear against the enemy. Next to this is another scene of a fierce battle engaged between the saint and the Pagans, many armed angels fighting for the victory of the former. Here Spinello produced many things worthy of consideration in that day when art had not yet the ability nor any good method of expressing the ideas of the mind in colour in a lively manner. Among many other things in this composition are two soldiers, who have seized each other by the beard, and are endeavouring to kill each other with the naked rapiers which they hold in their disengaged hands; their faces and all the movement of their limbs show the desire of victory, their proud spirits being without fear and of the highest courage. Also among those who are fighting on horseback there is a finely executed knight who is fastening the head of an enemy to earth with his lance, the other having fallen backward from his terrified horse. Another scene shows the saint presented to the Emperor Diocletian, who is questioning him about the faith, and who afterwards consigns him to the torture, putting him in a furnace in which he remains uninjured, whilst the servants who are very ready on every side are burned in his stead. In short, all the acts of the saint are shown, to his beheading, after which his soul is carried to Heaven. The last scene shows the transportation of the bones and relics of St Petitus from Alexandria to Pisa. The whole work in its colouring and conception is the finest, most finished, and best executed of Spinello's paintings, and this is shown by its present excellent state of preservation, for its fresh appearance excites the wonder of everyone who sees it. When this work in the Campo Santo was completed, Spinello painted in the church of S. Francesco, in the second chapel from the high altar, many stories of St Bartholomew, St Andrew, St James, and St John the apostles, and he might perhaps have remained longer at work in Pisa, because his paintings were admired and rewarded there, but seeing the city thrown into an uproar and turned upside down through the murder of M. Pietro Gambacorti by the Lanfranchini, who were Pisan citizens, he once more removed to Florence with all his family, for he was by this time an old man. He remained there for one year only, and in the chapel of the Macchiavelli in S. Croce, dedicated to SS. Philip and James, he did many stories of the life and death of those saints. The picture of the chapel he did at Arezzo, and sent it on from there in the year 1400, for he was anxious to return to his native place, or, to speak more correctly, to the place which he looked upon as such. Having thus returned thither at the age of seventy-seven or more, he was lovingly received by his relations and friends, and remained there, much loved and honoured, until the end of his life, which was in the ninety-second year of his age. Although at the time of his return to Arezzo he was quite an old man, and had enough property to enable him to live without working, yet he could not remain idle, since he had always been accustomed to work, and undertook to do some stories of St Michael for the company of S. Agnolo in that city. These are roughly drawn in red on the plastered wall, as was the most ordinary method of the old artists, and as an example he did a single scene in one corner, colouring it entirely, which gave considerable satisfaction. Having afterwards agreed upon the price with the wardens, he completed the entire front of the high altar, representing Lucifer establishing his seat in the north, and the fall of the angels who change into devils as they rain upon the earth. In the air is St Michael fighting with the serpent of seven heads and ten horns, and in the middle of the lower part is Lucifer already changed into a hideous monster. It gave Spinello so much satisfaction to make him horrible and distorted that it is said (so great is the power of imagination) that the figure in the picture appeared to him in a dream, and demanded when the artist had seen him so ugly, asking why he did him so great an indignity with his brush. Spinello awoke from his dream speechless from fear, and shook so violently that his wife hastened to assist him. Yet he ran considerable risk of dying suddenly, through the failure of the heart, owing to this misfortune, and it caused his death a short while afterwards, until when he lived in an utterly dispirited manner with wide open eyes. He died greatly lamented by his friends, and left the world two sons—one called Forzore was a goldsmith, who did some admirable work in *niello* in Florence; the other, Parri, who followed his father and pursued the art of painting, far surpassing Spinello in design. The Aretines were much grieved at this sad chance, although Spinello was old, at being deprived of ability and excellence such as his. He died at the age of ninety-two, and was buried in S. Agostino at Arezzo, where there is a stone with a coat of arms made after a fancy of his own, containing a hedgehog. Spinello was far better able to design than to put his thoughts into practice, as our book of designs shows, which contains two Evangelists and a St Louis by his hand, all very fine. His portrait given above was taken by me from one which was in the old Duomo before it was pulled down. His paintings were executed between the years 1380 and 1400.

GHERARDO STAMINA,
PAINTER OF FLORENCE.

Certainly those who travel far from home to dwell in other parts very frequently do so to the advantage of their temperament, for by seeing divers customs abroad, even if they be of rather an extraordinary nature, they learn to be reasonable, kind and patient with considerably greater ease than they would have done had they remained at home. Indeed those who desire to refine men in their worldly conversation need no other fire and no better cement than this, because those who are naturally rough become gentle, and the gentle become even more gracious. Gherardo di Jacopo Stamina, painter of Florence, though rather hasty than good-natured, being very hard and rough in his dealings, did more harm by this to himself than to his friends, and it would have been even worse for him had he not remained a long time in Spain, where he learned to be gentle and courteous, for he there became so changed from his former nature that when he returned to Florence a very large number of those who had mortally hated him before his departure, received him with very great friendliness and continued to cherish a great affection for him, so gentle and courteous had he become. Gherardo was born in Florence in the year 1354, and as he grew up and was naturally bent to the art of designing, he was put with Antonio da Vinezia to learn to design and to paint. In the space of many years he not only learned the art and practice of colours, but had shown his ability by some things produced in a good style; accordingly he left Antonio and began to work on his own account. In the chapel of the Castellani at S. Croce, which was given to him to paint by Michaele di Vanno, an honoured citizen of that family, he did in fresco many stories of St Anthony the abbot and of St Nicholas the bishop, in such a good style that they attracted the attention of certain Spaniards then staying in Florence on business, and ultimately led to his being invited to Spain to their king, who saw and received him very gladly, there being at that time a great lack of good painters in that country. Nor was it a difficult matter to induce Gherardo to leave his country, for as he had had hard words with some men after the affair of the Ciompi and the appointment of Michele di Lando as gonfaloniere, he was in considerable danger of his life. Accordingly he went to Spain and did many things for the king there, and became rich and honoured by the great rewards which he earned for his labours. At length becoming desirous of showing himself to his friends in his improved estate, he returned home and was warmly welcomed and received in a very friendly manner by all his fellow-citizens. It was not long before he was employed to paint the chapel of St Jerome in the Carmine, where he did many stories of that saint, and in the story of Paul, Eustace and Jerome he represented some of the Spanish habits of the day with very happy invention and an abundance of fashions and ideas in the attitudes of the figures. Among other things, in a scene where St Jerome is receiving his earliest instruction, he represented a master who has caused one boy to mount upon the back of another and strikes him with the whip in such a manner that the poor child is twisting his legs with pain and appears to be crying out and trying to bite the ear of the boy who is holding him. The whole is executed with much grace and lightness, and Gherardo appears to have delighted in these touches of nature. In like manner, when St Jerome, being at the point of death, is making his will, he has hit off some friars in a delightful and realistic manner, for some are writing, others listening attentively and looking about, observing all the words of their master with great earnestness. This work won Stamina much fame and a high rank among artists, and his courteous and mild manners gave him a great reputation, so that his name was famous throughout Tuscany and indeed in all Italy. Being at this time invited to Pisa to paint the chapter-house of S. Niccola in that city, he sent in his place Antonio Vite of Pistoia, because he did not wish to leave Florence. Antonio, who had learned Stamina's style under him, did the Passion of Jesus Christ there, completing it in its present form in the year 1403, to the great delight of the Pisans. Afterwards, it is said, he finished the chapel of the Pugliesi; and as the works which he did there at S. Girolamo greatly pleased the Florentines, because he had expressed in a lively manner many gestures and attitudes which had not been attempted by any painters before his time, the Commune of Florence in the year that Gabriel Maria, lord of Pisa, sold that city to the Florentines for 200,000 scudi (after Giovanni Gambacorta had stood a siege of thirteen months, although even he at length agreed to the sale), employed Stamina to paint on a wall of the Palazzo di parte Guelfa, St Denis the bishop, with two angels, and below it an accurate representation of the city of Pisa. In the execution of this he displayed such diligence in every detail, especially in the colouring in fresco, that notwithstanding the action of air and water and a northern aspect, the picture has always remained in excellent condition, and even now it has all the appearance of having been newly painted, an achievement worthy of high praise. Gherardo having by this and other works acquired a great reputation and much renown both at home and abroad, death, the envious enemy of virtuous deeds, cut off at the height of his powers the great promise of much better things than the world had yet seen from him; and having come to his end unexpectedly in the forty-ninth year of his age, he was buried with much pomp in the church of S. Jacopo sopra Arno.

The pupils of Gherardo were Masolino da Panicale, who was at first an excellent goldsmith and then a painter, and some others whom it is not necessary to mention, as they did not possess any remarkable talent.

The portrait of Gherardo occurs in the story of St Jerome, mentioned above; he is one of the figures who are standing about the dying saint, represented in profile with a hood about his head and a mantle buttoned about him. In our book are some designs of Gherardo done with the pen on parchment, which are of considerable excellence.

LIPPO,
PAINTER OF FLORENCE.

Invention has been, and always will be considered the true mother of architecture, painting and poetry, as well as of all the superior arts and of all the marvels produced by man. By its aid artists develop their ideas, caprices and fancies, and are able to display more variety, for all those who work at these honourable professions always seek after a laudable diversity, and possess the power of delicate flattery and of tactful criticism. Lippo, then, painter of Florence, who was as varied and choice in his inventions as his works were really unfortunate and his life short, was born at Florence about the year of grace 1354; and although he took up the art of painting somewhat late, when he was already a man, yet he was so far assisted by natural inclination and by his fine talents that he soon distinguished himself brilliantly. He first painted in Florence and in S. Benedetto, a large and fine monastery outside the gate of the Pinti belonging to the Camaldoline order, now destroyed; he did a number a figures which were considered very beautiful, particularly the whole of a chapel, which affords an example of how close study quickly leads to great performances in anyone who honestly takes pains with the desire for fame. Being invited to Arezzo from Florence, he did for the chapel of the Magi in the church of S. Antonio a large scene in fresco in which they are adoring Christ; and in the Vescovado he did the chapel of St James and St Christopher for the family of the Ubertini. All these things were very fine, for the invention displayed in the composition of scenes and in the colouring. He was the first who began, as it were, to play with his figures, and to awaken the minds of those who came after him, a thing which had never been done before, only attempted. After he had done many things in Bologna and a meritorious picture at Pistoia, he returned to Florence, where he painted the chapel of the Beccuti in S. Maria Maggiore in the year 1383 with scenes from the life of St John the evangelist. Following on from this chapel, which is beside the principal one, on the left hand, six scenes from the life of this saint are represented along the wall, by the same hand. Their composition is excellent and they are well arranged, one scene in particular being very vivid, namely, that in which St John causes St Dionisius the Areopagite to put his vest on some dead men, who come to life again in the name of Jesus Christ, to the great wonderment of some who are present who can hardly believe their own eyes. The foreshortening of some of the dead figures shows great art and proves that Lippo was conscious of some of the difficulties of his profession and endeavoured to some extent to overcome them. It was Lippo also who painted the wings of the tabernacle of the church of S. Giovanni, where are Andrea's angels and his St John, in relief, doing some stories of St John the Baptist in tempera, with great diligence. Being very fond of working in mosaic, he did some in that church over the door leading towards the Misericordia, between the windows, which was considered very beautiful and the best work in mosaic produced in that place with them. In the same church he further repaired some mosaics which had been damaged. Outside Florence, in S. Giovanni fra l'Arcora, without the gate leading to Faenza, he painted a number of figures in fresco beside Buffalmacco's Crucifixion, which was considered very beautiful by all who saw them. In certain small hospitals near the Fænza gate and in S. Antonio inside that gate near the hospital, he did some poor men, in fresco, in some varied styles and attitudes, very beautifully executed, and in the cloister within he made, with beautiful and new invention, the vision of St Anthony of the deceits of the world, and next to that the desires and appetites of men, who are drawn hither and thither to divers things of this world, the whole of the work being executed with much consideration and judgment. Lippo also did mosaic work in many places of Italy, and in the Guelph quarter at Florence he made a figure with a glass head, while Pisa contains a number of his productions. Yet in spite of all this he must be considered a really unfortunate man, since at the present time the greater part of his works have disappeared, having been destroyed in the siege of Florence, and also because his career was terminated in a very tragic manner; for being a quarrelsome man and liking turmoil belter than quiet, he happened one morning to say some very insulting words to an opponent at the tribunal of the Mercanzia, and that evening as he was returning home, he was dogged by this man and stabbed in the breast with a knife, so that in a few days he perished miserably. His paintings were produced about 1410. There flourished at Bologna in Lippo's time another painter whose name was also Lippo Dalmasi, who was a worthy man, and among other things he painted a Madonna in the year 1407, which may still be seen in S. Petronio at Bologna and which is held in great veneration. He also painted in fresco the tympanum above the door of S. Procolo, and in the church of S. Francesco in the tribune of the high altar, he made a large Christ, half length, and a St Peter and a St Paul, in a very graceful style. Under these works may be seen his name written in large letters. He also designed very fairly, as may be seen in our book, and he afterwards taught the art to M. Galante da Bologna, who afterwards designed much better than he, as may be seen in the same book in a portrait of a figure dressed in a short coat with wide open sleeves.

DON LORENZO, MONK OF THE ANGELI OF FLORENCE, PAINTER.

I believe that it is a great joy to a good and religious person to find some honourable employment for their hands whether it be letters, music, painting or other liberal and mechanical arts which involve no reproach but are on the contrary useful and helpful to other men, for after the divine offices the time may be passed with the pleasure taken in the easy labours of peaceful exercises. To these advantages we may add that not only is such a monk esteemed and valued by others during his life-time, except by such as are envious and malignant, but he is honoured by all men after his death, for his works and the good name which he has left behind him. Indeed whoever spends his time in this manner, lives in quiet contemplation without any danger from those ambitious stirrings which are almost always to be seen among the idle and slothful, who are usually ignorant, to their shame and hurt. If it should happen that a man of ability acting thus is slandered by the malicious, the power of virtue is such that time will reestablish his reputation and bury the malignity of the evil disposed, while the man of ability will remain distinguished and illustrious in the centuries which succeed. Thus Don Lorenzo, painter of Florence, being a monk of the order of the Camaldolines in the monastery of the Angeli (founded in 1294 by Fra Giuttone of Arezzo of the order of the Virgin Mother of Jesus Christ, or of the Rejoicing friars as the monks of that order were commonly called), devoted so much time in his early years to design and to painting, that he was afterwards deservedly numbered among the best men of his age in that profession. The first works of this painter monk, who adopted the style of Taddeo Gaddi and his school, were in the monastery of the Angeli, where besides many of the things he painted the high altar picture, which may still be seen in their church. When completed it was placed there in the year 1413 as may be seen by the letters written at the bottom of the frame. He also painted a picture for the monastery of S. Benedetto of the same order of the Camaldoli, outside the Pinti gate, destroyed at the siege of Florence in 1529. It represented the Coronation of Our Lady and resembled the one he had previously done for the church of the Angeli. It is now in the first cloister of the monastery of the Angeli, on the right hand side in the chapel of the Alberti. At the same time, and possibly before, he painted in fresco the chapel and altar picture of the Ardinghelli in S. Trinita, Florence, which was then much admired, and into this he introduced portraits of Dante and Petrarch. In S. Piero Maggiore he painted the chapel of the Fioravanti and in a chapel of S. Piero Scheraggio he did the altar picture, while in the church of S. Trinita he further painted the chapel of the Bartolini. In S. Jacopo sopra Arno a picture by his hand may still be seen, executed with infinite diligence, after the manner of the time. Also in the Certosa outside Florence he painted some things with considerable skill, and in S. Michele at Pisa, a monastery of his own order, he did some very fair pictures. In Florence, in the church of the Romiti (Hermits), which also belonged to the Camaldolines, and which is now in ruins as well as the monastery, leaving nothing but its name Camaldoli to that part beyond the Arno, he did a crucifix on a panel, besides many other things, and a St John, which were considered very beautiful. At last he fell sick of a cruel abscess, and after lingering for many months he died at the age of fifty-five, and was honourably buried by the monks in the chapter-house of their monastery as his virtues demanded.

Experience shows that in the course of time many shoots frequently spring from a single germ owing to the diligence and ability of men, and so it was in the monastery of the Angeli, where the monks had always paid considerable attention to painting and design. Don Lorenzo was not the only excellent artist among them, but men distinguished in design flourished there for a long time both before and after him. Thus I cannot possibly pass over in silence one Don Jacopo of Florence, who flourished a long time before D. Lorenzo, because as he was the best and most methodical of monks, so he was the best writer of large letters who has ever existed before or since, not only in Tuscany but in all Europe, as is clearly testified not only by the twenty large choir books which he left in his monastery, the writing in which is most beautiful, the books themselves being perhaps the largest in Italy, but an endless number of other books which may still be found in Rome and in Venice and many other places, notably in S. Michele and S. Mania at Murano, a monastery of the Camaldoline order. By these works the good father has richly deserved the honours accorded to him many years after he had passed to a better life, his celebration in many Latin verses by D. Paolo Orlandini, a very learned monk of the same monastery, as well as the preservation of the right hand which wrote the books, with great veneration in a tabernacle, together with that of another monk, D. Silvestro, who illuminated the same books with no less excellence, when the conditions of the time are taken into consideration, than D. Jacopo had written them. I, who have seen them many times, am lost in astonishment that they should have been executed with such good design and with so much diligence at that time, when all the arts of design were little better than lost, since the works of these monks were executed about the year of grace 1350, or a little before or after, as may be seen in each of the said books. It is reported, and some old men relate that when Pope Leo X. came to Florence he wished to see and closely examine these books, since he remembered having heard them highly praised by the Magnificent Lorenzo de' Medici, his father; and that after he had attentively looked through them and admired them as they were all lying open on the choir-desks, he said, "If they were in accordance with the rules of the Roman Church and not of the Camaldolines, I should like some specimens for S. Peter's at Rome, for which I would pay the monks a just price." There were, and perhaps still are, two very fine ones at S. Peter's by the same monks. In the same monastery of the Angeli is a quantity of very ancient embroidery, done in a very fine style, with excellent designs by the fathers of the house while they were in perpetual seclusion, with the title not of monks but of hermits, and who never came out of the monastery as the nuns and monks do in our day. This practice of seclusion lasted until 1470. But to return to D. Lorenzo. He taught Francesco Fiorentino, who, after his death, did the tabernacle which is on the side of S. Maria Novella at the head of the via della Scala leading to the Pope's chamber. He also had another pupil, a Pisan, who painted in the chapel of Rutilio di Ser Baccio Maggiolini, in the church of S. Francesco at Pisa, Our Lady, a St Peter, St John the Baptist, St Francis and St Ranieri, with three scenes of small figures in the predella of the altar. This painting, executed in 1315, was considered meritorious for a work done in tempera. In our book of designs I have the theological virtues done by D. Lorenzo's hand in chiaroscuro, with good design and a beautiful and graceful style, so that they are perhaps better than the designs of any other master of the time. Antonio Vite of Pistoia was a meritorious painter in Lorenzo's time, and is said to have painted, among many other things described in the life of Stamina, in the palace of the Geppo of Prato, the life of Francesco di Marco, who was the founder of that pious place.

TADDEO BARTOLI, PAINTER OF SIENA.

Those artists who put themselves to a great deal of pains in painting in order to win fame, deserve a better fate than the placing of their works in obscure and unhonoured places where they may be blamed by persons whose knowledge of the subject is not considerable. Their productions ought to be so prominently placed with plenty of light and air that they may be properly seen and examined by every one. This is the case of the public work of Taddeo Bartoli, painter of Siena for the chapel of the palace of the Signoria at Siena. Taddeo was the son of Bartoli son of the master Fredi, who was a mediocre painter in his day, and painted scenes from the Old Testament on a wall of the Pieve of S. Gimignano, on the left hand side on entering. In the middle of this work, which if the truth must be told was not very good, the following inscription may still be read: *Ann: Dom 1356 Bartolus magistri Fredi de Senis me pinxit*. Bartoli must have been young at the time, for there is a picture of his of the year 1388, in S. Agostino of the same district, on the left hand side on entering the principal door. The subject is the Circumcision of our Lord with certain saints, and it is in a far better style both as regards design and colouring, some of the heads being really fine although the feet of the figures are in the ancient style. In fact many other works of Bartoli may be seen about that district. But to return to Taddeo, as the best master of the time, he received a commission, as I have said, to paint the chapel of the palace of the Signoria for his native place, and he executed it with such diligence, with consideration for so honoured a place, and he was so richly rewarded by the Signoria, that he greatly increased his glory and renown. Thus not only did he afterwards make many pictures for his native land, to his great honour and benefit, but he was invited and asked of the Signoria of Siena as a great favour by Francesco da Carrara, lord of Padua, to go there, as he did, and do some things in that most noble city. He did some pictures and other things there, notably in the Arena and in the Santo with great care, to his own great honour and to the infinite satisfaction of the said lord and of the whole city. Returning subsequently to Tuscany he did a picture in tempera in S. Gimignano, which is something in the style of Ugolino of Siena and is now behind the high altar of the Pieve facing the choir of the priests. He next went to Siena, but did not remain long there as he was summoned to Pisa by one of the Lanfranchi, a warden of the Duomo. Having proceeded thither he did for the chapel of the Nunziata the scene where the Madonna is ascending the steps of the temple, where the priest in his pontificals is awaiting her, a highly finished work. The face of the priest is the portrait of the man who had invited him, while his own is hard by. On the completion of this work, the same patron induced him to paint over the chapel in the Campo Santo, the Coronation of Our Lady by Jesus Christ, with many angels, in most beautiful attitudes and very finely coloured. For the chapel of the sacristy of St Francesco at Pisa, Taddeo also painted a picture in tempera of the Madonna and some saints, signing his name to it and the year 1394. About the same time he did some pictures in tempera at Volterra, and another picture at Monte Oliveto, while on the wall he did an Inferno, following the arrangement of Dante as regards the division of the damned and the nature of their punishment, but as regards the site he either could not or would not imitate him, or perhaps he lacked the necessary knowledge. He also sent to Arezzo a picture which is in S. Agostino containing a portrait of Pope Gregory IX., the one who returned to Italy after the papal court had been so many decades in France. After these things he returned to Siena, but did not make a long stay there as he was invited to Perugia to work in the church of S. Domenico. Here he painted the whole of the life of St Catherine in the chapel dedicated to that saint, and did some figures in S. Francesco beside the sacristy door, which may still be discerned to-day, and are recognisable as being by Taddeo, because he always retained the same manner. Shortly after, in the year 1398, Biroldo, lord of Perugia, was assassinated. Taddeo accordingly returned to Siena, where he devoted constant work and steady application to the study of art, in order to make himself a worthy painter. It may be affirmed that if he did not perhaps attain his purpose, it was not on account of any defect or negligence on his part, but solely because of an obstructive malady which prevented him from ever realising his desire. Taddeo died at the age of fifty-nine, after having taught the art to a nephew of his called Domenico. His paintings were done about the year of grace 1410. Thus, as I have said, he left Domenico Bartoli, his nephew and pupil, who devoted himself to the art of painting, and painted with superior skill. In the subjects which he represented he exhibited much more wealth and variety in various matters than his uncle had done. In the hall of the pilgrims of the great hospital of Siena there are two large scenes in fresco by Domenico, which contain prospectives and other ornaments, composed with considerable ingenuity. It is said that Domenico was modest and gentle and of a singularly amiable and liberal courtesy, which did no less honour to his name than the art of painting itself. His works were executed about the year of our Lord 1436, and the last were in S. Trinita at Florence, a picture of the Annunciation and the high altar picture in the church of the Carmine.

Alvaro di Piero of Portugal flourished at the same time, and adopted a very similar style, but made his colouring more clear and his figures shorter. In Volterra he did several pictures, and there is one in S. Antonio at Pisa and others in various places, but as they are of no great excellence it is not necessary to mention them. In our book there is a sheet of drawings by Taddeo, containing a Christ and two angels, etc., very skilfully executed.

LORENZO DI BICCI,
PAINTER OF FLORENCE.

When those who excel in any honourable employment, no matter what, unite with their skill as craftsmen, a gentleness of manners and of good breeding, and especially courtesy, serving those who employ them with speed and goodwill, there is no doubt that they are pursuing to their great honour and advantage almost everything which can be desired in this world. This was the case with Lorenzo di Bicci, painter of Florence, born in Florence in the year 1400, at the very moment when Italy was beginning to be disturbed by the wars which ended so badly for her, was in very good credit from his earliest years; for under his father's discipline he learned good manners, and from Spinello's instruction he acquired the art of painting, so that he had a reputation not only of being an excellent painter, but of being a most courteous and able man. While he was still a youth, Lorenzo did some works in fresco at Florence and outside to gain facility, and Giovanni di Bicci de' Medici, having remarked the excellence of his style, employed him to paint in the hall of the old house of the Medici, which afterwards was left to Lorenzo, natural brother of Cosmo the Ancient, after the great palace was built, all those famous men who may still be seen in a fairly good state of preservation. This work being completed, Lorenzo di Bicci was anxious, like the doctors who experiment in their art on the skins of poor rustics, to have practice in the art of painting in a place where things are not so closely criticised, and for some time he accepted everything which presented itself; hence, outside the gate of S. Friano at the ponte a Scandicci, he painted a tabernacle, as it may now be seen, and at Cerbaia under a portico he painted very agreeably a Madonna and many saints on a wall. Afterwards a chapel in S. Marco at Florence was allotted to him by the family of the Martini, and on the walls he painted in fresco a number of scenes from the life of Our Lady, and on the altar picture the Virgin herself in the midst of many saints. In the same church over the chapel of St John the Evangelist, of the family of the Landi, he painted in fresco the angel Raphael and Tobias. In the year 1418 for Ricciardo di M. Niccolo Spinello, on the piazza front of the convent of S. Croce he painted a large scene in fresco of St Thomas examining the wounds of Jesus Christ in the presence of all the other apostles who are kneeling reverently at the sight. Next to this scene and also in fresco he did a St Christopher, twelve and a half braccia high, which is a rare thing, because with the exception of the St Christopher of Buffalmacco, a larger figure had never been seen, and although the style is not good it is the most meritorious and best proportioned representation of the saint. Besides this the pictures were executed with such skill that although they have been exposed to the air for many years, and being turned to the north, they have suffered the violence of rain and storm, yet they have never lost the brilliancy of their colouring and are in no wise injured by these accidents. Lorenzo also made a crucifix with many figures inside the door which is in the middle of these figures, called the door of the knocker, at the request of the same Ricciardo and of the superior of the convent, and on the encircling wall he did the confirmation of the rule of St Francis by Pope Honorius, and then the martyrdom of some friars of that order, who are going to preach the faith to the Saracens. In the arches and on the vaulting he did some kings of France, friars and followers of St Francis, drawing them from life, as well as many learned men of the order, distinguished by their several dignities of bishop, cardinal and pope. Among these are the portraits from life of Popes Nicholas IV. and Alexander V., in medallions. For all these figures Lorenzo made the grey habits, but with variety owing to his skill in workmanship, so that they all differ from one another, some inclining towards red, others to blue, some being dark and others more light, so that all are varied and worthy of consideration. What is more, it is said that he produced these works with such facility and speed that when the superior, who paid his expenses in designing, called him one day, when he had just made the colour for a figure and was beginning it, he answered, "Make the soup and I will come when I have finished this figure." Accordingly it is said with a great show of reason that no one ever exhibited such quickness of the hands, such skill in colouring, or was so resolute as he. By his hand also is the tabernacle in fresco which is beside the nunnery of Foligno and the Madonna and saints over the door of the church of that nunnery, among them being a St Francis espousing Poverty. In the church of Camaldoli at Florence, he painted for the company of the Martyrs some scenes of the martyrdom of certain saints, and decorated the chapels on either side of the principal chapel. As these paintings gave considerable satisfaction to the whole city, he was commissioned on their completion, to paint a wall of the church in the Carmine for the family of the Salvestrini, now almost extinct, there being so far as I know, no other surviving member than a friar of the Angeli at Florence, called Fra Nemesio, a good and courteous monk. Here he did the martyrs, when they are condemned to death, being stripped naked and made to walk bare-footed on thorns sown by the servants of the tyrants, whilst they are on the way to be crucified, and higher up they are represented on the cross in varied and extraordinary attitudes. In this work, the largest which had ever been produced, everything is done with great skill and design, according to the knowledge of the time, being full of the expressions showing the divers ways of dying of those who are put to death with violence. For this cause I am not surprised that many men of ability have made use of some things found in this picture. After this Lorenzo did many other figures in the same church, and decorated two chapels in the screen. At the same time he did the tabernacle on the side of the Cuculia, and the one in the via de' Martelli on the wall of the houses, and over the knocker door of S. Spirito he did a St Augustine in fresco, who is giving the rule to his brethren. In S. Trinita in the chapel of Neri Capponi he painted in fresco the life of St John Gualbert. In the principal chapel of S. Lucia in the via de' Bardi he did some scenes in fresco from the life of St Lucy for Niccolo da Uzzano, whose portrait he introduced there from life together with those of some other citizens. This Niccolo with the assistance and model of Lorenzo, built his own palace near the church, and began a magnificent college or studium between the convent of the Servites and that of S. Marco, that is to say, where the lions now are. This truly magnificent work, rather worthy of a prince than of a private citizen, was not completed, because the immense sum of money which Niccolo left in his bank at Florence for the building and endowment of it were expended by the Florentines on war and other needs of the city. Although Fortune can never obscure the memory and greatness of the spirit of Niccolo da Uzzano, the community suffered a great loss by the non-completion of the work. Therefore, let anyone who desires to help the world in such a manner, and to leave an honourable memorial of himself, do so himself in his life-time, and not trust to the faithfulness of posterity and of his heirs, as it very rarely happens that a thing is carried out where it is left to successors. But to return to Lorenzo. Besides what has been already mentioned, he painted a Madonna and certain saints very fairly in a tabernacle on the ponte Rubaconte in fresco. Not long after, Ser Michele di Fruosino, master of the hospital of S. Maria Nuova at Florence, a building founded by Folco Portinari, citizen of Florence, proposed, as the property of the hospital had increased, to enlarge his church outside Florence, dedicated to St Giles, which was of small importance. Accordingly he consulted Lorenzo di Bicci, his close friend, and on 5th September 1418 he began the new church, which was completed in its present form in a year, and then solemnly consecrated by Pope Martin V. at the request of Ser Michele, who was the eighth master and a member of the family of the Portinari. Lorenzo afterwards painted this consecration, at the desire of Ser Michele, on the front of the church, introducing the portrait of the Pope and of some cardinals. This work was then much admired as something new and beautiful. For this cause Lorenzo was judged worthy to be the first to paint in the principal church of his native city, that is S. Maria del Fiore, where, under the windows of each chapel, he did the saints to which they are dedicated; and afterwards, on the pillars and through the church, he did the twelve Apostles with the crosses of the consecration, as the church was solemnly consecrated in that very year by Pope Eugenius IV. of Venice. In the same church the wardens, by a public ordinance, employed him to paint on the wall in fresco a deposition, finished in marble, in memory of the Cardinal de' Corsini, whose effigy is there, upon the sarcophagus. Above this is another like it, in memory of Master Luigi Marsili, a most famous theologian, who went as ambassador with M. Luigi Giuccardini and M. Guccio di Gino, most honoured knights, to the Duke of Anjou. Lorenzo was afterwards invited to Arezzo by D. Laurentino, abbot of S. Bernardo, a monastery of the order of Monte Oliveto, where he painted scenes from the life of St Bernard in fresco for the principal chapel for M. Carlo Marsupino. But as he was about to paint the life of St Benedict in the cloister of the convent, after he had painted the principal chapel of the church of S. Francesco, for Francesco de' Bacci, the elder, where he alone did the vaulting and half the tympanum, he fell sick of a chest affection. Accordingly he caused himself to be carried to Florence, and left instructions that Marco da Montepulciano, his pupil, should do these scenes from the life of St Benedict in the cloister, from a design which he had made and left with D. Laurentino. These Marco did to the best of his ability, completing them in the year 1448 on 24th April, the whole work being in chiaroscuro, and his name may be seen written there, with verses which are not less rude than the painting. Lorenzo returned to his country, and, having recovered, he painted on the same wall of the convent of S. Croce, where he had done the St Christopher, the Assumption of Our Lady surrounded in Heaven by a choir of angels, and below a St Thomas receiving the girdle. In the execution of this work, as Lorenzo was sick, he was assisted by Donatello, then quite a youth, and by means of such effective aid it was completed in the year 1450, so that I believe it to be the best work both in design and in colouring that Lorenzo ever produced. Not long after, being an old man and worn out, he died at the age of about sixty years, leaving two sons who practised painting, one of whom, named Bicci, assisted him in many of his works, and the other, called Neri, drew the portraits of his father and himself in the chapel of the Lenzi in Ognissanti, in two medallions, with letters about them giving the names of both. In this same chapel Neri did some stories of Our Lady, and took great pains to copy many of the costumes of his day, both of men and women. He did the altar picture for the chapel in tempera, and painted some pictures in the Abbey of S. Felice, of the Camaldoline order, on the piazza of Florence, as well as the high altar of S. Michele of Arezzo of the same order. Outside Arezzo, at S. Maria delle Grazie, in the church of S. Bernardino, he did a Madonna with the people of Arezzo under her mantle, and on one side St Bernardino is kneeling, with a wooden cross in his hand, such as he was accustomed to carry when he went through Arezzo preaching; and on the other side are St Nicholas and St Michael the Archangel. The predella contains the acts of St Bernardino and the miracles which, he performed, especially those done in that place. The same Neri did the high altar picture for S. Romolo at Florence, and in the chapel of the Spini in S. Trinita he did the life of St John Gualbert in fresco, as well as the picture in tempera which is above the altar. From these works it is clear that if Neri had lived, instead of dying at the age of thirty-six, he would have done many better and more numerous works than his father Lorenzo. The latter was the last master to adopt the old manner of Giotto, and accordingly his life will be the last in this first part, which I have now completed, with God's help.

BIBLIOBAZAAR

The essential book market!

Did you know that you can get any of our titles in large print?

Did you know that we have an ever-growing collection of books in many languages?

Order online:
www.bibliobazaar.com

Find all of your favorite classic books!

Stay up to date with the latest government reports!

At BiblioBazaar, we aim to make knowledge more accessible by making thousands of titles available to you- *quickly and affordably*.

Contact us:
BiblioBazaar
PO Box 21206
Charleston, SC 29413